PREDATORS

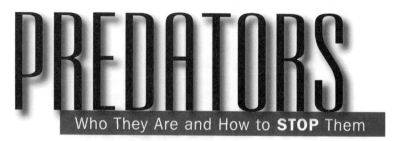

PREDATORS

Who They Are and How to **STOP** Them

GREGORY M. COOPER
& MICHAEL R. KING

with Thomas McHoes

PB Prometheus Books

59 John Glenn Drive
Amherst, New York 14228–2197

Published 2007 by Prometheus Books

Inquiries should be addressed to
Prometheus Books
59 John Glenn Drive
Amherst, New York 14228–2197
VOICE: 716–691–0133, ext. 207
FAX: 716–564–2711
WWW.PROMETHEUSBOOKS.COM

11 10 09 08 07   5 4 3 2 1

Library of Congress Cataloging-in-Publication Data

Cooper, Gregory M., 1954–
    Predators : who they are and how to stop them / by Gregory M. Cooper and Michael R. King with Thomas McHoes.
        p. cm.
    Includes index.
    ISBN 978–1–59102–506–1 (alk. paper)
    1. Victims of crimes. 2. Criminal behavior. I. King, Michael R. II. McHoes, Thomas. III. Title.

HV6250.25.C68 2007
362.88—dc22

                                                                    2007001598

Printed in the United States of America on acid-free paper

CONTENTS

FOREWORD

by John Douglas

In 1995 I selected Greg Cooper as a new criminal profiler for the Investigative Support Unit at the FBI Academy in Quantico, Virginia. We worked together for five years and have enjoyed a close personal and professional association since that time. Greg was a quick study and excelled as a criminal profiler. Because of my confidence in his abilities, he was given an opportunity usually reserved for senior agents—to testify as an expert witness in criminal behavior analysis. I highlighted this case in my *New York Times* best-selling book *Mind Hunter* (Simon & Schuster) as an example of the effective use of criminal investigative analysis in linking cases to common offenders. It wasn't long before Greg was promoted to Program Manager of the Violent Criminal Apprehension Program and as my principal relief supervisor. When I retired, he served as the acting unit chief and eventually returned to Utah as a chief of police.

Greg has continued to serve in other public safety–related positions, but his focus has remained in consulting, training, research, and publication in the public safety venue. Greg and his coauthor, Mike King, a retired twenty-five-year law enforcement veteran, have traveled internationally instructing law enforcement audiences in criminal investigative analysis, criminal behavior, prescriptive interviewing, and cold-case methodology. For example, Greg and Mike claim to have solved the coldest case in history in their book *Who Killed King Tut?* (Prometheus Books). Their case became a Discovery Channel documentary titled *The Assassination of King Tut*, which was shown in 33 languages and 144 countries. Greg and Mike have also coauthored two college course textbooks titled *Analyzing Criminal Behavior* and *Cold Case Methodology*. They recently published a professional article in the *Journal of Forensic Nursing* titled "Interviewing the Incarcerated Offender Convicted of Sexually Assaulting the Elderly." Mike was a contributing author in a book titled *Profilers* (Prometheus Books), and Greg is also a contributing author in the first and second edition of the classic best seller *Crime Classification Manual* (Jossey-Bass). The *Crime Classification Manual* provides a standard system for investigating and classifying violent crimes. His chapter "Prescriptive Interviewing: Interfacing the Interview and Interrogation with Crime Classification" reveals how classifying the crime from a behavioral perspective, first, will most effectively prepare the interviewer to understand the motive of the crime and, subsequently, prepare for the best interview approach.

When Greg told me about this project and their desire to educate both the public safety professional and the general public about the principles of victimology, I was happy to endorse it. Victimology, or the "study of the victim," is often the key to solving crimes for the investigator, and it is also the key to crime prevention for the public.

This book effectively illustrates the role of victimology in analyzing several factors in criminal investigations, including why a particular victim was selected, the motive for the crime, and personality characteristics of the unknown offender. Conducting a victimology from an investigative perspective will result in allowing the investigator to lead the investigation rather than react to it. It will also assist the investigator in concentrating on probabilities over possibilities when attempting to identify offender typologies. Moreover, a thorough understanding of such things as the victim's lifestyle, recent activities, associations, personality characteristics, and so forth, will provide significant insight into preventive measures to be taken for future consideration. It has often been our contention, as profilers, that if the general public understood the principles of victimology, certain types of crimes could be drastically reduced. These principles are effectively illustrated in this book.

Greg and Mike enlisted the help of Tom McHoes, a former investigative reporter, to dramatically present their insights and observations. If you are going to truly understand a work of art, there is no substitute for talking to the artist who created it. The same holds true for understanding criminal behavior. I always encouraged the profilers that I trained and supervised to go to the experts. Greg and Mike spent hundreds of hours interviewing offenders and have presented their findings and insights into the criminal mind. To really understand the criminal personality and their crimes, the best source is the criminal. I taught the profilers under my direction that there is no better source from which to learn. Greg and Mike have carried on that tradition.

Another unique approach utilized in this book is to provide, whenever possible, an understanding of the crimes from three different perspectives—the profiler or investigator, the offender, and the victim. Typically, books of this genre provide only one of these perspectives. But Greg, Tom, and Mike's approach reveals some extraordinary discoveries for both law enforcement and people who desire to protect their loved ones.

You will find the information in this book interesting, entertaining, and even alarming, but most important, you will find it to be educational. In the final analysis, if you and your loved ones improve the safety and quality of your lives, then the mission of the authors has been accomplished. So sit back, read, enjoy, and above all, learn.

INTRODUCTION

The balance between paranoia and common sense is a delicate one. When we think about our safety, it is easy to get so overwhelmed that it can seem like the only way to keep ourselves and our loved ones safe is to lock ourselves up in the house and never come out.

We turn on the TV and see countless news stories about killers who strike randomly and at will; serial rapists who, seemingly without cause, break into houses at night and attack their victims; or predators who snatch our children off the streets or get to them through the Internet.

We see this in and around our communities, and we wonder if we will be next. We see a kidnapping on the news, note the victims' similarities to ourselves, and wonder how we could prevent that from happening to us. It can, indeed, be very overwhelming at times.

That is why we decided to write this book.

With more than fifty years of combined experience, not only are Greg Cooper and Mike King two of the most experienced criminal investigators in the country, but also they specialize in getting into the minds of predatory criminals and retracing their steps. They know how criminal predators think—whether they are solely opportunistic, what opportunities they look for, and the type of people they seek as potential victims.

More important, through these experiences, Cooper—who will serve as the voice of the book—and King also know how to help you minimize those opportunities.

Our hope is that, as you read this book, you will feel a greater sense of urgency to make lifestyle changes that will further protect you and your loved ones. In reading about these crimes, you may feel very uneasy at times—an uneasiness that creates a knot in your stomach. What we hope happens, however, is that we are able to help you untie those knots by teaching you some simple lifestyle changes that will make you safer.

Of course, we are not naive enough to think that we have all the answers for stopping every predatory criminal. That's just not possible. What is plausible, however, is that you can greatly reduce the risk of being victimized simply by knowing whom you're up against and eliminating the easy opportunities predators routinely look for. Putting a stop to the predator's opportunities is what, by and large, puts a stop to the predator.

One thing we do not want is for you to come away thinking that you can't trust anyone. That is simply not true.

We do want you to be able to recognize when it is most safe for you to put your trust in someone and when it is least safe to do so. We also want you to be able to feel a sense of control over situations you put yourself and your loved ones in. Many times, victims hand control of their security—or the safety of their loved ones—to someone who shouldn't be trusted. We hope that, by the end of this book, you will have a greater sense of whom can be trusted and when.

Finally, in writing this book, we confront the task of revisiting criminal cases without revictimizing the victims. Many have moved from the areas where the crimes took place, and they are trying to start new lives.

What we absolutely do not want to do, if at all possible, is disrupt their attempts to rebuild their lives. To prevent that, we have done everything possible to protect their identities. In cases where it was feasible, we have changed their names, the names of their assailants, the names of some investigating officers, the locations of the crimes, and certain details that might be used to identify the victims. In some instances, we have combined two or three cases into one. The point is to use the case as a teaching tool.

It is important to emphasize, however, that some cases garnered so much media attention that the victims' identities are impossible to conceal. Unfortunately, no matter where they go, someone is probably going to recognize them.

We also spoke to a number of predatory criminals who agreed to divulge their strategies for public benefit only on the condition that their identities be concealed. Because we think the information that they provided is so valuable, we feel it is of the utmost importance for us to honor those requests. This way, other inmates will be more likely to divulge facts about their crimes—information that will be extremely useful in helping prevent future crimes—that only they can provide.

It is also important to note that we have taken some creative license in order to reconstruct events not known by anyone other than the individuals involved. Any such dialogue or reconstruction of the events in these cases is purely speculative on our part but based on facts of these cases. We do this only to give you a more complete picture from which to learn.

Again, our aim is not to sensationalize these cases but to use them as a means to teach you, the general public, how to avoid being victimized by criminals of opportunity—or, as we like to call them, predators.

1

VICTIMOLOGY AND THE PREDATORY MIND

Honey, where did I put my keys?"

The young husband and father of two was running a little behind this particular morning, anxious to leave for work by 6 a.m. as he did every weekday.

"They're on the counter," his wife called. "Remember, you put them there last night so you could grab them on your way out."

"Oh, yeah," he said, racing downstairs before giving his striking young wife a quick kiss good-bye. "What would I do without you?"

"You certainly wouldn't have that clockwork lifestyle that keeps you tickin'," she replied with a laugh.

"Aren't you funny," he retorted. "Remember, we have dinner with my parents tonight, so I'll be home at five, right—"

"I know," she interrupted with a smile. "Right on the dot."

"Am I that predictable?"

"And then some," she said. "Let's just say if you were a book, you'd be illustrated with *Sesame Street* characters."

"Ha, ha. It is to laugh," he shot back. "Have a good day. I love you."

"I love you, too," she said, giving her husband a kiss good-bye.

"Can I have a kiss, too, Daddy?" the cute little four-year-old asked, her tone unnecessarily pleading. She knew her father could never resist her smile and bright blue eyes.

"You want a kiss, too?" the doting father teased. "Well, I guess I can accommodate my other sweetheart."

With that, he bent down and gave his daughter a quick peck on the cheek before heading out.

In a way, he was predictable. He definitely preferred to have everything scheduled and executed at precisely the right time. Keeping a tight schedule enables one to maximize his time and productivity and is the mark of a responsible person.

The only problem, however, is that you never know who is keeping your schedule with you.

Outside their home that day, hiding just across the street, was the man who would change this young couple's lives in a very tragic way. Slumped behind a row of bushes, Antonio Baptista observed the same thing he had spied every weekday over the last six weeks in this quiet Provo, Utah, neighborhood.

The young woman, so beautiful with her long, blond hair and natural warm smile, would always give her husband a quick kiss at the side door right at 6 a.m. It was a joy for this uninvited observer to watch her routine.

Shortly after her husband left for work, she would strap her two small children into the buggy, which she normally did around 7 a.m. for her daily run. Like her husband, she, too, liked to keep things on a schedule. She ran almost exactly two and a half miles every morning. The first leg of the run was a northerly ten-block jaunt up 900 East, before turning west for another three blocks, then heading back down toward her house on 600 East for another ten blocks and the stretch run home. Sometimes, if the unsuspected stalker had the time, he would follow her, admiring the perfectly contoured curves of her body. He quietly thrilled at the motions her body made as she jogged.

It was summertime, and she wore shorts, baring her irresistible legs for only him to see. In his mind, he was her only audience.

Or was he exclusive?

There was the matter of her husband, a man who obviously had little appreciation for his wife's beauty. If he did, the kisses he gave her in the morning wouldn't be so rushed, and he certainly wouldn't be in such a hurry to leave her.

The stalker wondered if this fool rushed their lovemaking. Was he so anxious to waste another precious minute to be productive in his career that he took for granted the beauty of the woman he was with?

"Idiot!" the stalker muttered to himself. "It's time for her to be with a man who will appreciate her for her true beauty. It's time for her to be with a real man!"

The stranger bolted from his hiding place to the couple's back bedroom window and forced his way into the house. He looked for a place to hide, wanting to confront his fantasy lady without her seeing him and without children in the room. As he was searching, he heard her voice. He quickly tried to find a place to hide, but it was too late. As he turned the corner, she had already made her way down the hall, and the stunned young woman found herself at a loss for words as the stranger stood before her.

"Hi," he said nervously. "It's me. We finally get a chance to be alone."

"E-excuse me?" she stammered. "Alone?"

"Yeah," he said, somewhat disappointed that she didn't share his enthusiasm for the encounter. "You know, alone. We finally get to be together, away from that man you live with, from that boring life you want to get out of."

"I—I think you must have me confused with someone else," she said, as she backed away. "I'm very happy with my life."

"Come on, Sara, you're acting like you don't even know me. We see each other every day. We want to be together. I've seen it in your eyes, the way you look at me."

"I'm sorry," she said, still backing away. "I don't know what you're talking about."

She frantically began to look for the telephone. Where had she left it?

"What are you doing?" he demanded. "What do you mean you don't know what I'm talking about? Oh, I see. You've just been messing with me all this time. Is that it? You're just using me to make him jealous. Well, I'll tell you what. Nobody uses me. I hate women like you. I hate you!"

With that, she bolted from the bedroom into the hallway, but she didn't get far. He wrapped his hand tightly around her ponytail and dragged her to the ground, slamming her head against the bedroom door.

"I can't believe how ungrateful you are!" he shouted. Then, a noise came echoing through the kitchen, a sound that sent shivers up the woman's spine.

"Mommy?" said the tiny girl's voice. "Mommy? Who's here?"

He quickly pulled her back into the bedroom and shut the door. "Get rid of her," he demanded in a whisper.

"Nobody, honey," she gulped. "Just go back and—and, check on the baby for me, OK, sweetie?"

"OK, Mommy."

In an instant, the little girl skipped away and the sound of pitter-pattering feet quickly faded.

"Please don't hurt my babies," she pleaded.

"Nobody? Is that what I am to you? After all those moments we've had, and that's all you can say about me? You really are a user. You're a taker!"

"I'm sorry," she cried. "You must have me confused with someone else. I've never seen you before in my life."

"Confused? Neither of us is confused," he said, grabbing a pillow from the bed and shoving it into her face. "You know exactly who I am, and now you're trying to blow me off like I'm some nobody!"

She struggled to get the pillow off her face, but it only angered her attacker. He grabbed her and turned her onto her stomach. For a moment, she just lay on the floor, trying to catch her breath and relieved he hadn't suffocated her with the pillow. He seemed out of breath, too, so she thought she would try to smooth things over.

"No, no," she said, trying to use the most reassuring voice possible. "I swear. I'm not trying to blow you off. I just don't know who you are. I think there's just been a misunderstanding. Maybe I look like someone you know. I don't know. But, I promise, if you leave, I won't say a word to anybody. I promise. Please, just don't hurt us."

"If I leave? Don't hurt you? I can't believe you're saying this to me," he said. "You're just like all the rest of them. I'm sick and tired of you chicks thinking you can just lead me on all the time and get away with it."

"Leading you on? I don't even know you!" she shouted, losing her composure. She wanted to hit him, but her arms were pinned underneath the weight of her own body. "What gives you the idea I could have been leading you on? Please, just leave me alone. Stop doing this to me!"

"Stop doing what to you? What about what you're doing to me?"

"What? What did I do to you?!" she cried. "I'm sorry for whatever I've done. Just let me go."

"Like you don't know," he barked. "You married chicks are all the same. You have your nice little perfect husband and family, your safe little world for everyone to see. Then, you see a guy like me and make your slutty eyes at me and have your slutty fantasies about me. You know what those little smiles mean. What, do you get off on making me want you then slamming the door in my face when I finally make my move? We both know what you want. I'm tired of being nice about this. I came here for something, and I'm taking it."

With that, he grabbed a fistful of her shorts and underwear and pulled them down to her knees. She struggled to pull them up but he swiftly backhanded her, sending her reeling for a few precious seconds, seconds he used to tear the rest of her clothes off. She tried to sit up and fight back but a punch, then another, knocked her out for another minute, maybe two. When she came to, she realized she was being raped, but she lacked the strength to do anything but cry.

"What are you crying about!" he yelled before slapping her again. "Don't cry! Don't you dare cry. You know you wanted this. You know you—"

"Mommy?" the little voice interrupted. "Why are you yelling? Who's here, Mommy?"

"You know you wanted this," he whispered in her ear. "If you say a word to anybody about me, I'll kill you."

He got off her, pulled up his pants, and climbed out the window.

The bedroom door opened, and the little girl shrieked.

"Mommy!" shrieked the girl. "Get up, Mommy. Please get up! The baby is crying. He needs you."

Instinctually, the young mother took her daughter's hand and caressed her face, trying to calm her.

"You need to be a big girl and get the phone for Mommy," said Sara, summoning what little strength she had left.

I had gotten an early wake-up call at home to come to the scene of one of the most brutal rapes I have ever investigated.

All my years as an FBI profiler, and here I was as the chief of police in the relatively peaceful community of Provo, Utah, being briefed about a blatant attack on a young mother of two in a quiet neighborhood. I had certainly seen more brutal attacks but never anything quite as unexpected or utterly shocking as this.

That morning, pure innocence met sheer evil.

"I got here as quickly as I could. How is the victim?" I asked Mark Sheridan, one of the detectives assigned to the case.

"She's in pretty bad shape, chief," he answered.

"They've taken her to the hospital," said Jim Weston, another detective. "But it looks like she's going to pull through."

This was one of the worst cases either detective had ever been involved with. Both had been around a while, and they were definitely people I trusted implicitly. They both had that rare combination you see in people who are driven to excel, yet they possessed a lot of compassion.

Weston had a wife and family, and even though I'm not sure he would have admitted it then, he had a difficult time separating his personal feelings from the case, probably wondering about the safety of his family.

"Well, it looks like you guys have this covered," I said. "I've got some things to do at the office. If there is anything you need, give me a call."

"OK, chief, will do," they responded.

"Did you get a chance to talk to her at all before they took her out?" Sheridan asked Weston.

"No," answered Weston. "Like I said, she was in pretty bad shape when we got here. But I think there's something you need to see. There, in the bedroom, it looks like our guy had to force his way in. He climbed over the bed, grabbed a pillow, and walked over to where he raped the victim. And check this out. He left footprints on the carpet, and he wasn't wearing any shoes."

"Bare feet, huh?" Sheridan said. "It looks like our perpetrator might have lived pretty close by. I think we need a sketch on this one before we start talking to too many people. We should get Carrie involved."

Carrie Specter was one of the best sketch artists in the valley, maybe the whole state. She was also a very good officer. We were lucky to have her on this case because her talents would prove vital in solving it.

"It's just not your typical rape," Weston observed. "Seven in the morning, a decent neighborhood, a young housewife—and the worst part, there was a four-year-old girl and a baby in the house at the time. The little girl might have seen some of it. We've got Annie with her now to find out."

"This is horrible. Have we notified the husband?" Sheridan asked.

"Yeah, we had to send someone to pick him up," Weston answered. "He's in total shock. Apparently, he'd just gotten to work when this happened. He should be here in a few minutes."

"OK, let me contact Carrie, then we'll see how much of this poor lady's memory we can jog. In the meantime, you talk to the husband," Sheridan said.

The detectives picked up several pieces of evidence around the house that helped them develop a profile of the rapist.

"The window was pretty flimsy, not much of a lock, so it looks like it didn't take much for him to push it open," Weston observed. "Was there any sign of a weapon used on her?"

"No," replied one of the medics. "It looks like it was a straight-up brutal beating."

"Hmm. Then whoever it was, he had to be pretty confident that the woman's husband wasn't going to come back anytime soon," Weston continued, analyzing the victim's possible relationship to her attacker. "That's an indication that either our perpetrator knew the victim, or he had staked this place out over time. If it was a stakeout, then it has to be someone who lives relatively close by, probably within a six-block radius. That would also explain the bare feet. It's just not feasible for someone who lives much farther away than that to be able to have gotten the couple's schedule down so accurately."

"So do you think it was someone who knew her?" asked one officer. "Like, maybe a family friend?"

"We won't really know until we get more information on the victim, but it probably wasn't someone who knew her that closely," answered Weston. "A family member or close friend would have access but probably wouldn't take the chance of being seen by the children. But I'm guessing that this was definitely someone she had encountered before. This was something the perpetrator planned. Let's talk to the husband and anyone else close to the victim. See if she either had any other romantic interests or anyone she felt threatened by. And let's get a list of any registered sex offenders in the area. Also, talk to the neighbors and see if they saw any strange people or strange vehicles in the area."

"OK, detective," the officer said. "Will do. I think I heard them bring in the husband. Do you want to talk to him?"

"Yeah, I'll be right there."

When Weston walked into the living room, he saw a frazzled young man sitting on the couch.

"Mike, I'm Detective Jim Weston," he started. "We're investigating the attack on your wife. Can I ask you a few questions?"

"How is my wife? Where is she? What happened?"

"She's at the hospital," said Weston. "She's hurt, but she should be OK. We'll have somebody take you to see her as soon as we're finished here, OK?"

"Yeah, OK," he said. "But can we please make this quick? I need to see her."

"We'll be as brief as possible," Weston assured the young man. "Is there anyone you can think of, maybe even from your wife's past, who would want to hurt her?"

"No. Everybody loved Sara. I can't imagine why anyone would want to hurt her."

"What about anyone strange to the area? Have you seen or has your wife mentioned having seen anyone strange around the neighborhood lately?"

"No, not that I can think of. Definitely nothing way out of the ordinary, or I'm sure she would have said something to me. Are we almost done? I'd really like to see her now if I could."

"We're just about there," said Weston. "Just one more thing, and it's nothing personal, just standard procedure. We need to get a list of people from you who can confirm you were at work at the time this happened."

"Am I a suspect or something?"

"No, we just need to completely eliminate you as one," Weston told him. "Like I said, it's just standard procedure. We're not saying this is the case here, nor, frankly, do we think it is, but in many cases, an attack like this is the result of domestic violence. When we've ruled you out, I promise, we'll take you to your wife, OK?"

He agreed and soon was on his way to the hospital. The next part was the toughest.

The detectives went to talk to the little girl—Amy—to see if they could get a good description of her mother's attacker. They were hoping she had seen something, but odds were, if she got a look at him, it wasn't a long one. And if he had even suspected that she had seen him, I don't think she would have been left behind to talk.

As they began to talk to her, Weston and Sheridan were surprised
by how composed she was. Most adults, let alone children, have a
tough time dealing with that kind of trauma. As always, Annie
Thompson, our victims' assistance specialist, had done a great job of
settling her in and making her feel safe and comfortable around the
detectives.

They met with Amy in her bedroom for a couple reasons: one, the
room was located in the portion of the home furthest away from the
attack, and two, it was a familiar place in which the child was going
to feel most at ease.

"Well, hi, guys," Annie said as she saw the detectives approaching.
Then, she turned to the little girl. "Hey, sweetie, you're in luck. It's not
everybody who gets to meet the two best policemen in the city. I'll bet they
even have a treat to go with your new teddy bear. Would you like that?"

The girl, cute as a button, nodded.

Not wanting to be too imposing, Sheridan knelt down and reached
into Annie's treat bag.

"Well, look what we've got here," Sheridan said. "Smarties. My
favorite. They're also Detective Weston's favorite, but you can probably tell because he has such a big belly."

By the look on his face, Sheridan could see that Weston wasn't too
happy with his attempt at humor, but it got a giggle out of the little girl,
and Weston quickly turned his attention toward the task at hand.

"Do you like this kind, or do you want something else?" he asked
Amy.

She didn't say anything but reached out her hand and took the
candy.

"You know, sweetie, these policemen are here to find out how your
mommy got her owies," Annie continued. "Do you think you could
answer a couple questions for them?"

Again, she nodded.

"Well, Amy," began Sheridan, his six-foot-four, 250-pound frame
planted on the floor amid a variety of Barbie dolls and Care Bears.
"Did you see anybody in the bedroom with your mommy?"

"Uh-huh," she said. "He was climbing out the window."

"Oh, I see. Could you tell me what color hair he had?"

"I'm not sure," she said.

"Well, maybe this will help," the burly detective offered. "Was his hair dark or light?"

"It was dark," she responded.

"How about his clothes? What color were his clothes?"

"Blue," she stated matter-of-factly. "He had a blue jacket on and blue pants."

"Kind of like these?" Sheridan asked, pointing to Annie's jeans.

"Yeah, just like those pants. Is my mommy coming home soon?"

"She should be able to see you soon," Annie answered. "She's at the doctor's, and he's making her better."

Amy looked around her room for a moment with a stare that suggested she knew she would never see it the same way. Never again would this humble home represent safety and tranquility for this child—or for her mother and father.

"Can I keep the teddy bear?" she asked.

"You bet you can," Sheridan said. "In fact, you did such a good job answering our questions, I think you deserve another treat. What do you think, Detective Weston?"

"You better believe it," Weston replied. "This is the best I've ever seen anybody do. In fact, she deserves a treat for getting Detective Sheridan to play with dolls."

"Hey, I like to play with dolls," Sheridan said, playing along to get another giggle from the four-year-old. As he handed the girl another package of Smarties, the burly detective began to get up off the floor and said, "Thank you for talking to us, Amy. Maybe we can visit again someday, OK?"

"OK," she said sweetly.

As the detectives watched Annie take the girl over to her father, Sheridan pulled Weston aside.

"There's no need to keep talking to the girl until we can gather more evidence," said Sheridan. "We've got a solid partial description from her for now, and I'm sending Carrie to talk to the victim. I'm hoping she can get a description from her, and I want to see if we can get an accurate sketch of our perpetrator. In the meantime, let's talk to the neighbors and find out if anyone saw him running from the house."

While they covered the neighborhood, Carrie and Annie dealt with one of the most difficult aspects of any case—talking to the victim to see if they could get a workable description of the attacker.

We hoped she would be well enough to talk to Carrie. But Annie and Carrie were surprised by Sara's composure. Again, Annie had done a great job of settling her in and making her feel safe and comfortable.

Sara's case perfectly illustrates the reason I felt strongly about establishing a victim's assistance division within the department. Usually the first people any victim sees are investigating officers. If it is an especially traumatic crime or if children are involved, it is extremely important that there is someone on the scene to hold the victim's hand and gently guide him or her through the investigative process. It helps law enforcement during the investigation, and it helps reduce the level of intimidation the victim might feel. Annie was the best I ever saw at doing just that.

"Hi, Carrie," Annie said as she saw her approaching. "I'd like to introduce you to Sara. Sara, this is Carrie Specter. She is one of our officers and also the sketch artist in our department."

"Hi, Sara," said Carrie. "Do you mind if I ask you a few questions, just to see if we can get a good picture of the man who did this to you? Do you think you're up to that?"

The woman, brutally battered and bruised, stared off in the distance for several seconds. For a moment, it didn't look like we were going to be able to get anything from her. Then, she turned and looked straight at Carrie.

"Will it help you get the monster who did this to me?" Sara responded, her lower lip quivering.

"Depending on how detailed the description is, yes, it could help a lot," Carrie said softly.

"Then, yes, I'm up to it," she said, this time her voice more determined. "He put a pillow over my face, but I knew that if he let me live—"

Sara wasn't able to finish the sentence before she began to cry.

"I'm sorry," she said through her tears. "It's just so hard. I can't believe this happened."

"It's all right," Annie assured the young woman. "You're doing great. And you're not alone in this. We're going to be with you every step of the way."

"I know," Sara answered. "Thank you. I'm ready to keep talking. I did get a look at him. What do you need to know?"

"We just need to know what you saw," Carrie said. "We'll just take it a step at a time. Let's start with his facial features. What color were his eyes?"

"They were brown," Sara answered.

"Would you say they were more almond shaped or more of a true round shape?"

"Definitely narrower, like an almond."

"What about his hair? Was it long or short?"

"It was long and black. And it was wet, as if he had just gotten out of the shower."

The questions continued, and the young woman bravely answered every one of them. Before long, Carrie had completed the sketch.

"Is there anything else you remember?" Carrie asked. "Any smells or any other features that stood out to you?"

"Yes," Sara said. "He smelled like smoke. He wasn't wearing any shoes. And his hands were rough."

"You mean 'rough' as in 'calloused'?" Carrie asked.

"Yes. His hands were calloused."

At the end of the question-and-answer session, Carrie had what she hoped was an accurate sketch of our suspect.

"I think we've got it," Carrie said softly. "But I'm going to have to ask you to do one more thing, OK?"

"OK. What?"

"I'm going to have to show you the final draft of the sketch I've drawn and have you confirm that this is the person who attacked you," she said. "Do you think you can do that for me?"

"I think so."

"OK, then," said Carrie, turning the sketch to Sara's view. "Is this him?"

Tears began to well up in Sara's eyes, and for a few seconds she was unable to speak.

"Yes!" she suddenly blurted. "That's him. That's him."

"You did great," Carrie said, taking Sara's hand. "This will help us find him, OK?"

Sara nodded then stared into the distance. I think she knew she had a long road ahead of her. I hoped we could help her take the first step by getting her attacker off the streets and assuring her that he would never threaten her again.

Our investigators questioned people in the neighborhood, but no one could recall having seen anything out of the ordinary. It appeared we had hit a snag in the investigation. Because of the calluses the victim described, we knew that he probably worked in construction, so we kept our eyes peeled for residences that had construction paraphernalia out front. As expected, the husband was cleared, and our team became more and more convinced that our rapist was someone who lived in the neighborhood. Sure enough, when we spoke to the manager of a nearby apartment complex, he immediately recognized the man in the sketch.

"Yeah, I know him," the apartment manager said. "That's Antonio, Antonio Baptista. He's a real quiet guy, kind of keeps to himself."

"That's great," Weston said to the manager. "Will you do us a favor?"

"Sure," he answered. "Whatever you need."

"Don't say anything to Mr. Baptista about us being here. But will you please look for him, and when you see him return home, will you call us immediately?"

"You bet."

As it turned out, Baptista had served four years in prison for sodomizing a woman in Salt Lake City a few years earlier. He had moved to Provo and rented an apartment located about four blocks from the victim's home. He worked at a local machine shop.

When Baptista returned home from work, Weston and another officer paid him a visit, finding a very nervous suspect when they knocked on the door.

"Hello, are you Antonio Baptista?" Weston asked.

"Yeah, that's me," Baptista answered. "What do you guys want?"

"Do you know why we're here, Antonio?"

"You want to see if I got my registration papers," he said. "I've got them, man, so you don't need to keep hassling me, OK? You guys were just here a couple weeks ago. What, are you going to come every week?"

"It would be great to see your papers, Antonio, but that's not exactly why we're here," Weston said. "You know, a lady was raped just a few blocks from here."

"Give me a break, man! What, every time something happens around here, you're going to think it has to do with me? Man, I served four at the Point for something I didn't do, and I ain't going back for something else."

"Calm down, Antonio, we aren't looking for any trouble," Weston warned. "We just want to ask you a couple of questions and get a little DNA sample, that's all. If you're innocent, you've got nothing to worry about, right?"

"Yeah, whatever!" Baptista spouted. "You'll make something up, just like you always do. I ain't letting you do nothing 'til I see my lawyer, man."

"Fine, but we've got enough reasonable suspicion to take you in for questioning," Weston said. "With or without your lawyer, the evidence won't lie."

Baptista settled down and agreed to let us take him. He gave us a DNA sample, and, of course, when the test came back, Baptista's DNA was a complete match. We had our guy.

*   *   *

I've thought a lot about this case and wondered what this family could have done, if anything, to prevent this from happening. In terms of what they had been taught about safety, they did all the right things and certainly should never feel as though they hold any responsibility for this attack.

But as I think about it, we as a society have been trained to do certain things to protect ourselves. At most, we lock our doors and shut our windows at night (though a lot of people don't even do that). We don't go out too late, and if we do, we know we shouldn't go alone. Sometimes we carry pepper spray or mace to thwart our attackers. You can pick up a pamphlet at your local police station that will give you a laundry list of things you should do to ensure your safety.

The problem is, it just isn't enough anymore.

As so often seems to be the case, the bad guys are at least one step ahead of the good guys. While they continue to enhance their skills and learn to work their way around the system, we haven't updated our way of thinking to prevent ourselves from being victimized. In other words, while we continue to use the same locks on our doors that we've used for the past twenty or thirty years, criminals have been using more modern tools and schemes to break through those locks, both literally and figuratively. In fact, even those of us who use the most updated security systems sometimes find that some determined savvy criminal has cracked the code.

That is why we want to share with you an investigative technique I learned as an agent in the FBI's Behavioral Analysis Unit, the unit portrayed on the CBS drama *Criminal Minds*.

It's not only a great technique for criminal investigators but also something you can use as a practical tool to keep yourself safe. We will use this technique as a risk-reducing template throughout this book.

The technique is called victimology.

Victimology, simply stated, is nothing more than a comprehensive study of the victim, a way for authorities to narrow a list of probable types of suspects. One important component is something we call the Risk Continuum, a tool used for determining how much a person was at risk for a particular crime. The Risk Continuum gauges different aspects of a person's life (career, lifestyle, relationships, etc.) as being anywhere from low risk to high risk or somewhere in between. If understood and utilized properly, it can be a valuable resource in helping you evaluate your life and reducing the likelihood of either yourself or your loved ones being victimized.

When I was an FBI profiler, whenever we investigated a crime, the first thing we did was a thorough study of the victim. We went through all the basics. We looked at the victim's age, sex, race, place of work, friends, family, and so forth. From this, we could determine probable types of suspects based on correlations we drew between the crime and the victim's lifestyle/risk level. Something about that person's life would lead us to the perpetrator, so we looked for aspects of the victim's lifestyle, circumstances, or behavior that put him at high risk for that crime.

For example, if a murder victim is a prostitute or a drug dealer, we know that person's career/lifestyle puts him or her on the high end of the Risk Continuum. By virtue of what that person does to make a living, he puts himself in the path of the people who would be most likely to commit murder or some other heinously violent crime.

On the other hand, a housewife is among the least likely to become a victim of a violent predatory crime because she generally spends her time in a safer environment. Now, does this mean housewives are never attacked, while prostitutes are always doomed to that fate? Of course not. As you saw in Sara's case, anyone can be a violent criminal's target.

Does this mean that high-risk individuals are to blame for their own victimization? Absolutely not. No one deserves to be a victim, especially of a vicious predatory crime. Victimology and the Risk Continuum do not place blame. Instead, these tools help us assess risk. And they can help you determine your own risk level and evaluate your lifestyle so that you can take steps to reduce your risks.

With these tools, let's use a probable example to show how, even by no fault of her own, a low-risk-lifestyle person can quickly become a high-risk victim. Then we will put some strategies in place to help her reduce her risks.

Let's say a middle-class housewife gets a phone call at 1 a.m. Her sister, who lives four hours away, has an emergency and needs her there as quickly as possible. Unfortunately for the housewife, this emergency occurs while her husband is out of town on business, so she leaves her sixteen-year-old son in charge of the other kids. But while en route to her sister's house, her car breaks down on a lonely stretch of freeway where there is no cell phone coverage. To top it off, there are no services for several miles in any direction, so walking isn't a feasible option. The woman, who is now stranded on a highway at three in the morning, immediately becomes an easy target for any opportunistic predator looking to strike. She is now at the mercy of whomever stops. While in such a high-risk situation, she must take steps to reduce her risk level.

But how?

First, she could have done a number of things to ensure her safety before she even left the house. She could have told her son that she would call at an estimated time of arrival. She also could have left that information with her sister, giving both parties strict instructions to call the authorities if they did not hear from her past a certain time. In addition, she could have mapped her exact route to her sister's home. This way, if she were late, her family could call the highway patrol and have them look for her vehicle on specific stretches of road.

Second, in such a precarious situation, there are actually two things she could do: One is to stay with the car. The other is to lock it and make herself as invisible as possible by walking several yards off the highway to watch the car yet still remain unseen. This way, if anyone with predatory intentions does stop near her vehicle, she won't be a sitting duck. In addition, if she took the correct steps before leaving, the highway patrol will spot her car and help her. If she reduces her visibility, then she decreases her risk of being sighted by a predatory criminal looking to seize an easy opportunity. And even if she did fail to take the proper pretravel steps, she could, at the very least, lay low until daylight and hope a highway patrol trooper passes her way.

This certainly is not the ideal situation, but at least it lowers her chances of being victimized. And reducing one's risks is exactly the point of this book.

The fact is, because of our complex society and the many ways we are put at risk, there is no one checklist of easy answers. We just don't live in a place or time when locking our doors and windows is enough anymore. You could build a fortress around your house, and predators could still get to you and your loved ones using countless methods. For example, the local news is filled with stories on Internet crime, a medium that requires only a willing, naive participant.

The bottom line is, because there are infinite ways to be victimized, there are also infinite ways to reduce your risks—so many, in fact, that it would be virtually impossible to list them all.

That is why we decided to write this book.

We think the most effective way to enhance your safety is through the way you live and the way you think. We're not talking about becoming paranoid or making drastic lifestyle changes. We're talking about educating yourself, analyzing your life as it pertains to safety, then making commonsense changes. Our job is to educate you, and yours is to employ the common sense.

To do that, you must put yourself in two pairs of shoes.

One is in the mind of the criminal, where you can understand how he thinks. Ask yourself what he looks for, how he targets his victims, and how he knows which victims will most likely succumb to his wishes.

The other pair of shoes belongs to the criminal investigator. Instead of trying to imagine all the precautions you would need to take, try to imagine yourself as the detective investigating a crime that has already been committed against you.

To do this, all you need to know are the basics of how an investigator approaches a crime and what he looks for. Throughout the rest of this chapter, we will take you through the investigative thought process. In chapter 2, we will take you through the mind of the criminal. The remainder of the book will focus on specific crimes, the kinds of criminals that commit them, and how they are investigated. We will go through real-life cases and take you through the mind-set of the predators who committed them, how criminal investigators used those thought patterns to solve cases, and, most important, what could have been done, if anything, to prevent these horrible crimes.

We know it is impossible to prevent all crimes. Indeed, the most determined criminal is the one who offends without worrying about the potential consequence. But we hope that what we share with you will allow you to protect yourself from the vast majority of criminals—the opportunists. Remember, it is always easier to retrace one's steps (to work backward, if you will) than it is to try to predict what could happen. In other words, it's easier to play the Monday morning quarterback than it is to actually *be* the quarterback.

So, with that in mind, please allow us to start by taking you through Criminal Investigation 101 and share some of the investigative techniques taught at the FBI training academy located in Quantico, Virginia.

Sir Arthur Conan Doyle, author of the famed Sherlock Holmes stories, built what I think is the perfect foundation for investigative technique. In *The Sign of Four*, Holmes says, "When you eliminate the impossible, whatever remains, however improbable, must be the truth."

I love that quote because the ultimate aim of any investigation is to solve the mystery, answer the questions, and reveal the truth. When I taught at the FBI National Academy, that is exactly what we taught—how to get to the truth. The following is a summary of the material that I used at the academy. I will add commentary to apply these principles to Sara's case so you can have a better idea of how you can apply them to your own life.

To start, it is important to realize that, in any investigation, revelation of the truth is the primary and critical foundation to solving the case. Without the truth (meaning the indisputable facts), a conclusion will never be reached. Or hasty conclusions might be drawn, and unless they are based on accurate and reliable data, the answer remains open to conjecture, fallibility, and false claims. That is not what we want. We want to be sure that the community and the victim know beyond a reasonable doubt that the person we put away is truly the criminal who committed the crime.

But for that to happen, the criminal investigator must be absolutely committed to the discovery of the truth first, which will then lead to a successful and accurate judgment. For you, this means being absolutely truthful with yourself in regard to your lifestyle and level of risk.

If the detective develops a theory before gathering all the facts, his conclusion could be prone to critical error. In this sense, the investigator's job is much like a doctor's. Imagine a patient who complains of headaches to his physician. The doctor impulsively prescribes a new set of glasses for impaired vision, only to later discover that the patient is suffering from a brain tumor. Much like the doctor who writes a misdiagnosed prescription before even conducting an examination, the detective might make a faulty arrest if he rushes to his diagnosis. Regrettably, a number of innocent people have been falsely accused, tried, convicted, and sentenced. When additional evidence was discovered, they were subsequently released after several years of confinement, their lives ruined. These errors reek of the highest injustice and unnecessary folly in the criminal justice system.

That said, the key to avoiding those pitfalls and providing accurate crime analysis lies in the science of victimology. By examining who the victim is, we begin to unravel and eliminate an often perplexing web of misguided leads. A thorough understanding of the victim can often lead the investigation toward a probable suspect rather than a reaction to an endless pool of less likely possible candidates. Likewise, as you examine your life, you will unravel potential chinks in your armor and be empowered to repair them.

As investigators, this is the approach we took in ultimately finding the man who beat and raped Sara. We couldn't possibly have hoped to have found Baptista if we had marched into the victim's house and began coarsely interrogating her husband. Yes, statistics show that most rape victims are also victims of domestic violence, and being that the neighborhood was not a high-crime area, it was reasonable to hypothesize that this was probably a domestic crime. It would have been a plausible theory. But, as it turned out, it wasn't a domestic assault at all.

Had we allowed the probabilities and our theories to lead the investigation instead of doing a proper study of the victim, we never would have found Baptista. Had we conducted a stern interrogation of the husband, for example, we would likely have alienated the victim, thereby not getting her to cooperate with the sketch artist. That would have cost us valuable time—time that Baptista would most likely have used to pack his things and move out of the area. We never would have apprehended him without first trying to find out what really happened. Worse yet, he probably would have victimized someone else had our team not conducted a proper investigation, starting with the study of the victim.

LEARN TO ASK YOURSELF
THE RIGHT QUESTIONS

He who asks the questions cannot avoid the answers.
—Cameroonian proverb

The next step to discovering the truth in any criminal investigation is, as the preceding proverb says, to ask the appropriate questions. With the prospect of cascading leads, there is a need to focus on the probable while eliminating the possible. Asking the right questions is the most effective way of utilizing scarce departmental resources. In a sense, we conduct a personality autopsy of the victim.

Asking questions is a good way for you to focus on the probable ways that predators could get to you. As we take you through the various predatory crimes, it is our hope that you will continue to note the probable ways in which, living how you are now, you could be open to victimization.

Of course, with victimology, the primary question should always be "Who is the victim?"

In Sara's case, we didn't start our investigation by gathering a list of probable suspects. That's great if you have only an hour on a TV show to solve a crime.

No, we started by trying to figure out who Sara was. We made it a point to get to know her social, economic, and marital status. We needed to know if she knew her attacker before their brutal encounter that morning.

Keep that in mind as you read the rest of this text. According to the FBI's *Crime Classification Manual*:

> Victimology is often one of the most beneficial investigative tools in classifying and solving a violent crime. It is a crucial part of crime analysis. Through it the investigator tries to evaluate why this particular person was targeted for a violent crime. Very often, just answering this question will lead the investigator to the motive, which will lead to the offender. Victimology is an essential step in arriving at a possible motive. If investigators fail to obtain complete victim histories, they may be overlooking information that could quickly direct their investigations to motives and to suspects.

Likewise, if you overlook aspects of your entire life, you, too, could be overlooking information that could be used to protect yourself and your loved ones.

A perfect example of the importance of victimology, as it relates to gathering crucial investigative information, is illustrated in the Chandra Levy case.

In 2001 the twenty-four-year-old Modesto, California, woman disappeared in Washington, DC, while working as an intern for Congressman Gary Condit. As the days passed, the investigation began to point toward Condit, who had admitted to having an affair with the victim. As a result, the public scrutiny on him was intense, to say the least, as was the pressure on authorities to resolve the case. Still, there was not enough evidence to try the congressman, or anybody else, for the young woman's murder or abduction.

Then, more than a year after her disappearance, Levy's badly decomposed body was discovered in Rock Creek Park near Washington, DC. Unfortunately, because so much time had elapsed, any evidence was difficult to come by.

Mike King and I appeared on Greta Van Susteren's show, *On the Record*, to discuss some of the investigative aspects of the highly publicized cold case. Because it had been more than a year since Levy's disappearance, Greta had a number of questions for us, most important of which was how to determine who killed Chandra Levy.

Greta asked us how it would be possible for investigators to build a case against anyone. Guess what we started with?

You got it. Victimology.

"Even though the case is cold, you have the opportunity to 'interview' the young woman from a forensic standpoint," Mike said. "From there, you can get an idea of the sophistication level of the offender and the offender's comfort level with the location of the crime scene."

Greta then made an observation that most people would make if they were on the outside looking in: "It's almost like looking for a needle in a haystack."

"It is," I told her. "Until you look at the victimology. Once you look at her behavior and what was going on in her life just prior to the crime, you can get a clearer picture of what might have happened. For example, we know she had packed up just before her disappearance, which suggests she was leaving. So, then, you can legitimately ask, if she was preparing to leave, why did she go to the park? What drew her there? Did she go to meet someone?"

Those are the questions that can lead your investigation if you take the time to study the victim first. Again, examine your life (your victimology, if you will) to see what crimes could be most easily committed against you. As you do this, it's important to understand that, from an investigative standpoint, the more violent, complex, bizarre, and/or perplexing the crime (as was the case with Chandra Levy's disappearance and subsequent death), the greater direction a victimology will provide. You must assess where each aspect of your life falls on the risk scale.

The following victim characteristics may serve as a guide to construct a comprehensive study of your life as it pertains to the potential for being victimized. As you look through this list, assess your situation and ask yourself how each characteristic could make it easier for a predator to get to you:

VICTIMOLOGY CHARACTERISTICS

Age/description

Sex

Race

Marital status

Religion

Scholastic achievement/academics

Lifestyle

Personality style

Demeanor

Employment/occupation

Social status

Friends/associates (type/number)

Income (level/source)

Domestic relations/environment

Alcohol/drug use/abuse

Dress style (typically/proximate to crime)

Handicaps (physical/mental)

Transportation

Dating status/sexual habits

Criminal history

Initial contact/abduction site between victim and offender

Residence in relation to crime scene

Employment in relation to crime scene

Victim's last known sighting and activities

Significant events before the crime

Crime scene

Sexual assault

Disposal site

Physical injuries

You can now attempt to answer the related questions of what, when, where, why, and how, reconstructing a virtual crime committed against you or a loved one.

Age, for example, is the first characteristic on the list. How does knowing a victim's age help us understand that person in relation to a crime? Well, if the victim is elderly, we can reasonably deduce, if we base our deduction on age alone, that he was probably a victim of opportunity. Most crimes against the elderly are predatory opportunities.

Incidentally, in chapter 5 on crimes against the elderly, we will introduce you to a man named Terry Donnelly, who is serving life in prison for brutally strangling five elderly women. You will get a clear picture of this man's thought process, as he agreed to talk to Mike and me for a criminal analysis project we worked on a few years ago.

You may have noticed that in Sara's case, after finding out more about her, the detectives' next step was to ascertain her potential relationship to the attacker. They knew that because she lived a low-risk lifestyle, the probability was high that either she knew the offender or he knew her, possibly through casual contact. As they later found out, the contact was very casual—he saw her sun bathing. Once they got to that point, the investigators narrowed the list of possible answers to other pertinent questions, one of the most critical being *why* she was victimized. This is crucial for any investigation because the answer leads to the criminal motivation.

Often, the offender will inadvertently reveal himself through behavior committed during a crime, an element of criminal profiling known as signature behavior. That's how we, as criminal profilers, know what we're dealing with.

You may have seen TV shows that discuss M.O., or method of operation. It's important to realize that there is a big difference between M.O. and signature. An M.O. can change, and often does, because predators get more proficient and organized with time. If a killer is messy in committing a murder, for example, we know he hasn't had much experience. If, however, he is well organized, then we know he has done it before. Baptista was very well organized and had done this before.

Signature, on the other hand, is that which gives the criminal a sense of psychological gratification from his crimes. It seldom changes. For example, later in the book we will take you through a case in which a notorious serial killer's signature was the excessive bondage and photographing of his victims, a facet of the case that eventually allowed authorities to catch this monster, who may be responsible for the murders of nearly fifty more victims.

This is why the signature diagnosis in any case assists the investigator during the initial stages of formulating a probable motive and reasonable suspects. It points to a predator's unique behavior. This aspect of the Risk Continuum is extremely important for you to understand because as you begin to comprehend the criminal mind, you will also begin to know what to look for in protecting yourself from these criminals.

To relate this point to analyzing your situation, you might ask yourself a number of questions (the same kinds detectives ask about the victim during the course of an investigation) that can help you see things a potential offender might do to assert control over you, based on your current circumstances, situation, or environment. These include:

- Why was I (the victim) selected by the offender?
- Why was the crime committed in this location?
- Why was the crime committed in this manner?
- Why did the offender approach the victim (me) in a particular manner?
- Why did the offender assault the victim (me) in this particular manner?
- Why did the offender use/choose a particular weapon?
- What was the precrime association/contact between the victim (me) and the offender?
- Was the victim (I) a victim of opportunity?
- Was the victim (I) specifically targeted?
- Did the victim (I) somehow contribute to his/her (my) victimization? If so, was it through ignorance, innocence, and naiveté, or was it through recklessness, negligence, and disregard?
- What was the degree of preplanning, premeditation, and forethought?

- Was this a crime of passion, impulse, and spontaneity?
- What was the level of criminal experience and sophistication?

As it related to Sara, asking these questions was critical in helping us solve her case. Because the detectives had already determined that she was healthy mentally and emotionally—she was happily married, exercised regularly, was involved in her community—they quickly ascertained that Sara had no prior relationship with the assailant. Therefore, they knew that, in order for him to attack her without fear of anyone intruding, he had to have staked out her house for at least a couple weeks. There was no other explanation for how he could have examined the couple's lifestyle so thoroughly. And, in order for him to maintain some kind of sustenance, there was no way he would have been able to stake the couple out unless he lived nearby. There was also little chance that he would have encountered Sara at all had he not lived nearby. The evidence obviously indicated that he knew who she was, but she certainly didn't know him.

From a risk-reduction perspective, the only precautions ever taught to this young couple were to lock their doors and windows. Indeed, they did everything they were taught to do.

But, again, so much more can be done, and while it requires little, if any, physical or monetary expense, it does require a good degree of thinking, planning, and awareness.

For example, no one told this family that it would be a good idea to alter their routine once in a while. The young father left for work at exactly the same time and in exactly the same manner every weekday. Now, that can't always be helped, but it doesn't hurt to turn around and make a pass by the house maybe once or twice a week. Because a predator typically relies on predictability, a random return trip or two would at the very least make him think twice about attacking.

Another valuable point is that Sara went running about the same time she always did, using the exact same route. As it turned out, Antonio Baptista had observed this family's routine for five or six weeks. And, as we mentioned, he encountered the family as he walked through the neighborhood one afternoon and saw Sara sun bathing through the back-yard fence. On another occasion, she was out in the yard with her daughter and had simply said hello and smiled at him as he passed by. Being the deviant person he was, he obviously interpreted those friendly gestures to mean a lot more than they were intended.

There is a lot to be learned from this family's situation. We need to change the way we approach our safety. Be proactive. In this case, Sara could have adjusted her running schedule from time to time. Maybe reinforcing the locks on the bedroom windows would have bought her a few precious seconds. Keeping a mobile or cell phone with her might have given her more time to get help and maybe even scared him into abandoning his plans.

With advances in technology, engineering, and especially thought process, we have updated our lives in every facet except for where our personal security is concerned.

Think about it. In all likelihood, your place of employment is equipped with a computer, but twenty years ago it wasn't. That computer probably has Internet access, something it most likely would not have had just twelve to fifteen years ago. And in terms of hiring competitively, your company probably offers some 401(k) plan due to the instability of Social Security. None of this was taking place twenty years ago.

Still, when you look at our approach to personal safety, it's so far behind.

For example, when you think of fire safety, do you think of Dick Van Dyke telling us to "Stop, drop, and roll"? When you think of preventing crime, do you think of McGruff the Crime Dog telling us to "take a bite out of crime"? When you think of preventing forest fires, do you think of Smokey the Bear? While they all send good messages, all those slogans were created at least twenty-five to thirty years ago! Yet here we are still using them, not just as rule of thumb, but as the hard-and-fast rules for safety. We're not keeping up in the area we need to most.

That is why we hope to help take you to the next level. Decreasing your risk is exactly the point of this book. We want to take a look at cases such as Sara's and empower you to take control of your personal safety, as well as the security of those you care about.

The next chapter is titled "There's Always a Story" because we want to impress upon you that there is always more than meets the eye, and it's not hard to train yourself to see beyond the obvious. Again, it doesn't require a whole lot of effort, just some simple lifestyle changes. In order to do that, however, you need to know a little about how various criminals think. It's important to know what motivates them, what they look for, and, ultimately, what will most likely scare them off. That is why we will take you through the most common—and vicious—predatory crimes and into the heads of those who commit them.

The vast majority of predatory crime consists of crimes against children, sexual assault, domestic violence, kidnapping, crimes against the elderly, homicide, and terrorism.

Yes, there is great security technology out there, but I fear that most people, because they can't afford it, give up on their safety and fall back to the status quo instead of using the most effective security tool they have—their minds.

To me, that's sad because the one resource that costs nothing to use and can be more effective than any security device is the human mind. In my ten years as a criminal profiler in the FBI, I spent a lot of time tracking serial offenders of all kinds—killers, arsonists, kidnappers, rapists, and so on. In so doing, I learned a lot about the criminal mind and how to counter it. Mike King has more than twenty years in law enforcement and is extremely proficient in the art of criminal profiling. He will tell you the same thing.

From this experience, we have learned, above all, that criminals are simply predators looking to find a weakness they can expose in their prey. They are creatures of opportunity who can exist only if the opportunities present themselves.

Well, guess who largely controls whether they get these opportunities? That's right—you.

Throughout the rest of this book, we will talk about how you can minimize your risks by cutting off access to yourself and your loved ones and by eliminating, or at least limiting, the opportunities these would-be offenders have to victimize you.

Remember, there are important questions you need to ask as if they had already happened:

- Why did an offender select me as a victim?
- Why was the crime committed in my house?
- Why was the crime committed in this manner?
- Why did the offender approach me in a particular manner?
- Why did the offender assault me in this particular manner?
- Why did the offender inflict these particular wounds on me?
- Why did the offender use/choose a particular weapon?

We know these are uncomfortable questions to ask, but again, it is much more comfortable to ask them hypothetically than it is to have to ask them after something has really happened.

2

THERE'S ALWAYS A STORY

We walked out of the cozy old house in the country and into another gray Washington day. As we approached our car, my mind kept playing through different scenarios. How was the baby taken? Who took him and for what purpose?

A raspy voice suddenly interrupted my thoughts.

"There's a story here, Cooper," said Dean Stager, a senior FBI agent who had just been assigned to serve with me in the Washington State area.

"Huh?" I said, wondering what he meant.

"There's a story here," he repeated. "Something doesn't add up about that girl or what she's saying. I can't quite put my finger on it, but I don't think she's telling us the whole truth. She's holding something back."

"I've got that feeling, too," I agreed. "What do you think it could be?"

"I don't know," he said. "But I've been in this business a long time, and if there's one thing I've learned, it's that no matter how things seem, there's always a story—always."

On that day, we had just talked to a fifteen-year-old girl in a rural area of Washington State. Her baby, a five-month-old boy, had been missing for over a week, and a frantic search had ensued. She'd been on every TV news station in the state, pleading with the kidnapper to bring her baby back. As you can imagine, the community was in an uproar and had come together to search for the child.

I had been an agent in the bureau for ten months, and during that time, I was assigned to cover four counties and five Indian reservations in the area. The local sheriff's office had been trying to solve this case for several days when they asked me to assist.

I knew Dean was transferring to the area soon and that he was coming to set up his new office. When he arrived, I had asked him to help with the investigation. He was a large man, a burly six-foot-four, and his hair—including his mustache—was peppered. The thing I liked most about Dean was his confidence in his investigative abilities, and he had good reason. Experience is one of the best teachers for an FBI agent, and after eighteen years with the FBI, Dean had seemingly learned it all. And if he hadn't, he did not have many lessons left to learn.

When I met with the young lady, her future father-in-law and mother-in-law, as well as their teenage son, were all present. The first words out of my mouth were, "We're going to get to the bottom of this, and we're going to find your child, but I need your help."

As I talked to the young lady, I discovered that the baby's father was in the navy and at sea when the baby went missing. He had been gone for some time, and his family had taken his fiancée in to help with the baby. As we spoke, I decided the best approach would be to go over her daily morning routine to see if anything was out of the ordinary that day.

"Take me through your routine," I said. "What do you do to get ready each morning?"

"I usually start by changing the baby and feeding him," she began. "Then, while I get ready for school, my fiancé's parents watch him so I can get dressed and stuff."

She took me through the rest of the routine then explained what had happened the morning the baby disappeared. Right away, I noticed one important difference. Instead of waking the parents, she woke up the teenage boy and asked him to look after the child.

As I questioned him, he hadn't remembered being woken up by the young lady.

"I honestly don't remember," he pleaded. "She must have woken me up, and then I fell back asleep. I feel so bad, like it's my fault. If I just hadn't gone back to sleep, none of this ever would have happened."

According to the time line, the child was taken between the time he was fed and the time his mother finished getting ready for school. The teenager felt like he was asleep when he should have been watching the baby. That was a heavy burden for anyone, much less a boy his age, to carry.

I asked the young lady to show me her bedroom, the place from where the child was taken. In the room were her bed, the baby's crib, and a chest of drawers. There was a window with a large bush in front of it.

As we spoke, she suddenly did something I thought was extremely unusual for the situation. She lay back on her bed and stretched her arms above her head, revealing her midriff to me. I realized that fifteen-year-olds tend to be somewhat flirtatious, but this was an odd time to be flirting, especially with the agent who is trying to help you find your child.

When I left the house that evening, I thought about why she would do that.

After talking to the family, Dean and I knew something wasn't right. We thought it would be a good idea to bring the girl to the local sheriff's substation for questioning, get her out of the house.

"She had to have something to do with this, Cooper," Dean said. "Not a lot of people would have the guts to come in and snatch a baby in broad daylight, especially in the middle of an isolated rural area like that."

"I agree," I said. "Let's see what we can get from her at the station."

When we sat her down at the office, Dean quickly reprised the role of bad cop in our good cop–bad cop interrogation strategy. Because I had built a good rapport with the girl and her family, I got to be the good cop.

"Listen, young lady," Dean said gruffly. "You'd better start talking to us."

"What do you mean?" she asked, taken aback.

"You know exactly what I mean," he shot back.

"No, I don't. Are you saying I had something to do with my baby being taken? How dare you."

"I'm saying that you had *something* to do with this, and you'd better tell us what happened."

Just as the young lady was at her wit's end, I intervened and applied a strategy I had learned from a book about Ted Bundy, who spoke of his crimes in hypotheticals.

"Look, why don't we calm down and take a breath for a second," I suggested. "We're just trying to find out what happened. Remember that I told you we were going to get to the bottom of this?"

"Yes."

"OK then. But, remember, I told you we would need your help, OK?"

"OK. What can I do?"

"Well, why don't we talk about some hypothetical scenarios that could have occurred in a situation like this? We're not talking about you right now but a case just like this. Do you understand?"

"Yeah, I think so."

"OK, good. Then, what are some ways that a baby in a house in a rural area could end up missing in a matter of just a few minutes?"

She began by throwing out a couple kidnapping-related scenarios, then she said something that caught Dean's attention and mine.

"Or the baby could have died accidentally."

Dean and I paused for a moment, then I asked her, "That's what happened to your baby, isn't it?"

At first, she didn't say anything, then Dean, sensing she was close to talking, got up and said, "Since Cooper is your friend, I'm going to step outside and let you two talk."

I leaned over, put my hand on her shoulder, and said, "You'll feel better if you get this out."

Over the next half hour, she laid out the whole shocking story.

"I woke up at about four in the morning," she started. "He messed his diaper really bad, and I went to bathe him in the sink, over in the kitchen. I rinsed him off a little bit, then I put him in the little baby tub and started to fill it up. The water runs so slow, and I had such a headache. I was so tired."

At that, she began to choke up but then regained her composure.

"I didn't mean to fall asleep. I just needed to lie down for a minute. I didn't mean to leave him there. Usually, if I lie down for just a minute or two, my headache goes away. But I never fall asleep. Never! I can't believe I fell asleep."

As she began to cry, I reached over and handed her a handkerchief. "Take your time."

She took a deep breath and, after a moment, continued.

"When I found him, he wasn't breathing. I tried to get him to start, but he just wouldn't. He was so blue. I've heard of people turning blue, but I've never seen it. I was so scared. I didn't know what to do. Then, I heard my fiancé's mom in the back bedroom. She was getting up to go to the bathroom or something. All I could think of was I didn't want her to see the baby that way. So I wrapped him in his little blanket, put him in a bag, and took him outside."

"Where is he now?"

"He's still in the back, over in the bushes behind the house."

Tears began to stream down her cheeks. It was clear that the torture of the past few days had taken its toll.

"Why did you take him outside?"

"I don't know," she said. "I just panicked. I guess I didn't want anybody to think I hurt my baby. But I did. I did hurt him. I just let him lie there in the water and drown to death. My own little baby—I just let him suffer. How could I have done this? How could this be happening?"

"Things like this just do sometimes," I said, trying to comfort her.

With each word she spoke, my heart ached for this girl. She had her whole life in front of her, and in five minutes, everything spun out of control and collapsed right from underneath her. She stacked one bad decision on top of another, and now, at fifteen, instead of chasing boys and going to high school, she was locked in the worst kind of prison imaginable, incarcerated in a lifetime of regret and sorrow.

We called a team to search the yard, and, sure enough, the baby's body was found right where she said it was—in the bush outside her bedroom window. No one had thought to conduct a search for a body on the property because everyone was busy looking for a kidnapper.

That's the lesson I pulled from this experience, as well as others I had over the time I worked with Dean: There's always a story.

No matter how obvious something seems or how much we might think we know, there is almost always something lurking behind the scenes. And sometimes, it jumps right out and bites us when we least expect it. That's why I wanted to write this book. I've spent twenty-five years talking to victims of some of the most heartbreaking crimes imaginable, and it seems 90 percent of them tell me they never saw it coming. I don't want that to happen anymore. I want people to be able to recognize at least some of the more common dangerous situations so they can be empowered to avoid them.

The old adage "Expect the unexpected" is probably the best defense against the predators of today. Now, was this girl a predator? Of course she wasn't, at least not in the sense that she intended to harm anybody. But by virtue of the circumstances surrounding this case, something very important was taken from the people of that community. Innocence was replaced by skepticism. When word of the missing baby first spread, people came together in a way you don't see very often. They organized searches in an effort to find the child, much the same way the people of Salt Lake City did for Elizabeth Smart. Ordinary people were taking shifts around the clock to look for the baby boy. Not one minute went by in which someone wasn't looking for the lost child. Volunteers across the state and in neighboring states were posting pictures of the baby along city streets. Media outlets were leading with daily updates to find a child who, as it turned out, was not missing at all but rather the victim of a tragic accident.

Unfortunately, situations such as this are why police start any kidnapping investigation by questioning family members. Whenever a kidnapping is reported, believe me, no officer likes to put anyone who has legitimately lost a child through this line of questioning, but it has now become a necessary evil. I guess you can say that in this instance, the community became a victim of a predator called deception, which caused some of its members to lose their trust. More than likely, the next time a child is truly abducted in this community, some will remember what happened the last time and won't make the same efforts. What a shame.

On the other hand, there is a positive lesson we can learn—expect the unexpected in a resourceful manner, in a way that will help us reduce our risks.

Remember that, in order to follow the predator's thought processes, you have to keep in mind that there is always a story behind the offender, his victim, and the circumstances that brought them together.

Take, for example, the tragic experiences of two young women and their families who were victimized several years ago by the same man in a Southern community.

Donna Hansen and Denise James, two mildly learning-disabled women in their early twenties, were enjoying the social side of young adulthood. Each had a hard time in high school, and each had been befriended by some ladies at their respective places of work and would regularly go out on the weekend to a local club.

At first, Donna's parents showed concern about her newfound social life, but seeing a bounce in their daughter's step offset any worries they had.

"I'll be back at eleven," the young lady told her parents as she walked out the door one night.

"OK, sweetheart," said her mother. "Have a nice time."

"It's good to see her happy, isn't it?" her father said.

"It sure is a far cry from high school," she replied. "The girls there could be so mean to her. I'm so grateful for those people she works with. They've really taken her under their wing and included her."

At the club, Donna and her co-workers were having a great time.

"You're quite a dancer, Donna," said one of her friends as they headed back to their table. "Where did you learn moves like that?"

"I don't know," the embarrassed young lady said. "My dad used to dance with me in our living room."

"Well, your daddy must have been a good teacher because I'm not the only one who noticed your moves. Look over there. I think that guy is checking you out."

"No, he's looking at you," Donna said coyly.

"I don't think so. In fact, don't look now, but I think he's making his way over here as we speak."

"Hello," said the young man to Donna. "Mind if I buy you a drink?"

"Uh, yeah, I guess. Sure."

"What's your name?"

"D-Donna," she stuttered, taken aback. "But my friends call me Dawn."

"Ask him his name," Donna's friend whispered in her ear.

"Oh, yeah," she said, giggling. "What's your name?"

"Carl," he said. "I'll tell you what. Why don't we grab a dance or two first, then we'll get that drink. What do you say?"

"Sure," she said, and off they went to the dance floor. The surprised young lady looked back at her co-workers, who were waving at her to have a good time with the young man.

"So what do you do?" he asked her as they danced.

"I'm a receptionist for a real estate agency," she answered. "How about you?"

"Oh, I'm in business for myself," he said. "I do mostly consulting work for general contractors."

As the night wore on, Donna's friends could tell she was enjoying herself, but it was time to go.

"Should we grab Dawn and give her a ride home?" one co-worker asked.

"I don't know if she wants to be grabbed," giggled another. "At least not by us."

At that, the group of young ladies howled with laughter.

"Well, let's at least let her know we're going."

"OK, I'll go tell her."

"Hey, Dawn," the young lady interrupted as the couple danced. "We're going now. Do you want to come, or will you be OK?"

"I'll give her a lift home," said Carl as Donna nodded in approval.

"OK. Have a good time. We'll see you Monday at work."

With that, the group, minus Donna, headed home. The young lady, meanwhile, was having the most romantic night of her life. Finally, a relatively good-looking young man had taken an interest in her. Not only that, he had singled her out from among dozens of other women at the club. She couldn't believe it. Here she was dancing with someone who thought *she* was pretty. After all those cruel years during adolescence when she didn't have a prayer in the world of getting this kind of attention, now someone found her attractive and beautiful and special. And it wasn't just anyone. It was a handsome man with an irresistible smile. At that moment, she felt like she was living a fairy tale.

Unfortunately, her dream night would quickly turn into an unimaginable nightmare.

"Hey," Carl yelled to Donna over the loud music. "Why don't we get out of here and go someplace where we can be alone and talk?"

"OK," she hollered back.

Soon, they were in his truck, driving down the moonlit highway.

Donna was on cloud nine. Had she finally broken out of her shell? Would this be the man she would marry? She couldn't wait to tell her mom and dad about her fairy-tale night.

All of a sudden, Carl abruptly pulled onto a dirt road and parked the truck behind a row of tall bushes. In an instant, the young man's friendly smile disappeared, replaced by a monstrous look.

"Get out of the truck," he demanded. "We're going for a walk."

"Huh?" she said. "Why? What's wrong?"

"I said, get out!" he shouted as he reached across her lap, opened the door, and shoved her out.

She tried to get up and run, but he rushed around and grabbed her.

"Where the hell do you think you're going?" he barked.

"Ouch! Stop, you're hurting me."

"Oh, am I hurting you?" he queried sarcastically. "Then how does this feel?"

With that, he shattered her nose with a single punch to the face.

"Did that hurt, too?" he mocked.

All Donna could do was sob, and the more she sobbed, the more he hit and tore at her.

"What are you crying about?" he continued. "Oh, I know. I must not be the prince charming you were hoping for. Is that it? I thought you wanted a good time. Well, let me show you what a good time is."

He ripped her skirt clean off her body. Then, he tore her panties, blouse, and bra off, taking chunks of skin with them. Then, he beat her some more.

"Why are you doing this to me?" she cried.

"Why?" he screamed at her. "Because you're disgusting, that's why!"

Then he kicked her repeatedly between the legs. All Donna could do was tremble and try to control the sobbing that seemed to draw more of his ire. At this point, she could only hope to get out of this alive.

"Why is this happening to me?" she thought. "Why is he being so mean? I didn't do anything to him. I should have gone home with my friends."

"Please don't hurt me anymore," she mumbled to her attacker.

"Don't hurt you?" he mocked. "Don't hurt you? You should be thanking me. You're finally gonna get laid."

He knelt on top of the terrified girl then wrapped his hands around her throat before repeatedly banging her head against the ground until he had strangled the life out of her.

Then he raped her and savagely beat her some more.

He repeated his crime three months later, following nearly the same M.O. with a young lady named Denise James. The crime occurred just a few miles from where he had dumped Donna's body. It was sickeningly uncanny how similar the circumstances between the two murders and victims were. With the instinctive skill of a wild predator, he had sniffed out two young women he knew would make easy prey. In just minutes, he had identified victims he knew he could lure into his hands and have his sickly way with.

But it wasn't long before the authorities caught up to Carl Steven Moseley.

Witnesses who saw him with Donna and with Denise were able to place him at the club during the nights in question, while others had seen him drive away with each girl. Combined with physical evidence collected at the respective locations, prosecutors had Moseley nailed for each murder. Or did they?

Even though the homicides took place so close to one another, they were committed in separate counties, and in a prosecutor's world, jurisdiction is everything. That meant that prosecutors would have to find a way to connect the homicides in order to try him as a serial killer instead of trying the cases individually.

Without the ability to link Donna's case to Denise's, the evidence that the state could present against Moseley would be much weaker. That could mean reduced sentences, and no one wanted to see this guy walk—ever.

That's where I came in.

As an FBI profiler with the Investigative Support Unit, my testimony was used to tie the two crimes together. And even though that in and of itself was significant from a legal perspective, it was the fact that I would be able to confront this cowardly monster in open court that gave me the most satisfaction. And when the day came, believe me, I was ready.

In a packed courthouse, I took the oath, sat down in the witness chair, and immediately made it a point to make eye contact with Moseley. I locked in on him and refused to let him look at anything other than my face.

"Mr. Cooper," began Eric Saunders, the deputy district attorney, in a pronounced North Carolina drawl. "By whom are you employed?"

"The Federal Bureau of Investigation," I stated.

"In what capacity, sir?"

"I am a criminal investigative analyst assigned to the National Center for the Analysis of Violent Crime at Quantico, Virginia, at the FBI Academy," I answered.

"And as an agent in the Investigative Support Unit, can you tell the court what some of your duties are there?"

"We provide consultation services for any legitimate law enforcement agency internationally. Specifically with regard to repetitive violent crimes, we provide any type of services from investigative techniques, prosecution strategy, interrogation techniques, and the analysis of the crime to identify particular personality characteristics of an unknown offender."

"What does that entail?"

"When we analyze a crime, we request the specific information on a crime to assist us in re-creating the crime so that we can vicariously experience being both the victim and the offender," I explained. "The procedure involves the basic following process: We will request initial police reports of the crimes and investigative reports, including the crime-scene photographs, the autopsy photographs, and forensic medical examiner's reports. In addition, we'll request, at times, maps to identify the locations of the crime scene, the abduction, or the initial contact site, as well as the disposal site."

"And what are you hoping to determine from that analysis?"

"What we attempt to determine," I responded, squarely fixing my gaze on Moseley in an attempt to gauge his response, "are specific behavioral characteristics that we see at a crime scene to assist us in translating the personality characteristics of an unknown offender. It's one of the services we provide."

As I continued speaking, I could see that Moseley was growing a little uneasy, but he still had an air of smugness about him. I was determined to suck that right out of him.

"In addition to that," I continued, "we attempt to identify common characteristics between crimes to assist agencies in identifying whether or not there may be a serial offender in the community, identifying unique characteristics of a crime scene to determine whether or not they suggest that the same person may have committed those crimes."

Over the next several minutes, Saunders asked me about the criminal-profiling procedure. I could tell that Moseley was interested, but he didn't seem overly concerned about my testimony, at least not until Saunders began asking me about the victims.

"Did you study the victimology of Donna Hansen and Denise James?"

"Yes, I did," I answered.

"Would you tell the court what you found?"

"Sure," I replied. "Both the victims were very small in stature. Both also possessed birth defects affecting their speech patterns, and both received medical treatment previously in their lifetime for that particular condition. They also were both living at home in a somewhat dependent relationship with their parents."

As I continued talking about the lives of these young ladies, I could almost see a smirk running across Moseley's face. He obviously had little remorse for what he had done, and I was ready to wipe that underlying smirk off his face. But I knew I had a job to do, and I couldn't let myself get caught up in emotion if I was going to give an effective testimony, so I simply continued with my answer in a matter-of-fact fashion. Besides, I knew that the best way to rattle him was to expose his innermost personality in open court—and that is exactly what I intended to do.

"Both had no steady serious relationships in terms of a boyfriend," I continued. "Both attended the nightclub unattached, and both were considered friendly and trusting and unsuspecting. As an example, James, as I recall, was asking strangers for a ride home the evening of her disappearance. In addition, Hansen was dancing with people whom she was not known to have known before that evening."

"And what did that tell you about the victimology between the two girls?" Saunders asked.

"From the perspective of the offender, looking for a particular victim to commit this type of violent crime," I answered, now glaring at Moseley, "he's looking for somebody he can easily dominate, control, and manipulate—somebody who is high risk, as far as he's concerned, when they cross his path."

As I talked about the victims, I added commentary about the offender. I spoke of what kind of a small man would do something like this to two friendly, innocent girls. I could see beads of sweat forming on Moseley's forehead. His jaw began to lock, and his nostrils flared. I was beginning to get to him. He was taking my comments personally, which told me that he was definitely the perpetrator. Why else would he take testimony about a general criminal profile so personally?

"The offender in a case like this is typically referred to as a predator," I said, still staring straight into Moseley's eyes. Now I was the one with the invisible smirk.

"Predator?" Saunders asked. "Why a predator?"

At this point, I paused for effect. I wanted to make sure Moseley hung on my every word as I dissected him psychologically. Nothing drives a serial killer crazier than being told exactly what he was thinking as he planned and carried out his crimes. Serial killers are notorious for their arrogance in that regard.

"Because he's out stalking, looking for somebody, for a victim that fits his particular profile. He wants someone who will reduce his risk of identification yet enhance the exposure to his crimes. Basically, he wants to make news, but he doesn't want to get caught."

As I was speaking, I noticed Moseley becoming increasingly uncomfortable in his chair. I knew it was time to turn up the heat, and my goal was to shatter his self-image, to utterly destroy the world he had created for himself.

And Saunders's next question opened the door for me to do just that.

"In addition to identifying the person the offender is looking for, how does the victimology affect the individual victim?"

"From our perspective, the victim is trusting, unsuspecting. There is no reason for her to believe she is exposing herself to any particular kind of risk," I said before pecking away at Moseley's self-image.

"Typically, the offender in these types of cases will use what is referred to as the 'con approach,' meaning he will appear to be very innocent. He will use the ruse that he wants to help the victim, which helps him manipulate her into his own environment where he can control her."

As I dissected Moseley's cowardly strategy, I could see that I was destroying his self-image. In his mind, he was an ingenious giant. In the dark fields of North Carolina, he could dominate two helpless young ladies. But in open court? He didn't stand a chance. He could only sit and listen as I laid out—and professionally belittled—what he thought was a clever plan. In court, he had power only to sit—sit and listen to the truth, which was simply that he was nothing more than a cowardly bully. With each piece of testimony I gave, his self-image was imploding for all to see—and it was eating him up inside.

I concluded my testimony by hammering the final nail in his coffin.

I attempted to portray how a predatory criminal garners all his self-esteem from thinking he can destroy lives and terrify a community, while never being held accountable for it, and how he views himself as a puppet master—an unknown entity who controls an entire community at the push of a button. But in reality, I testified, he is just a small man who has accomplished nothing of consequence in life and therefore has to resort to taking the lives of innocent people. And most often, he is so inept that the only people he can prey upon are those who are among the weakest in the community—in this case, two small, learning-disabled young women who could scarcely defend themselves.

By the time I concluded my testimony, Moseley was red-faced, and beads of sweat poured down his brow. He wanted so badly to hop over the table and come after me. Of course, he never would have. Even if there had been no armed guards in the courtroom, he wouldn't have. He didn't have enough depth of character to ever attack someone out in the open, face-to-face. That's why he committed the assaults in such a cowardly way.

In fact, my testimony shook him so much that the guards who ushered him to and from court told me that when he saw me several months later at his trial for the second homicide, he said, "That's the S.O.B. who's gonna try and get me for this one, too!"

Another thing I noticed while in the courtroom was the families of the two young ladies. I think about them every so often and wonder what could have been done to prevent this horror. Again, it goes back to being prepared for certain situations and recognizing that things aren't always what they seem. Perhaps these young ladies could have been taught to be more cautious. Instead of being willing to accept rides from strangers, they should always have gone with friends or family. And they never should have agreed to go alone with him.

But maybe it's not so obvious that the two young ladies should have gotten Moseley's phone number instead of freely giving away information about themselves. This way, they would have been in control of any second meetings that took place, possibly as a group, where he wouldn't have them isolated. By having that control, they would have been empowered to tackle any attacks this young man had planned. I know they were having the time of their lives, but even a simple phone number would have allowed them to make further contact with the young man while still keeping a safe distance. At that point, maybe they could go out with a group of friends or have him over for dinner with Mom and Dad. Friends or family members may have been able to detect something strange about him and help the young ladies take steps to terminate any further contact with him. Again, this is no indictment of these young ladies' friends and families. Really, how were they to know? While this information has been out there, it has been overshadowed by TV shows and movies that romanticize chance meetings and encourage people to just jump in. It's OK to have a romantic life. You just need to realize that it's not OK to hand your well-being over to someone you just met at a club.

Again, we don't want to make anyone other than the man who committed these murders to feel responsible for these young ladies' deaths. We simply bring up these points to prevent this from happening to someone who might face a similar situation.

This is where knowing the mind of a criminal can help you.

Look at your home, your circle of acquaintances, your place of employment, your daily routine, and other life circumstances. Then, analyze your situation as if you were going to commit a crime against yourself. Ask yourself, "What are my points of vulnerability? What kind of crime would be easiest to commit against myself? Of all my weaknesses, which is the one I would take advantage of first?"

Keep those questions in mind as we explore the mind of a man who raped seventy-five women in eleven states throughout the western United States.

Brad Morrison, who is currently serving fifty years to life in prison for those rapes, never beat his victims. He never tied them up or hand-cuffed them. He never even threatened them with a weapon. So how was he able to do this once, let alone seventy-five times? You may be saying to yourself, "If it was me, I would have kicked him or punched him. There is no way I would have gone down without a fight."

While that may be true, keep in mind that Morrison planned his crimes before even stepping one foot into his victims' homes. In almost every case, he hadn't even seen his victims before he knew he would be successful. So how did he do it?

The best way to explain it is to describe a little about Brad's history.

Mike King was an investigator with the Weber County Attorney's Office in Utah when Brad was taken into custody. Mike and I got to know Brad more intimately during the course of a criminal behavioral analysis study. We wanted to study as many different offenders as possible to help law enforcement better understand how they think. Of course, understanding the thought process of a predatory criminal is key to understanding how to catch one. During the course of this project, we were very intrigued with Brad because he seemed to have a unique perspective.

He started his criminal career for the same reason the vast majority of criminals do. He needed to support a drug habit, and he did so by burglarizing homes for six or seven years. Like most burglars, he became more efficient with experience, never stealing anything that he couldn't quickly use to support his habit. In fact, all he looked for during a burglary were pharmaceuticals and cash. He didn't target jewelry or other valuables because it would take too much effort to turn those items into the cash to buy drugs.

But, like most burglars, he began to get bored. Over time, he wasn't getting the same adrenaline rush he used to, and he began to look for something more. Interestingly, Morrison recalled that he was sexually aroused by the process of staking out a business or residence and then sneaking inside, ultimately stealing property and personal items. As his crimes intensified, he began finding sexual excitement and gratification in being in homes while people were sleeping.

One night, while in a woman's apartment, he had just finished taking what he needed when he noticed the woman sleeping on the couch. She had obviously fallen asleep while watching TV and was wearing only her panties.

"I kept looking at her," Brad told Mike and me during one of our interviews. "I just couldn't help but stare at her. I would say she was probably in her early twenties, and she was gorgeous. She had a great body. But I'll tell you what. I should have just taken what I came for and gotten out of there. If I wouldn't have kept staring at her and would have just gotten out of there, I wouldn't be sitting here [in prison] talking to you guys today."

But he did keep looking, and eventually, the temptation was too much for him.

He set his stuff down, kneeled over her, and put his hand over her mouth, startling her awake.

"If you do what I say, you won't get hurt," he told the woman. "Do you understand?"

The woman nodded.

"Now, if I take my hand off your mouth, you promise you won't scream?"

The woman nodded again.

"You're sure? Because, if you do, you won't like the consequences."

The woman nodded again, this time with more assurance.

"OK," he said. "You do exactly what I say, and I won't hurt you."

He took his hand off her mouth, removed her underwear, pulled down his pants, and raped her. Afterward, he warned her not to move, then he left the house on foot. Several minutes later, the woman called the police, but because Brad was on foot and had staked out the territory, he got to his car without any problem. He was right in figuring that the police wouldn't expect an intruder to park so far away from the crime. But thanks to law enforcement studies like this one, they do now.

From 1984 to 1988, Brad became one of the most notorious rapists in the Mountain West. The news coverage was intense, warning people to secure their homes and keep an eye out for anyone suspicious. Again, that was good advice, except for one problem: Brad didn't look suspicious. In fact, he looked so unsuspicious that on one occasion, the police actually let him help them search for the rapist. He was helping *them* search for *him*.

Just a few minutes after he had raped one victim, several officers descended on the crime scene and began searching for him. As usual, Brad had committed his crime in the wee hours of the morning and was on foot, but the police arrived quickly enough that they actually had him surrounded and were going house to house and yard to yard with searchlights.

"I thought for sure they had me," Brad told us. "They were actually within one house of finding me. But I got lucky and was able to duck into a garage."

As he was hiding and wondering what to do next, he got an idea.

"I just thought, 'I'll just pretend to fit in,'" he explained. "What did I have to lose?"

So he undressed down to his T-shirt and boxers, messed up his hair to give the appearance that he had just been woken up, then exited the side door and approached the police.

"Hey, what's going on here?" he called to one of the officers. "We're trying to get some sleep, and I've got to go to work tomorrow."

"We're looking for the Ogden rapist," the officer answered.

"Oh," Brad replied. "Hey, do you want me to help you look through my yard? I know exactly where he'll be hiding in if he's here."

"Sure," the officer said. "Let me get someone over here to assist me."

With that, Brad took the officers through a complete stranger's yard, as if it were his own, looking for the rapist. Because he looked clean-cut, no one even questioned it. When the search of the man's yard failed to produce any results, the officers thanked Brad and ordered him to go back into "his" house, upon which he reentered through the side garage door.

"I hid behind some stuff in the garage until about ten or eleven that morning," Brad recounted. "I even watched the guy who lived there get into his car and drive to work. When I finally left the house, I saw a police car still patrolling the neighborhood, but I just made the walk to my car as if I belonged there. No one ever even questioned me."

The lesson here is that, if trained professionals can be fooled, so can you. And the authorities had no idea who they were dealing with because he looked like an ordinary guy, unassuming and unsuspicious. On top of it, he had a pleasant way about him. He came across as a gentle, soft-spoken person, and in reality, that is his basic personality. That's why he didn't use any other forms of violence during the course of the rapes. He was just after the sex.

We will be discussing Brad Morrison more when we get into the sex crimes portion of the book. But, for now, suffice it to say that his experience is a great example of why you need to change your way of thinking in regard to what is suspicious or dangerous and what is not.

That is why putting up your guard against people who "look suspicious" isn't enough. Ted Bundy certainly didn't look suspicious. David Koresh, who we profiled when I was with the FBI and one whom we will go into later in this book, was extremely charismatic, well liked, and well spoken. Too often, people base their safety on a whim instead of on principles or training. We say, "Don't talk to strangers," but what we really practice is the philosophy "Don't talk to strangers who look or act weird."

That's not enough. Most predatory criminals don't look weird or act strangely at all. They are opportunistic and make "fitting in" a crucial part of their criminal strategy.

In that regard, they are much like the predators of the wild. Crocodiles, for instance, will lie in wait for an entire day, calmly waiting for their prey to drink from the swamp. They have to. They are much too slow to have any hope of catching their prey on foot, so they become expert in blending in with the vegetation and muck that line the swamp's shoreline. Before taking a drink, unsuspecting animals try to keep themselves safe by searching the shore, looking for any sign of danger. When they deem it safe, they approach the water, and snap! Before they even know what's happening, they find themselves in the fatal jaws of the crocodile.

Sound familiar?

All predatory criminals use the same strategy in some form or another. If they don't want to be seen or caught (and, believe me, they don't), then they must invoke a strategy that will allow them to go undetected. Hence, the vast majority of predatory criminals are opportunists. They want to achieve whatever satisfaction they are looking for with the least resistance possible, so they become experts at analyzing people and situations. They are simply looking for the easiest opportunity to satisfy their desires.

Over time, Brad also became very effective at casing his targets, often parking at least a couple miles away from the neighborhoods he would eventually prey upon. This way, no vehicle could be tied to the crimes he committed. Once he arrived in his chosen neighborhood, he would begin to look for signs of easy prey. Of course, someone who didn't lock her doors or windows was the easiest, but beyond that, he looked for other, more subtle signs. (This is where you need to examine your situation.) He searched for people who would be least likely to put up a fight should they wake up during a burglary or rape. He also looked for people who were most likely to have what he was looking for, namely, cash and pharmaceuticals.

And you know what? He found them. Single women, who were recently divorced or separated and had children, were his ideal targets.

"They were depressed, so they usually had medication for their depression," he told Mike and me during one interview. "And because they were depressed, they were too worn out to put up much of a fight. And whatever fight they did have in them, I could quickly end by holding their kids' safety over their heads. You would be surprised what a woman is willing to do to keep her kids safe."

That last statement is chilling, to be sure.

Of course, not every woman he raped had children, in which case he would threaten their personal safety. Remember, he had already targeted them, so he knew that in all likelihood, they would be too emotionally drained to fight.

Which brings us to a point that we mentioned before. We know that there are many of you who are saying, "If anyone broke into my place and tried to rape me, he would be in for it. I'd fight him like he'd never been fought before."

We will go into this in more detail when we discuss sexual assault, but keep in mind that all of us—and we mean all of us—go through periods when we are more confident and at our strongest. But we also go through times when we are more down and at our weakest. If you happen to be in a good place in your life right now, that is great. We are truly happy for you. But please do not make the mistake of thinking that you won't hit a low point when you won't have it in you to fight. Those down periods are when we are most vulnerable, and predators know how to sniff that out. So if you are at your most confident, now is the time to prepare and make the changes that we have discussed. When you do hit a bump on the road of life, you will still be able to prevent, or at least reduce the likelihood of, becoming the victim of a predatory criminal.

I guarantee you that most, if not all, of Brad's victims had times in their lives when he would not have targeted them—and not just when they were in a healthy relationship and had a man around the house, so to speak. There were probably times when they felt confident and ready to take on anything, including a would-be rapist.

But that's not when he attacked them.

No, he assaulted his victims when they were down, when they were at their lowest points. And the scary part is that he could tell they were in that frame of mind just by looking at their homes.

"Usually, I could tell just by looking at either their car or at the way they kept their yard or their house," he told us. "Like, if things were cluttered, or the grass hadn't been mowed for a long time, and you could tell that there was no man living in the house, I knew they were either too depressed or too run-down to put up much of a fight. If they were too tired and didn't have the energy to clean up, then they weren't going to have it in them to fight me off."

But if you happen to be at a low point in your life, there is hope. Remember, most predatory criminals are opportunists, so if you don't provide the opportunity, they won't even try to commit the crime. And it's not that hard to at least present the appearance that your residence is not safe for them to attack.

For example, if you are a single woman living in an apartment, put a dusty old pair of construction boots out front. Or get a dog—even a small one makes enough noise to inconvenience the opportunistic predator. Or put something masculine, like a rusty old tool set, in your car so that it can easily be seen. Again, predators want the easiest possible opportunity. A fight makes things too difficult for the predatory criminal.

"Anything that would draw attention to me is not what I wanted to see," Brad said. "If there was going to be any kind of commotion, then forget it. I would pass right on by and look for the next house."

Of course, not every offender is like Brad. Some people will stop at nothing to get what they want. But we use Brad as the primary example for this section because he represents the vast majority of criminals. Even the violent ones, as you will see later, look for an opportunity that will require the least effort and provide the least likelihood of getting caught. In other words, if you analyze your life and see where you can take away the easy opportunity, you have just reduced your risk of victimization by more than 50 percent. If you were a business owner and found that you could cut your costs by such a margin, then that would be a very significant savings. Shouldn't the same hold true for your personal safety?

Using a more positive example of these principles, let's contrast

the Brad Morrison case with the first-person account of a branch manager I interviewed after his Los Angeles–area bank had been robbed.
The gunmen had fled with the money, but no one was harmed, and the
quick-thinking manager was the primary reason for that.

"Nobody move!" the taller of the two hooded bank robbers
shouted. "Just put the money in the bags and nobody will get hurt!
Who's in charge?"

"I am," the manager calmly replied. "What do you want us to do?"

"Get out of that chair and make sure your people don't do anything
stupid," the gunman said.

"OK, we'll give you everything you want," he said. "None of us
care about the money. It's the bank's. The only thing we care about is
getting home safely to our families. So just tell us what you want and
how you want it, and we'll do exactly what you say."

"I want your tellers to put every bit of cash they have behind that
counter in these bags," the robber replied in a much calmer, though
still demanding, tone. "And do it fast."

"OK, we've got it covered. Do you want me to get back there and make
sure it gets done, or do you want me out here where you can see me?"

"Stay out here," the gunman growled.

"All right, guys," the bank manager said. "You heard him. Let's
get going. Empty your drawers."

Within two minutes, the bank tellers gave the gunmen what they
wanted, and the robbers fled the scene. To me, this bank manager was
the truest kind of hero. He didn't put anybody's safety at risk, and, most
important, he wasn't caught by surprise. He expected the unexpected.

Of course, in a bank scenario, managers and employees typically
have several hours of training in regard to robbery protocol and personnel safety. Still, in this case, the manager had gone the extra mile.
Having rehearsed several scenarios such as this in his mind, he was
able to accomplish two things: One, he ensured everyone's safety by
keeping all involved calm, including and especially the bank robbers.
Two, he was able to help us capture the perpetrators because he was
observant.

When the two men walked in, they weren't wearing masks or hoods. In fact, they looked like a couple of clean-cut college kids. But they did some subtle things that caught the manager's attention. Upon entering the bank, they made a distinct effort to keep their faces turned away from the camera. Instead of walking straight to the desk where the deposit slips were located, the men wandered over in a sideways motion. They wore jackets with the hoods flapped backward in a way that would be easy to flip over their heads. You might think that this is an obvious tip, but what made this move subtle is that the gunmen weren't wearing thuggish coats, the sweat-jacket type you see a typical armed robber typically wear. These men were sporting nice mesh Windbreakers you see at Nordstrom or Macy's.

Upon noting the men, the manager took special care to memorize their faces in the event that something did happen. He had seen suspicious movement like this several times before and had taken similar note, yet there had never been a robbery. Most people experiencing an armed robbery for the first time understandably would have panicked, but this man remained calm and did the right things because he had taken a few moments each week to go over safety guidelines and rehearse some potentially dangerous situations with his staff. In short, he was being proactive in regard to his safety and that of his employees.

He was reading the story behind the story.

To help you to be like this bank manager, we have a list of basic questions you should ask yourself. They won't cover every situation, but they will help you eliminate opportunities for the majority of predators looking for easy targets. And, more important, they will help you start thinking in the right direction.

- Do I securely lock my doors and windows at night or when I'm away?

- When I am away on vacation or business, do I have a friend gather my mail and newspapers?

- Do I keep the lights on at night to give the appearance of being home?

- If I live alone, do I add things to my home and vehicle that make it appear that someone lives with me?

- Do I advertise or make known the fact that I have pharmaceuticals in the house? If I do have them, do I keep them in a location other than a medicine cabinet that is concealed and out of reach of young children?

- Do I have the authorities run background checks on people who have access to my children?

- Do I regularly change my routine and travel route?

- Do I keep a means of communication (a cell phone, for example) on or near me at all times?

- Do I let people know where I am headed and approximately when I will arrive when I travel long distances?

- Do I put myself or my loved ones in vulnerable positions with strangers or people I don't completely trust (despite their appearance or demeanor)?

- Do I have plans in place for myself and my children in case potentially dangerous situations (strangers, burglars, stalkers, etc.) should arise?

- Do I at least occasionally role-play with my children so they will know how to react in those situations?

- Do I role-play scenarios (at least in thought) on my own so that I will know how to react in potentially dangerous situations?

Thus far we have spoken of preventing predatory crimes in general terms. We did this to lay a foundation, but from this point on, we will deal in specifics. We hope that as we take you through the most common yet vicious crimes in our society, you will see how applying the principles we have outlined can improve your ability to keep yourself and your loved ones safe.

3

CRIMES AGAINST CHILDREN
THE WORST KIND OF CRIME

ally, it's time to get your shoes and socks on," called Stacy Peterson, the mother of a dawdling little girl. "You don't want to be late for Jenny's ice-skating party, do you?"

"No, Mommy," she replied. "But I can't find my blue socks."

"Why do you want to wear your blue socks? The pink ones will match better with your outfit."

"What's this I hear about an ice-skating party?" interrupted James Peterson, the girl's father, upon arriving early from work. "You get to go ice skating?"

"Uh-huh," said Sally.

"But my sweet little number-one girl couldn't already be big enough to ice skate, could she?" he teased.

"Sure I am! I'm this many!" she proclaimed, holding up two fingers.

In reality, the bubbly little girl with the golden curly hair was six, but the developmental disability had made it difficult for her to comprehend things like time and age. She was well behind other children her age in academic and social progress, but the disability also gave her a sweetness that made her stand out from the rest of her peers.

"Yep," interjected Stacy. "She sure is. And she is going to have a great time, aren't you, sweetheart?"

"Yep!" Sally adamantly agreed.

"But we won't be able to go anywhere if you don't find those shoes and socks," reminded her mom. "Why don't you go look under your bed, OK?"

"OK," agreed the little one, scampering to her bedroom.

"Is she really going ice skating?" James quietly asked. "I thought we weren't going to let her do anything that could embarrass her in front of other kids. I would think ice skating would be one of the last things we would want her to do."

"No, of course not. We're not going to let her get on the ice unless there's an adult with her," Stacy answered. "It's just that the Spencers invited Sally to Jenny's ice-skating competition. Jenny has a meet, then there's an open skating session afterward. She has invited some of her friends from the neighborhood to watch her and then have a little party afterward. Lila didn't want Sally to feel left out, so they're going to lend her a pair of Jenny's old skates and let her walk across the carpeted area with them so she can at least feel a part of things. Then, if we get a chance, I'll go out there with her."

"Oh, OK. Well, that's good," James replied.

"What, you don't trust me?" Stacy asked with a wink. "Remember who takes her to most of her doctors' appointments?"

"I know. I know," James said sheepishly as he crossed the living room. "You know I trust you. I just wanted to make sure. It's the worrisome papa in me."

James stared out the window.

"You know, we are so lucky to have neighbors like that," he finally said. "Everyone's been so good to Sally since we moved here—even the other kids. It's not often you live in a place where people know how to treat kids like our Sally. I am so glad we moved here. It has really been a blessing."

"It sure has," his wife agreed. "And she is so excited that she gets to go to this."

Just then, Sally skipped back into the living room.

"Well, it looks like our little girl has found her shoes," Stacy said. "You ready, princess?"

"Yep!"

"OK, then let's give Daddy a kiss and go have some fun!"

"I love you, Daddy!"

"I love you, too, sweetheart," said James. "You have a great time. And don't show the other girls up too badly, OK?"

"OK, I won't!"

And with that, Stacy whisked her daughter out the door and to the ice rink. All the girls welcomed Sally warmly and made sure she was included in the festivities.

"Thank you so much, Lila, for inviting Sally," said Stacy to her neighbor as she watched her gleeful daughter tromp back and forth across the ice-rink carpet in her friend's old skates.

"Oh, it's my pleasure," Lila replied. "Sally is such a sweet girl and Jenny really likes her. We wouldn't have had it any other way."

The ice rink had a typical early 1980s disco layout—black carpet with fluorescent green, pink, and orange shapes spread out across the floor. Lighted disco balls hung above the rink, while skaters of every skill level glided, or stumbled (as was the case with many of the children), across the ice. The blaring music encouraged many skaters to do their best to stay balanced while trying to skate-dance to their favorite tunes. By all accounts, the atmosphere was festive, and everyone seemed to be having a good time, such a good time, in fact, that no one noticed the danger lurking from behind a nearby table.

And why would they?

The man, in his mid-thirties, was good-looking and clean-shaven with polite, gentle features. Besides that, he seemed to fit in quite nicely, as if he worked there and was maybe just taking a break.

"Mommy!" Sally interrupted in a clearly unhappy tone.

"Yes, sweetheart," replied her mother. "What's the matter?"

"My feet hurt," Sally said, frowning down at the skates.

"Well, why don't we take them off for a while and give those cute little feet of yours a break? OK, sweetie?"

"OK, Mommy."

"Oh, Lila, I forgot something," Stacy said as she helped her daughter remove the skates. "I was supposed to pick up some medication for Sally. Do you mind if I run to the pharmacy really quick? I promise to be back before the party ends."

"That will be just fine," Lila replied. "We would be glad to look after Sally. In fact, I think it's about time for cake and ice cream. Sally, would you like to help me get the cake and ice cream for Jenny?"

The little girl nodded.

"OK, then. It's all settled," said Stacy. "You be a good helper for Lila, and I'll be back in just a few minutes, OK?"

"OK, Mommy."

Stacy wasn't gone for more than forty-five minutes, long enough for the kids to eat their cake and ice cream and hurry back to the rink for more skating. Sally wanted to run out to the rink, too, but she remembered she had taken off her skates to give her feet a break. Then she remembered she wasn't supposed to go out on the ice without an adult.

Just then, she happened to see her skates lying on a bench nearby.

"I'll just put on these skates and go back and forth across the floor," she thought. "Then, maybe Mommy will take me out on the ice with her when she gets back."

While the grown-ups at the party watched the children make their way around the rink, they chatted with one another, and their attention soon drifted from Sally. Not sure whom to ask, the six-year-old wandered over to the bench where the skates lay, and she sat down and began to put them on. As she tried to lace up her ice skates, she fumbled with the laces. She had such a hard time remembering how to tie her shoes.

"Does the rabbit go in the hole first or around the tree?" she muttered. "No, wait. Maybe it goes under the tree, then into the hole. Oh, never mind, I'll never—"

"It looks like you're having some trouble with those laces there," interrupted a nearby figure. "Would you like some help?"

"Yeah, I guess," replied Sally, somewhat shyly. "I can't figure out how to do it."

"Oh, that's OK," said the man as he knelt down in front of her and began to tie the laces. "It took me a long time to figure out how to lace these things up when I was your age, too. It's not as easy as it looks. So how old are you, anyway? About nine?"

"No, I'm only six," said Sally, smiling and holding up two fingers.

"No way!" teased the very kind stranger, whom she had seen sitting at the corner table just a few minutes ago. "You seem a lot older than that to me. Are you sure you're only that many?"

"Yep," she replied.

"Well, you sure had me fooled," he said, squatting even lower to sneak a peak up her dress. "My name is Ben. What's your name?"

"Sally."

"Well, Sally, it sure is nice to meet you," said Ben, taking another look up her dress, this time a little longer. "Would you like to go get a treat with me?"

"My Mommy and Daddy say I'm not supposed to go anywhere with strangers."

"Oh, well, you must have a very smart mommy and daddy," he replied. "So why aren't you out on the ice with the other kids?"

"My mommy says I have to wait to go with her," Sally answered in a tone of disappointment.

"Oh, so you have to go with an adult?"

"Yep."

"Well, I'll tell you what. I'm an ice-skating teacher here, and it seems to me that you really want to learn how to ice skate," Ben said. "Would you like it if I took you out to the ice for a few minutes and showed you how to skate?"

"Yeah!" Sally exclaimed, then suddenly remembered she was supposed to wait for her mother. "But my mommy says I've got to wait for her to come back."

"Oh, well, that's good that you listen to your mommy," Ben said. "But I think your mommy would be OK with me taking you for just a few minutes, especially since I'm an ice-skating teacher. What do you think?"

"Well, Mommy says I should listen to my teachers, so I guess it would be all right."

"OK," said Ben. "Why don't we go out on the ice for just a few minutes, and we'll see if we can have a good time."

As the two headed to the ice, Ben Gerrish introduced himself as an ice-skating instructor to Lila and indicated that his specialty was in working with special-needs children.

"I'm just going to take her out on the ice and see if we can get her comfortable," he told Lila.

He seemed friendly and legitimate enough, so Lila gave him permission, assuming Stacy would be fine with the man's offer.

As Sally skated with Gerrish, he taught her how to move her feet and keep her balance. He even let her "pretend fall" so that she could "get used to the ice." Every time she fell, he picked her up and briefly fondled her. But the touching was not enough for Gerrish, and he began to fantasize about having a sexual relationship with the child. When they were done with their so-called lesson, Gerrish lavished the young girl with praise.

"Wow! You did great! Hey, if it's OK with your mommy, I would like to teach you some more. How does that sound?"

"Yeah!" squealed the little girl. "I'd like that a lot!"

"OK, then," replied Gerrish with a smile. "Let me find a pen and a paper so I can write a note to your mommy, and maybe I can give you a free ice-skating lesson. I'll be right back."

Before long, he returned with the note in hand.

"Now, you make sure to give this to your mommy," Gerrish said. "I've got to go home now, but you have her call me if she wants you to do this, OK?"

"OK," Sally affirmed, marching off in her skates toward Lila and the group of mothers.

When Stacy returned to the rink, she saw Sally with the note.

"Who gave you this?" asked Stacy.

"A man," replied Sally.

"A man?" said Stacy suspiciously. "Lila, did you see a man with Sally?"

"Oh, yes," Lila said. "I almost forgot to tell you. He is one of the skating instructors here. I've never seen him here before, but he said he works with special-needs children. He was a very nice man and did a great job with Sally. He only skated with her for a few minutes, but we watched them, and she did great. I hope that was OK?"

"Oh, yeah," responded Stacy. "As long as you were aware of it, then it's OK."

Stacy opened the note, which read, "My name is Mr. Ben Gerrish. I skate here at the ice arena and do some ice dance. Your daughter was here at the arena trying on the skates of a friend (another young lady). No harm done. She seems to be very interested in ice skating. If you approve, (I'll need a note) I'll rent her a pair of skates and go around for a little time with her, until she gets used to it."

"Mommy?" Sally interrupted.

"Yes?"

"The nice man wants to teach me how to ice skate. Can I? Please?"

"Well, we'll have to talk to your father about it and see what he says."

Later that night, the couple discussed Gerrish's offer.

"Well, if he's a professional who works with kids like Sally, it might not be such a bad thing," James said. "It could really build her self-esteem. Plus, didn't you say that Lila watched him and told you that he was good with her?"

"Yeah, she did," said Stacy. "I'm just not sure if Sally is ready for this, and Lila said she had never seen him there before, so she really doesn't know him."

"Well, why don't you take Sally down to the rink and meet him," James suggested. "And if you don't like him, we won't do it. If he seems OK to you, then we can go ahead and get her involved. After all, if it's anyone's judgment I trust, it's yours."

"I guess so," Stacy said. "I'll give this Mr. Gerrish a call tomorrow and see what happens."

The next morning, Stacy spoke to Gerrish and set up a meeting at the ice rink. It was a beautiful spring day, and Sally was as excited as ever. When they arrived, Gerrish met them at the front entrance. He was dressed in white slacks and a light-blue button-down shirt. Stacy was immediately impressed with his kindly demeanor and sense of style. Gerrish was clean-cut and well mannered and had a very friendly way about him. One got the feeling from the young man that, if he lived next door to you, he'd mow your lawn just to be neighborly.

"Mr. Gerrish, I'm Stacy Peterson, Sally's mom," she declared. "And, of course, you've already met Sally."

"Yes, of course. We had a great time yesterday, didn't we Sally?"

"Yep!" Sally responded.

"Well, why don't we sit down for a few minutes, and I can tell you how the program works," Gerrish began in the boyish tone he used to make people feel comfortable around him. "Would that be OK?"

"Absolutely," Stacy answered. "I'd like that."

"Well, the first thing I typically do with special children like Sally is to get them used to the ice," Gerrish explained. "I find that the biggest obstacle to skating is a fear of falling on the ice, so if I let them touch it, 'pretend fall' on it—as gently as possible, of course—then that tends to remove the fear, and they can concentrate on the skating. Of course, with Sally, she was a natural and didn't seem to have too much fear of the ice, so I think we could start right in by teaching her proper footwork and balance and such."

"That sounds like quite a program," Stacy said, feeling much more at ease. "What do we have to do to get started?"

"Well, this is something I've just started doing on my own time, so I'll give you the first two lessons free. After that, if you're still interested, we can discuss a fee. How does that sound?"

"Sounds great," Stacy answered. "When do we get started?"

"Well, I've actually got some time today. But only if you do. I usually take about four hours, with a lunch break in between."

Gerrish could see a concerned look cross Stacy's face as she thought about the time element of the lesson, and he quickly moved to put her mind at ease.

"I know that might seem like a long time," he continued. "But it's important that they get as comfortable with the ice and the footwork as quickly as possible. I find that if the first couple of lessons are longer, special-needs children adapt much more smoothly to the techniques."

"Well, I did have some errands planned for today," Stacy told him.

"If you'd like, you can leave her here while you do your errands," Gerrish said. "Of course, I'll understand if you're not comfortable with that. Safety is our biggest point of emphasis. That's why we have the parents sign a form. And we can always schedule this for another time if this doesn't work for you."

"Please, Mommy," Sally interrupted. "Can I do it today? Please!"

"Well, I guess so," Stacy said. "What time will I need to be back?"

"I'd say about two o'clock," Gerrish answered.

"OK," said Stacy. "Then, we'll see you at about two, maybe a little before then."

Stacy watched Gerrish skate around the rink with her daughter for a few minutes, just to see if Sally would be all right. As the two glided along the ice, the little girl squealed with delight.

"I haven't seen her this excited about something in a long time," Stacy thought.

Then, she noticed the time.

"Mr. Gerrish!" Stacy called out. "I'll be leaving now, but I'll be back just before two, OK?"

"Sounds great!" Gerrish called back.

And with that, Stacy left to do her errands, while Gerrish had Sally all to himself.

Gerrish made no attempt to assault Sally. His aim was to gain her mother's trust so he could have complete access to the girl for several hours. Because he still wasn't entirely sure that Stacy would be gone for the whole session, he kept himself in check.

Just before two, Stacy returned to a happy child and was delighted that things had gone smoothly.

"Well, it looks like someone had a good time," Stacy said. "How did she do, Mr. Gerrish?"

"She did fantastic, Mrs. Peterson," Gerrish replied. "I think you've got a natural here."

"Well, that sounds great," Stacy said. "So when would be the best time for the second lesson?"

"I've got a few hours tomorrow before my shift," Gerrish answered. "In fact, if you want to bring her back here around the same time, then that would work well for me. Would that work with your schedule?"

"Actually, that would be perfect," Stacy said. "I guess we'll see you tomorrow."

"Tomorrow it is, then."

"Oh, one thing," Stacy suddenly remembered. "I do have an appointment that might not be quite done by two. Would it throw your work schedule off too much if I was a few minutes late?"

"Well, my schedule is pretty tight," he replied. "You know, if it's all right with you, I could drop Sally off at your house after the lesson. You don't live too far from here, and, that way, I would be able to get back here in time for work."

"Yeah, I guess that would be OK," Stacy said. "Why don't we just plan on having you drop her off then?"

"Sounds like a plan. We'll see you tomorrow."

The next day, Gerrish was waiting diligently outside the ice-rink entrance when Stacy pulled up to drop her daughter off. As Sally got out of the car, Gerrish overheard Stacy say, "Do everything Mr. Gerrish tells you to do and make Mommy proud."

"I will, Mommy," Sally replied.

"I hope your appointment goes well," Gerrish called to Stacy.

"Thanks," she said. "And thank you again for being willing to drop Sally off."

"No problem," he replied.

Then a smile crossed the man's face as Stacy drove away. "I own this child!" he thought.

With one innocent instruction to her daughter, Stacy had inadvertently taken all her child's power away. Within minutes of watching Sally's mother leave, Gerrish turned to the little girl and whispered, "Before we get started, let's go for a ride."

He took Sally to a secluded park where he forced her to perform oral sex on him. Gerrish then French kissed her for some time and again forced her to perform the same sexual act.

After the assault, Gerrish dropped Sally off in front of the house. As she got out of his vehicle, he told her, "You were a really good girl. Your mom will be real proud of you. You don't have to worry about telling her anything. I'll tell her what happened and that you did what she told you to do."

Feeling a deep sense of shame, Sally couldn't get into the house quickly enough. Needless to say, she didn't want to go back to skating lessons, citing sore feet as the reason.

Gerrish assured the parents that it would take their daughter some time to get used to the skates and that maybe they could try again in a few weeks, when she was ready. "There's no reason to rush her," he assured Stacy and James. "Just let me know when she is ready to try again, and we'll give it another shot. This is perfectly normal for special-needs children."

Over several months, Sally never told her mother or anybody else about the assault. Sadly, she carried this burden, wondering for all that time if she were responsible—until one day at school. While watching a "Good Touch/Bad Touch" video in class, she finally garnered the courage to share the "secret."

Horrified, the teacher called Sally's parents and the local authorities.

Several days later, police questioned Gerrish. He confessed to the assault and was sent to prison for the remainder of his life.

For the purpose of combating child molestation, Mike King and I were able to develop a rapport with Oliver Ben Gerrish just a few years into his prison sentence. When it became apparent to him that he was going to spend the rest of his life in prison, Gerrish confessed to molesting more than five hundred children over a twenty-four-year period. As part of his therapy, he wrote down the incidents of his molestations, spoke to law enforcement groups, and shared his tactics for the purpose of preventing these crimes from happening to other children.

Yet, in Gerrish's own words, "There was a lot of heartache. For every child I molested, there were other victims—brothers, sisters, parents, aunts, uncles, and grandparents. I cannot comprehend the number of people I have affected by my selfish assaults."

Surprisingly, after watching Gerrish with Sally for only a few minutes after their first meeting, Stacy gave him permission to take her daughter for that day and the next. Keep in mind that this is the first time she had met Gerrish, yet she trusted him because he didn't "look like a child molester." It didn't take long for her to agree to release her child into his custody, and as you now know, the consequences were catastrophic for everyone involved.

What we learn from this family's experience is, again, to not judge a book by its cover. Just because it doesn't look like a rat or smell like one doesn't mean it's not a rat. Rats have the ability to clean up quite well when it serves their purposes.

The one positive thing about this case, however, is that, in developing a rapport with Gerrish, Mike and I were able to persuade him to share his experiences and techniques in order to help law enforcement better deal with child sex offenders. In fact, we got through to Gerrish so well that, upon his death, he bequeathed all his writings and drawings to us for the purpose of preventing further child molestation.

In January 2000, before a group of sixty-five police officers attending training on serial child sexual offenders, Gerrish offered the following statement regarding his depraved actions: "In the therapy I was in, it was extremely taxing, sometimes sixteen hours a day," Gerrish explained. "The staff supervises the discussions between the inmates and social workers, and because of that program, I can sit before you today and share these things. I reviewed my deviant behavior over a twenty-four-year period of time, which represented the amount of time I was offending, molesting little children before being sent to prison. The behavior is broken down into hours and years. One of our assignments in therapy was to re-create the amount of time involved in deviant thinking and/or behavior."

During the training session, Gerrish confirmed investigator suspicion that suggested a delicate "grooming process," in which Gerrish would prepare his victims—and their families—for the impending sexual assault. Like many serial predators, Gerrish was very careful and "organized" during the early years of his assaults. As time went on and the number of victims rose, Gerrish began to lose patience and failed to properly plan before each assault. In fact, Gerrish thought he was "smarter than the police" and that he "could get away with anything." Soon, his perversions became too powerful for even him to control, and he became "disorganized" in his selection of victim, assault location, and escape.

Just a few months before his death in 2001, he spoke of the countless victims left in the wake of his destructive perversions. During his thirty-five years of freedom, Gerrish admitted to sexually abusing more than five hundred children who ranged in age from three to thirteen years of age. The most common group he targeted was girls ages five to thirteen. Gerrish reported that he was questioned by police on only nine occasions and that he "walked" on all but the final two, which ultimately sent him to prison.

Included in the conference was a question-and-answer period in which law enforcement officials were given free reign. They were told they could ask Gerrish anything they wanted—and they did. When asked by police whether he felt he was ready for rehabilitation, the convicted serial offender left these words engrained in the memories of those in attendance:

Q: Can you look upon any child today without any sexually deviant thoughts?

A: To this day, at this time, no. The thoughts still occur. They come back. But the thing I am learning in therapy is not that the thoughts come back, but what I do with them.

Q: If you were released to an unrestrictive setting, how dangerous would you be due to the therapy you've gone through?

A: I think I would be dangerous, and that's a realistic appraisal at this time.

Q: How do you see your future as a result of this?

A: I have agonized over that for a long time before coming here today. To be absolutely blunt with you, I don't think I have a future.

Q: Were your desires so strong that, had you had your own children, would you have abused them?

A: Yes. I probably would have. I had no limits.

Q: Knowing yourself better than anyone else, if you were on a parole board, would you now let yourself out?

A: At this time, no, I would not.

Q: When considering the number of times you were questioned by police, do you know where they went wrong?

A: Yes! They believed me.

On the day of his burial in 2001, Gerrish's cremated ashes were placed in a "pauper's grave" on state ground near the Utah State Correctional Facility. He lived a miserable life where he left nothing but damaged children and their families in his wake. And in the end, no one was there to mourn his death or witness his burial. Yet the victims remained.

You may have noticed that we have a chapter designated for sex crimes, and you might wonder why we didn't include the discussion of child sex offenses there. The reason is that, although child molesters are technically classified as sex offenders, the psychology of someone who commits these crimes against children is different from that of someone who commits them against adults. Consequently, the ways in which one defends against a child molester are going to differ from those one would employ against an adult sex offender.

The sad truth is that the majority of crimes against children involve sex abuse. As you can imagine, someone who abuses children is in a whole different class psychologically and, therefore, needs to be dealt with in a much different way than you would deal with someone who commits these crimes against adults. This also means you need to prepare your children to protect themselves differently from this kind of predator than you would from any other kind of danger they might face.

Remember, these criminals are not going to look dangerous. If anything, they will disguise themselves to look quite the opposite.

One of the most valuable pieces of information that Mike and I elicited from Gerrish is a list of tactics he used to lure children—and their parents—into trusting him. As you saw in Sally's case, once he obtained her mother's trust, he was empowered to do practically whatever he wanted to. But he had to use certain techniques to gain their trust—and therein lies the secret to stopping the child molester. Learn the child offender's tactics, and you take the control away from the child molester and are able to give it to the child.

Keep that in mind as you read the list of grooming tactics provided straight from a career child molester himself. Gerrish includes not only his techniques but also ways in which parents and/or children could have countered his tactics.

We left the list exactly the way Gerrish wrote it, unedited. We didn't even correct his grammar. If you look closely, you will notice that you can glean certain psychological aspects through his writing style, the most notable being his sense of repetition. In fact, you may find this list somewhat redundant, but that's because child molesters are typically very cyclical in nature. Their desire to sexually abuse children usually has such a strong hold on them that they are seldom, if ever, able to break the cycle of abuse.

We will warn you now that what he wrote may be difficult to read. But if you want to protect your children from this kind of criminal, we strongly recommend that you—and every parent—read this.

GROOMING TACTICS of a Child Sex Offender WARNING FROM OFFENDER GERRISH: *This document contains graphic descriptions of various types of grooming tactics once utilized by me, a convicted child molester for the purpose of making my intended victims vulnerable for my sexual desires. It is hoped that this document will assist you, with detecting and halting the future molestation of other children. As a child molester, I depended upon absolute secrecy. I never molested a child who called attention to what was going on, because I was afraid of getting caught.*

TACTIC NO. 1
THREATS AND DIRECT
PHYSICAL COERCION

I began my career as a child molester, when I was age eight. My older Cousin and I forced his six year old Sister into the hayloft on our farm, where we made her do oral sex on both of us. My tactic then consisted mainly of cutting off her escape route. Once we had her in the hayloft, I pulled up the ladder so she couldn't get away from us. I am unaware of what tactics my Cousin used when they were at their home, however, they were effective; because she was always too scared to tell anyone about what we were doing to her. I suspect he threatened her.

Escape Tactics

Any child in this situation could escape by loudly screaming and drawing attention to what is going on. The last thing I wanted, was attention from others. I depended upon absolute secrecy, to commit my terrible acts against children. Screaming "FIRE!" loudly for a few times, is a good way to ensure others will pay attention.

TACTIC NO. 2
THREATS AND USE OF LIES
TO CONTINUE MY DEVIANCES

Shortly thereafter, when my little brother and I took our baths together, I began to force him to masturbate me. I would pin him into the corner of the tub and do the same to him. I used threats of physical abuse to keep him quiet and manageable. After the few times I got caught by Mom, I began to molest him in the hayloft and used the tactic of pulling up the ladder as learned when my Cousin and I molested his sister.

Escape Tactics

Any child in this situation could scream and call for help. Further, the child could tell adults what was going on. If the parent did not listen or scoffed at the child, the child could talk with other adults. Eventually, someone will step in and help the child avoid a dangerous situation.

TACTIC NO. 3
USE OF GUILT TRIPS;
FALSE FRIENDSHIP; THREATS

One day after the Elementary School let out, I saw a little girl playing by herself on the swings. She had a little dog with her. I asked her if she'd like for me to push her in the swing. After doing this awhile, I sat in a swing beside her and began talking with her. I told her how pretty she was. I deliberately guessed her age as older than she obviously was and acted surprised when she said: "Silly. I'm only five." I told her she looked older. We talked about pets. She let me know that her parents weren't home during the day and she was lonely a lot. When I asked about siblings, she said she had none. At this time I suggested I hold her and we could swing together. As we did, I allowed myself to become partially erect. She noticed this and when she innocently asked what it was, I told her: "It's something that boys have for pretty little girls to play with." When I told her again that she was pretty, I asked if she'd like to see it sometime.

When she said, "sure," I took her up onto the fire escape at the school and exposed my penis to her. As I held her hands on it and forced her to masturbate me, I asked her if she wanted to really make me happy. This was calculated to put her into an even more vulnerable position, because I knew she wouldn't want to make me feel bad. After all, I was her "new friend." This tactic was followed by me forcing her to do oral sex on me. After having my way with her, I told her that if she told anyone, I would find her and hurt her doggie. She was terrified and promised to never tell anyone our "secret." As far as I know, she never did.

Escape Tactics

Any child in this situation, could have avoided molestation by the use of any of the following escape tactics: 1) She could walk away; 2) She could scream for help; 3) She could say she wasn't supposed to talk to strangers; 4) She could go back inside the school and tell a Teacher about the strange man on the play ground.

TACTIC NO. 4
ACTED AS A FRIEND; USED KITTENS AS A LURE AND ENTICEMENT

Our house bordered an alley that a lot of kids used as a shortcut to the school play ground. One day, from my basement, I saw a little girl on her way to the play ground. I lured her over by asking if she wanted to see some little kittens. I knew her natural curiosity would prevail and when she came over, I took her into the basement with me. Inside, I asked her name and got to briefly know her as she played with the kittens. Then, as she played with them, I began to fondle her under her clothing. Afterwards, I told her that if her parents approved, I'd give her a kitten for her own when they were big enough. Two weeks later, I gave her the kitten. I now had placed this child in a position of feeling indebted to me; ensuring future molestations, which did frequently occur.

Escape Tactics

Any child in this situation could escape by: 1) Screaming and drawing attention to what was going on; 2) Telling parents and other adults; 3) Refuse to go into a stranger's yard or home; 4) Say she didn't like kittens; 5) Scream: "I'm going to tell the police."

TACTIC NO. 5
TICKLE GAMES AND
OTHER "INNOCENT" PLAY

Seeing several young girls playing in a park, I began talking with them about themselves; how they liked school; their ages and other general topics. I soon had their trust. Then I said to one: "I bet you are ticklish." When I tickled her, it evolved quickly into a general tickle session. During this activity, I was able to fondle each child both under and above their clothing, without it being noticed. I used this tactic countless times while I was actively molesting children.

Escape Tactics

Any child in this situation, could escape by: 1) Saying she wasn't supposed to talk with strangers; 2) Telling her friend it was time to go home; 3) Screaming and drawing attention to what was going on; 4) Telling me that if I didn't leave, they would tell their parents and Police.

TACTIC NO. 6
"PLAYING DUMB"

Many times when alone with a selected little girl that I wanted to molest, the following conversation would occur:

ME: "Hello."
SHE: "Hi."

ME: "You're a cute little boy."
SHE: "Silly. I'm a little girl."

ME: "Nah. You're a boy."
SHE: "I'm a little girl."

ME: "Prove it to me. Let's see if you look like a boy here." (I'd point to the genital area of the child's clothing.)

At this point, invariably the child would innocently expose herself. I would then feign disbelief and ask if I could touch her down there to see for myself. In all the times I used this technique, only one child ever refused to go along. Children want to please adults and the opportunity to show they are smarter, is hard to ignore. I knew this and preyed on it.

Escape Tactics

Any child in this situation could escape by: 1) Getting up and running away; 2) Saying they aren't supposed to talk with strangers; 3) Screaming to draw attention to themselves and what is going on; 4) Calling out to any nearby adults: "This man is trying to hurt me"; 5) After getting away, going to their parents or to the Police and telling what happened.

TACTIC NO. 7
"I NEED HELP"

In setting up this particular event, I spent several hours in what appeared to be aimless cruising. In reality, I was scoping out various areas near schools, parks, swimming pools and other public areas that were frequented by small children. I was locating areas that had few houses and other buildings around, so I could come there to obtain my victims. An example of how I used this tactic follows:

One hot summer afternoon, I parked in a secluded area that I knew little girls walked along on their way to the swimming pool. Getting out of my car, I put up the hood and as the child I had selected approached, I began tinkering around the engine. When the child came alongside the car, I dropped a screwdriver. I asked her if she'd please hand it to me. When she did, I told her I couldn't reach the item I needed to work on because it was out of my reach. I asked her if she would help me by holding the tool for me. Of course, she was too small to reach over the fender. I then asked if I could sit her up on the fender. Once there, I suggested if she'd spread her legs wide apart with her feet on the engine, she wouldn't slide off and get hurt. After she complied, I moved to the opposite side and looked up her dress. Soon thereafter, as I talked with her, I fondled her under her clothing. When finished, I gave her a ride to the swimming pool and told her what a "good girl" she was, to help a stranger. In events using this approach, I never had to use direct threats against my victim.

Escape Tactics

Any child in this situation could escape by: 1) Never walking down lonely streets, especially if they see someone parked in the loneliest part; 2) Never walking to the swimming pool alone; 3) Never stop to listen to a stranger who talks to them from his car; 4) Never agree to help any stranger who says he needs help. He can get help other ways;

5) Reporting the stranger to a parent, life-guard at the pool, policeman, teacher, or other adult the child knows; 6) If the child sees the same strange car in her area more than once, she should tell her parents and police right away; 7) The child should do anything to immediately draw attention to what is going on . . . screaming FIRE! is a good way to attract attention right away.

TACTIC NO. 8
LET ME HELP YOU

In this tactic, I choose victims who are by themselves and appear to be in distress and needing help. For example: One summer afternoon while resting in a local park, I heard a child crying. A three-year-old girl was limping on one foot and crying as she made her way across the park towards a path that went through the trees to a housing development. As she passed me I observed a cockle burr in her heel. I called to her to come over to me and I would help her. I removed the burr from her foot and then had her sit by me. I asked if she was happy now. When she nodded "yes," I asked if she would do something to make me happy. I forced her to masturbate me and then I pulled her onto my lap; moved her sun suit aside in the crotch area and rubbed my penis against her genitalia. After several minutes, I told her how nice she was and quit molesting her. I told her tha[t] since she no longer hurt anymore, she could go back to playing with her friends and didn't need to tell anyone how I had "helped" her. She nodded and scampered off. I used this tactic many times. Only once did it fail.

Escape Tactics

A child in this situation could escape by: 1) Play only in areas where a parent or play ground supervisor is present; 2) If hurting, seek help only from a person the child knows; 3) Never stop to talk with any stranger be it male or female; 4) Always go to and from play with a friend or group of friends; 5) Scream "FIRE" or "STRANGER" to draw attention to themselves and what is going on; 6) If they see a stranger who is paying too much attention to them, the child should tell a parent, policeman, teacher or other responsible adult, so steps can be taken to protect all the children.

TACTIC NO. 9
THE "SALESMAN" TACTIC

This tactic involved my obtaining a copy of a Directory as issued by some churches. These contained family photographs and names of all in the picture, with their telephone numbers! I focused only on families with little girls from ages three through six. I would then call a selected family; always at a time when I believed the adults would be busy or absent. If an adult answered, I hung up and varied the time I called until a child answered. The following event demonstrates how I victimized two helpless little girls; a complete family and several little boys I didn't even know, plus innocent others. Once a little girl took the call, I'd represent myself as a girls' underwear salesman from one of the local children's stores. I asked her name, age, and if she had any siblings. Once I had her interested, I asked her what color underwear she was wearing. After she responded, I asked about what her sister was wearing. In one instance, the victim responded that her three-year-old sister was outside playing with some boys. I asked her to go see what color her sister was wearing. After she came back and told me, I asked about the size. When she didn't know, I had her go out and take off her sister's underwear while the boys watched and bring it to the phone and read off the label to me. I told her that when she took it back, she should have the boys rub and play with her sister, "down there." When she returned, she said the boys were having fun. I told her to rub herself in that area and could tell by her response, she was doing it. When I finally heard an Adult female call out: "What's going on in there?", I hung up the phone. All during this type of event, I was getting off through fantasizing and masturbating as I talked with the little girl.

Escape Tactics

A child in this situation could escape by: 1) Hanging up the telephone; 2) Not talking to the person on the phone; 3) Calling a parent to take the call; 4) Not listening to the caller; 5) Telling a parent that a stranger was calling them.

TACTIC NO. 10
THE FAMILY PHOTOGRAPHER

During this time period, I was employed as a traveling Family Photographer. My company would arrange advance "shoots" for me in various towns and cities. When I arrived, I'd set up my studio in available space; complete with a table where the customers could sit and fill out the necessary forms. When I set up in small towns, I always had that table arranged so that the customers had their backs to me and couldn't see what I was doing. As they worked on the paperwork, I "got acquainted" with the children. If the child was between ages three thru six, I'd ask if she'd like to help me test the camera equipment. I'd lift them up so they could press the test fire button on my camera. They liked it when the flash would go off. Keeping an eye on the parent, I was able to fondle my victims without anyone being the wiser. I used this tactic countless times. The table set up was a grooming tactic aimed at the parents; whereas the camera test was used on the children.

Escape Tactics

A child in this situation could escape being molested by: 1) Staying with their parent until time for the actual sitting; 2) Telling the photographer that they didn't like to be touched by a stranger; 3) When touched wrong by the photographer, the child should tell a parent right away. Any parent who arrives for such a photo opportunity, should always: 1) Keep their child by their side until the paperwork is completed; 2) Never let the photographer work with the child out of the parents sight; 3) Always sit so that they can observe exactly what is going on at all times.

TACTIC NO. 11
THE SWIMMING POOL

I used several grooming tactics whenever I went swimming. One was to situate myself along the edge of the pool in water that was up to my shoulders. In most pools, small children will cling to the edges as they move up and down the sides of the pool. By being where I was, the water was too deep for them to get around without having to let go of the edge. I would "help" them by fondling them as I moved them from one side of me to the other side of the pool edge. I never once had any adult or life guard question what I was doing. By tickling and laughing with the victims, the entire event appeared perfectly normal. I counted on the fact that normal adults see what they expect to see: a friendly man, helping a child.

Other times, I would hold on to the exit ladder at the deep end as I went underwater. This way I could easily observe the little girls as they gathered by the ladder to leave the pool. In water, an otherwise tightly clinging suit will tend to float away from the body; allowing me to see their genitals. The general confusion by the ladder made it easy for me to fondle my victims without it being noticed. If a victim looked startled, I'd look at them and remark: "Oops. Sorry. I slipped off the edge." Without fail, the child giggled and ignored the touch.

Escape Tactics

A child in this situation could escape the molester by: 1) When being fondled, scream for help. At a swimming pool, screams for help are not ignored! 2) Go to the Lifeguard and tell them about the man who is blocking the edge of the pool; 3) Tell the Lifeguard that the man along the edge is touching you; 4) Tell a parent what is going on.

TACTIC NO. 12
CRUISING

In this tactic, I always looked for children by themselves as they walked to school. I'd drive around and look for a child who was late for school or involved in similar situations: in the rain or on wintry days, etc. Once I found a victim, I'd offer to give them a lift to school, so they wouldn't be "late"; "get wet"; "catch a cold"; the reasons given were endless and depended on the type of situation. The main theme presented was to keep the child from "getting in trouble." Once the child was in my car, I'd take the long way to school as I talked with them about various subjects all leading around to questions about sexual things. This led to my exposing myself and making the child touch me as I touched them. Experience had shown me that if I quit the instant the child became upset or alarmed and remained friendly, they apparently never told anyone.

Escape Tactics

A child in this situation could avoid molestation by: 1) Refusing to listen to the strange adult in the car beside them; 2) Screaming for help; 3) Telling the man: "I'm going to tell the Police; Mom; Teacher; Telling the school about the stranger who tried to pick them up on their way to school; 4) Always walking to school with a group of friends; 5) Never walking alone to school or elsewhere; 6) If the child sees a car following them or parking ahead of them with a stranger in it the child should turn around and go home or get help from a known adult.

Further: the child should be taught by their parents that they should never respond to strangers as they are going to school and NEVER go over to a stranger's car to talk to them or offer help. The strange adult can get help on his own . . . he doesn't need a child to help him!!!

TACTIC NO. 13
WOULD YOU LIKE TO . . . ?

Use of this grooming tactic involved my asking my selected victim if they'd like to do any number of various activities each geared to the specific situation and victim, such as: "Would you like to See the Chipmunks; Go for a ride; Learn to skate; Have your picture drawn; Be pushed in the swing; Go to the park; Learn to ride a bike; Have some fun learning about yourself" and so on. The list is virtually endless. In most of these situations, I'd take my victim to a secluded area and assault them sexually. Sometimes I sexually assaulted my victims right out in the open . . . which carried a heightened degree of sexual arousal for me.

Escape Tactics

A child in this situation could escape by: 1) Not getting into the situation in the first place; 2) Screaming and creating a spectacle of themselves to draw attention to what is going on; 3) Saying to the stranger: "I'm going to tell."

TACTIC NO. 14
SUMMER CAMP VOLUNTEER

In setting up this event, I groomed an entire church congregation. I moved to a new area where I was unknown and selected a church to "join." The selection was done with care because only those churches which had summer youth camps, would suffice. Once in the church, I began to let the members see only what I wanted them to see. They saw a man who eagerly volunteered to assist with upkeep of the building and grounds; a man who had a wealth of knowledge about the outdoors; a man who was active in Scouting and had been awarded both an Eagle and Life saving award; a man who was willing to share his knowledge and skills with anyone. In short: I groomed them as meticulously as an artist would detail a painting; covering up all my flaws and presenting "perfection."

When summertime rolled around, I was asked to assist with a Summer Camp for Youth. I volunteered to teach Canoeing, Wildlife and Outdoor Skills. At this first Camp, even though little girls were in attendance, I took pains to display exemplary behaviors. I was absolutely above reproach and conducted myself like a saint! This had the desired effect upon the entire congregation. The Pastor told me of a difficulty they were experiencing with an upcoming Camp and that it might be canceled due to lack of a Camp Nurse. He said that with my Paramedical background, if I volunteered, they could hold the Camp. He further mentioned that this Camp was for girls: ages six through eleven years of age (my preferred target range!). I volunteered.

Acting in the guise of a concerned medical person, it was easy to arrange being able to fondle various little girls. They never had a clue to what I was doing. I was selective and very careful, to not go beyond certain limits; that is, I never had the child disrobe. This would have been unacceptable to the Staff and a warning flag calling attention to what I was doing. For the next three years, I was highly sought after as a Camp Volunteer.

Escape Tactics

In such a situation, the entire congregation could avoid being victimized and manipulated by taking several actions: 1) Contact their local Police Department and requesting a background investigation into this "helpful" person; 2) Ask for and receive references from previous congregations and check these thoroughly yourself; 3) Check with your Church Headquarters regarding this person; had this been done in my case, they would have learned I'd been sexually active with children; 4) Be suspicious of any new male member who readily volunteers to help and ingratiates himself into the church community; 5) Be highly cautious of any male adult who appears to be overly friendly around and with children of any age! This should be an instant red flag; 6) A Camp Nurse should always be a trusted female; if needed, such can be located via local medical references. I the molester depended upon the inherent kindness and trusting nature of church members, knowing they would generally take me at face value.

DON'T DO THIS.

PROTECT YOUR CHILDREN; INVESTIGATE THIS PERSON!

Anyone who is being honest and straight forward, will not have objections to being checked out. Anyone who objects, should be watched and checked out very carefully because his actions indicate he has something he doesn't want you to find out.

TACTIC NO. 15
HAPPY BIRTHDAY

I found out which child in a large family was the "middle" child. Knowing this child probably didn't get the same amount of love and attention they did before the younger children came along, I set out to provide it. On her birthday I told her: "I'll have a special gift for you tomorrow." This set her up. I sketched a drawing of a sparrow sitting on a branch and gave it to her. The "gift" was the tactic and had the desired effect on the entire family. I was invited to their home for dinner. I groomed them all and became like a member of their family. Seeing that she always wore a dress, I manipulated her into exposing herself by telling her: "I like looking up your dress because you have beautiful legs." From then on, she always sat so that I could see up her dress. She had no idea that I was molesting her visually. Before long, I fondled her under her dress.

Escape Tactics

A child in this situation could escape being molested by: 1) Never accepting any gifts from anyone who is not a member of the immediate family; 2) Telling the parents immediately when a stranger tells them: "I have a gift for you"; 3) Telling the parents whatever the "new friend" says about the child.

The parents in this situation could escape such a tactic by: 1) Always being alert to what is going on with and around their children, especially the middle children in a large family. The molester knows such children often don't receive equal amounts of attention and love. In a very short time, the molester can tell which child is the one being deprived of needed attention and he is always there to provide it . . . to the detriment of the victim! 2) The parents need to be very cautious about letting new acquaintances give their children or family, any type of gifts. 3) The best escape is for the parents to contact their Police Department and request a background check on their new acquaintance. If nothing is wrong, the person will welcome the clean bill of health; if he protests, something is definitely wrong and he should be avoided!

TACTIC NO. 16
POOR ME

I used this tactic to set up an organization so I could literally rob them of goods. I presented myself to them as one who was in dire straits and had a desperate need for assistance. I told them I was just out of prison and didn't have enough funds for both food, rent and transportation, (even though I already had some funds). I was deemed eligible for their assistance. The official gave me a set of order forms and sent me to the distribution center. I altered the amounts on the forms and took excessive amounts of food and other goods. While I didn't sexually victimize anyone using this tactic, I still created victims of all who had donated to the organization in good faith. I took goods and food that could have gone to others who needed it more.

Variations on This Tactic

I was a member of a local church that had a sensitivity towards those in need. I groomed a specific family and became a family "friend." I spent spare time with the children in the family and one day, I used this friendship as a tactic to falsely obtain food. I hinted to the older kids, that I was out of food and it would be two weeks before I could afford to get more. She told her parents and they left a large box of food in my car . . . even though they didn't leave their names, it was easy to tell who did it by the actions of the kids.

Throughout the years, I used many variations of this tactic, to get my selfish wants met at the expense of others. I didn't care that others had worked hard to obtain that which they gave to me in good faith . . . I only saw them as fools who could be easily manipulated into giving me what I wanted. Usually in such circumstances, I had some funds available but was too stingy and selfish to use my own funds to provide for my own wants.

Escape Tactics

Anyone in this situation can escape being used by: 1) Having the local Police conduct a back ground check on the new person in your area; 2) Caution their children about accepting everything someone new tells them; 3) Continually warn the children about listening to strangers; 4) An official in such an organization, must always mail the order forms to the distribution point [and should] never give the forms to the recipient themselves. If the need is great, a simple meal will suffice until the forms reach the distribution area; 5) Families need to always be aware that some people make a profession out of appearing "in need of assistance" so they can live off the honest toil of others. This awareness will assist in preventing.

> REMEMBER: "As a child molester I depended upon absolute secrecy. I never molested a child who called attention to what was going on. I was afraid of getting caught."
>
> Oliver Benjamin Gerrish

Now that you have taken your journey through the mind of a child molester, you probably feel a sense of shock and sorrow. This is not how we want to leave you feeling.

Our aim here is to help empower you by teaching you, and ultimately your children, to take steps that will prevent would-be child molesters from harming them. We also hope that, by reducing the number of child molestations, our society will see fewer future child molesters. It's no secret that most child molesters were sexually molested when they were children. Or, in other terms, the children we feel sorry for today become the adults we despise tomorrow. We're hoping that this information contributes to seeing fewer despised adults in the world of tomorrow.

The way to do that is by remembering some important principles that we would like to share with you:

1. **Child molesters rely on absolute secrecy.** Teach your children that there is no such thing as a bad touch that is good, no matter whom it comes from. That includes family and trusted friends. Sadly, the majority of child sex assaults occur within a close circle of family and friends. Child molesters, regardless of how

they come into contact with their victims, will always try to intimidate children into keeping the "secret." Children need to be taught this principle so they are not caught off guard when a trusted member of that circle attempts to do something inappropriate to them. Better to lose a friend or family member than to have your child blame himself for something that is not his fault. Teach your children that if they are not comfortable being alone with a grown-up, then they do not have to be. Teach them that the only reason an adult would want to keep the touching a secret is because that grown-up knows he or she has done something wrong.

2. **Child molesters are afraid of getting caught.** This is where the real power comes from. Perpetrators often try to make their victims feel as if they share responsibility and shame for what happened. Teach your children that the reason they would be told such a thing is because the grown-up knows better and would only tell them that to stay out of trouble. Kids need to know that the adult is the only one who will be held accountable if they are assaulted. If you teach your children this principle, then they will have control over the would-be perpetrator, not the other way around.

3. **Child molesters abhor attention.** Teach your children to make as much noise as possible. Nothing halts a would-be offender like yelling and screaming, especially something specific like "fire!" This goes hand in hand with principle two. If a child calls attention to what is going on, the offender will do everything possible to disappear. Remember, Gerrish said he never molested a child who called attention to him.

4. **Empowerment from role-playing.** Verbally teaching your children these principles is good, but it's not good enough. We definitely encourage you to create an open dialogue with your

children in regard to this topic. That is where safety begins. But without role-playing, if a child finds herself in a potentially damaging situation, odds are she will freeze. If she has not been able to have the experience of yelling and screaming around an adult, even in a simulated situation, then she might feel so awkward about doing it under real circumstances that she ends up doing nothing at all. In our society, we teach kids to avoid raucous and loud behavior around adults, especially in a school or a church setting. If you role-play with your children in a variety of potential situations, odds are that their training will kick in if they ever do find themselves confronted by someone who tries to touch them or do inappropriate things to them, regardless of where it occurs.

5. **The power of telling parents, teachers, and other authorities.** This is the most vital principle, as well as the trickiest. It is vital because nothing can be done unless a trusted adult gets involved. It is the trickiest because, sometimes, one or more of these parties could be the offender or could be someone who does not believe the child. The key to teaching this principle lies in what we taught in principle one. There is no such thing as a bad touch that is good, regardless of whom it comes from—even an authority or a trusted figure. Teach your children this principle. Teach them that, if one authority figure dismisses or disbelieves what they tell them, then they need to go to another one and tell that person. If that one doesn't believe them, then go to another, and another, and another, until someone listens to their story and is willing to do something about it. As we mentioned earlier, the majority of child molestation occurs within a trusted family or friendship circle. It may, for example, be that the stepfather is committing these acts against his stepdaughter. The stepdaughter might tell her mother, and she might not believe her, accusing her of making up a lie simply because she doesn't like Mom's new husband.

At that point, the girl needs a list of authorities she can go to: another trusted family member, a teacher, a church official, the police, or a school nurse. Make sure your children know that they have a variety of people to go to for help. They do have options.

6. **Don't ever lie just to spite someone.** It is imperative that children know that making up such a story is very serious and will cause a lot of problems for not only the accused but also any children who really are victimized in the future. Children need to understand that this is a most serious and damaging lie. Having said that, please let your children know that, by all means, if they feel they have been violated, they are best served by going to a trusted adult who will help them. But only if it's the truth.

Overall, the point is to empower your children so they know what they can do to stay safe. As parents, we just can't be with our children 24/7. We can't account for every situation. With so many ways in which child molesters corner their victims, there is no way we could create a recipe book for staying safe. But we do cover the vast majority of them, and we hope that through these principles, your children can know how to keep themselves safe today better than they did yesterday.

Now, after all the insight on child offenders, you might still wonder about online predators. The scary thing about Gerrish is that he was successful as often as he was without the use of the Internet. Sadly, one way child molesters gain access to children today is through online chats. If you follow your local news, with so many stories about Internet predators, this probably isn't any surprise to you.

These people will enter any chat room commonly occupied by kids and begin a dialogue. The strategy is centered around the ego of the intended victim. Much like Gerrish's "Playing Dumb" and "Guilt Trips/False Friendships" tactics, the offender typically writes anything to make his victim feel "valued" or "important." This is how he becomes her "friend." He gives the appearance of leading a normal life with an occupation or hobby that makes her take notice. This way, he becomes someone his intended victim wants to be friends with.

He then tries to make his intended victim feel obligated to do what he asks. For example, he may invite the child to give him her phone number or set up a meeting. If she declines or wants to tell her parents first, the offender will say something like, "Why not? I thought we were friends. Don't friends trust each other? You don't do everything your parents tell you to do, do you? If you were truly my friend, you would give me your number."

Of course, for the offender, the guilt trip is just a measurement tool. He is merely trying to gauge the accessibility of his victim. If the child fails to fall for the guilt trip, then the offender just moves on to the next chat room. But if she takes the bait and gives in, then the offender gets what he came for.

The thing is, the ways predators hunt for children online are no different from what Gerrish did. They employ the same tactics—they simply use a different means to implement those tactics. What you do to combat that is to teach your kids the same principles we went over earlier. Only instead of yelling and screaming, they come and get you so you can see the computer screen. Remember, it's all about reducing the risk, and you can do that by anticipating what the predator thinks.

One other very important aspect of child molestation: As terrible as these random attacks are on children, what's worse is that the vast majority of child molestations occur at the hands of a family member or a trusted friend. Remember, Oliver Ben Gerrish's cousin and brother were among his first victims.

Unfortunately, because of the relationship dynamics involved, most of these crimes go unreported. The perpetrator uses the natural family relationship against the child, knowing that the victim has very little recourse or power to do anything. If he tells his parents, the reality of the situation is so difficult for most adults to handle that they either dismiss the child's claim or ignore it completely and hope the problem goes away, as Gerrish's mother did.

If you are a parent and your child tells you that the other parent is doing inappropriate things to her, please do not dismiss or ignore the child. At the very least, contact a child abuse hotline as soon as possible. They will talk you through what to do.

As a general rule though, it's best to get a trusted independent authority involved (a school counselor, a clergyman, or even a police officer, for example) than it is to hope the problem goes away. As difficult as it is to bring an independent person into your family's business, keep in mind that someone who is removed from the family relationship will be better able to assess objectively the situation and take any necessary steps to protect the child.

As we said earlier, if you are a child or a teenager, and you find that your parents are ignoring the problem or dismissing your story, then tell another trusted adult. We know it can be intimidating to bring to light the wrongdoings of a grown-up, but that is what the offending adult is counting on. The best thing for you to do is to find an adult authority figure who will have your best interest at heart throughout any opposition you might face.

The worse thing that can happen is complete silence. Silence puts your child at the higher end of the Risk Continuum.

If a child is taught to keep quiet, then all power has been taken away from that child, and he or she is sure to live a tortured life. Do not do that to your children. Teach them that they can come to you with anything, no matter how difficult. Role-play with them so that if the situation arises, they will feel empowered to at least take some kind of action.

Teaching them that the subject is off limits or taboo gives all the power to the abuser. Teaching children to talk openly gives the power back to the child.

As horrible as child molestation is, sexual assaults represent only one type of child offense, albeit the most common.

If we were to categorize them, then random violence, kidnapping, and domestic abuse would make up the other three general categories.

For purposes of this chapter, we will go into only random violence against children. We will, however, discuss the other two categories in our chapters that deal with domestic violence and kidnapping.

People who commit violent acts do so for one of two reasons: either they are hardened criminals, or they are using children as leverage to get something they want. In some cases, they do it for both reasons.

Either way, they think that by killing or mutilating a child, they send the message that they are capable of anything and that by so doing they can coerce people into giving them what they want.

These criminals thrive on shock and awe.

In their minds, being bad to the bone means they are stronger than anyone because they can stoop to the deepest depths of human behavior. Of course, the fact is they are the weakest humanity has to offer. And their weakness is the very reason they attack children, the most vulnerable members of our communities.

These predators are usually people who are down and out (at least emotionally) and feel like they need to do something that will create a reaction. They think that such a response—especially if it's public—will fill whatever void they have in their lives and make them feel important.

We all need a sense of validation. But instead of using legitimate means to fill a legitimate need, child predators—all predators, really—use illegitimate means.

Statistics show that the occasion is rare when a random person actually commits an act of extreme physical violence against a child. However, when such a crime does occur, the consequences reverberate throughout our society like the rings that spread after throwing a stone into a pond.

We are at a time in our society when, because of the deplorable actions of a few, adult authorities such as teachers, clergy, mentors, and others in similar positions of influence aren't allowed one-on-one contact with kids. In a lot of respects, that's a good thing because such policies keep our children safe. But in other ways, it's a sad thing, given the reasons for those restrictions.

Judge John Einhorn may have put it best when he sentenced child murderer Brandon Wilson to death for randomly selecting a nine-year-old boy at a Southern California campground, then slashing his throat while he was in the restroom.

"The death of a child by the means that we have seen through the course of this trial is an abominable occurrence," Einhorn told Wilson. "By your twisted and selfish actions, you have taken from us our country's most treasured asset—that is our children."

There isn't a more accurate explanation for why Wilson so brutally murdered Matthew Cecchi, an unassuming child who just minutes before was having the time of his life playing with his cousins at a family reunion.

Because of his assertion that he had been called by God to commit this act, Wilson was certainly twisted. But, more telling, because this drug-addicted outcast murdered to make himself feel important, he was the very essence of selfish.

All Wilson saw when he entered the bathroom were his own delusions of grandeur.

He didn't see an innocent boy who deserved to live his life to the fullest. He didn't see the pain his actions would cause the boy's family and friends. He didn't even care about the horror he would bring to that boy and the boy's family. All he cared about was his need to feel bigger than he really was.

In fact, he was so concerned with himself that, after he had been apprehended and had confessed to Matthew's murder, he asked homicide detective Chris McDonough, "Do you think this will make me some kind of celebrity?"

"Oh, yeah," answered McDonough, knowing he could seal the confession if he played up Wilson's delusions. "In fact, when we pull into the parking lot, there will probably be a ton of TV crews."

"Really?" Wilson responded.

"Oh, I'm sure," McDonough told him. "In fact, how do you want to do this? When we escort you into the office, do you want to be walking in front of us or behind us?"

"In front, for sure," Wilson replied.

Sure enough, Wilson was thrilled to find the cameras there, and McDonough, true to his word, escorted him from behind into the offices of the Oceanside Police Department.

That ego, however, would end up being Wilson's undoing.

McDonough, a veteran of more than 150 homicide investigations, certainly understood the killer's mind, which led to Wilson agreeing to fully confess to the murder on tape.

Before they had even discussed television cameras, McDonough, who was several inches taller than Wilson, made it a point to physically hunch down during his first encounter with Wilson.

"I knew I needed to lower myself below him," McDonough told us. "This was a person who needed to feel bigger than everyone else. That was the only way we were going to get anywhere with him. As a police officer, that's the only way you're going to get anywhere with anyone like him, really."

Indeed it was. And the veteran detective took full advantage of the young man's ego. When they got to the interrogation room, Wilson was excited, and McDonough continued to play him up, knowing there were two things he needed to get on tape. One, he needed Wilson to tell him about a stab wound to the victim's back, just under the right shoulder blade—a fact of the case investigators intentionally withheld from the public. If the perpetrator gave police this information, they had him, because only the killer could have known about that particular wound.

The other thing he needed was to have Wilson reenact the murder so a jury could see it. If he could keep this young man feeling on top of the world, he knew there was a good chance he would get both of those things. Essentially, the authorities were hoping Wilson would hang himself on camera.

McDonough started by getting Wilson to talk about the stab wound to the victim's back.

"Brandon," McDonough began. "How many times did you stab him? . . . Where did you stab him?"

"In the back," said Wilson. "Only once."

"Where [exactly] though? Let me see where."

"Right, like, right here," answered Wilson, pointing to the back of his right shoulder area.

"Right here?" the detective asked, pointing below his own shoulder for confirmation.

"Yeah. Right there, in the back," Wilson confirmed.

"So show me where at about the area."

"Like, right in there," Wilson said, demonstrating it on the detective's back.

"OK, why?"

"He was already dead, you know," Wilson said. "I mean, I just did it just to do it."

"OK, Brandon, let's say I'm the little kid," McDonough said, pretending to be Matthew. "Let's act this out. Are you with me on that?"

"Yeah."

"OK, let's say I'm here," McDonough demonstrated, moving to the far side of the interrogation room. "Brandon, come on over here and show me. Now, be gentle with me now, OK?"

"All right," Wilson snickered.

"OK, I'm the kid," McDonough continued. "What am I doing?"

"You're pissing," Wilson answered.

"OK. And what do you do now? Show me."

"OK. I walk around you this way, and you look at me," explained Wilson, standing a little behind and to the left of the detective.

"So I look over like this?" confirmed McDonough, looking over his left shoulder.

"Yeah. And I, and I, and I . . . you say nothing, but I kind of smile and I nodded [to disarm the boy]. You know me. [Then I say], 'I'm gonna kill you.'"

"Does he look back?"

"Yeah, he looks back."

"Then what happens?"

"I stop. I take out my knife—"

"OK," McDonough interrupted. "I noticed you pulled out your knife like that [from the front left side of your pants]. Is that where you had it?"

"Yeah. I had it right here."

"OK . . . now what happens?"

"I take it out like this," Wilson said, beginning to breathe more heavily. "I got it all figured out, got it put in the sheath the right way, so its sharp end is here . . . and I go up behind him . . ."

"Go ahead. Show me."

"OK. I grab him like this," Wilson said, his voice rising excitedly as he grabbed McDonough by the forehead with his left hand and pulled his head back to expose his throat. "Then I take him like this." He made a slashing motion across the detective's throat with his right hand.

"Right. Then what do you do?"

"I hold him like this . . . and he's startin' to sink down!"

"OK. Good. Then what happens?"

"[I stab him in the throat] one more time!"

"Then what happens?" asked the detective, feigning an excited interest in Wilson's story.

"He goes down. He goes all the way down!"

"All the way down?" reiterated McDonough, as he slowly re-enacted the fall to the ground.

"He's down on the ground!"

"Then what happens?"

"I'm leaning over him . . . and I take the knife . . . and I stab him [in the back, behind the shoulder] like this! One last time . . . and I pull the knife out."

"Right. What happens then?"

"He's dead. I stand up, start backing away, and I hear his mother's voice."

"Then what happens?"

"I think about what I'm going to do," Wilson continued, describing his subsequent encounter with the boy's aunt, whom he thought was Matthew's mother. "I'm going to kill her. I have to kill her. . . . She's screaming and screaming. And she sees me [with the knife] . . . and I run at her. . . . Then she runs. She's running a little ahead of me. And I run parallel to her, and she's screaming."

As you can see from this horrific confession, Wilson was definitely someone who craved acknowledgment, and he was willing to get it at any cost.

But how did he become like this?

It's important to know so that if you ever happen to encounter someone like Wilson early enough in his life, maybe you can see the warning signs and possibly intervene before it gets to this point.

Brandon Wilson, as he told it to investigators, was a drifter.

At seventeen, shortly after he graduated from high school, he began traveling. Over the next three years, he traveled to California from Wisconsin by way of Alaska and Washington. He was a self-described loner and hadn't really accomplished much socially in high school. He was, however, extremely intelligent from an academic standpoint, having scored in the top 15 percent nationally on the ACT exam.

He never had a serious girlfriend, and his parents had divorced just as he entered high school, the result of an affair his mother had with the high school wrestling coach, which caused him a lot of embarrassment.

Wilson had become so distraught and angered by the affair, he later told police, that he tried to work up the courage to kill his mother when he was sixteen. While she was doing the dishes, he approached her from behind, intending, coincidently, to use the very same knife he would end up using to kill Matthew Cecchi. The hunting knife was actually a gift his mother had purchased for him several months earlier. As it turned out, he wasn't able to go through with it, but it's an incident worth noting because some predatory killers find substitute victims in an effort to advance to their intended targets. We're not saying that's the case here, but we also can't rule out that possibility.

Add to all this that Wilson had absorbed drugs and pornography into his life—a definite recipe for disaster.

As he traveled the Northwest, Wilson committed a number of petty drug-related crimes and began making his way south, camping all the way. During this trip he had a "vision" while taking LSD.

In about four hours of testimony, Wilson delivered an emotionless description of the spiritual discovery that he claimed led directly to the killing. He also gave a detailed explanation of the thought process behind the slaying.

Its seed took root in high school, he related, when his mother broke up their idyllic home in rural Wisconsin. Wilson, already a confused teen, started using drugs—first marijuana, then mushrooms and LSD.

"A psychiatrist actually told us that Brandon was the angriest young man he had ever seen," McDonough later commented.

When he was sixteen, his only close friend died in a car accident. About a year later, Wilson received a $17,000 settlement after he was involved in a separate accident. During his three years of sporadic traveling, he regularly used LSD to "gain access" to parts of his mind that were normally unconscious.

His last trip began in August 1998. He went to Seattle, then to Colorado and Southern California. He camped in the desert east of San Diego. He also camped in Oceanside, a suburb in northern San Diego County.

"I guess I was trying to figure out what I wanted to do with the rest of my life," he testified. "[I was] trying to be a better person. Trying to live without materialism. The simple life."

His so-called spiritual breakthrough came November 12, 1998, two days before he killed Matthew. While camping in Borrego Springs, he took five doses of LSD, walked into the desert, and thought all night.

"I could see everything was related—everything was connected to God. It made me happy," he stated. "It made me feel like everything was going to be OK."

But he did not stop with the simple realization that God is in all things.

"I started to think about the relationship between God and the devil, good and evil," he said. "I realized that there was part of myself that was evil. God did this for a purpose."

Evil, he came to understand, is a necessary counterpoint to good. And those two together, along with everything else in existence, equaled God, he said. He also concluded that God is pure love, so everything else is love as well. Therefore, anything that Wilson did was good, he thought.

With all this in mind, he looked back on his life and redefined it. Bad things had happened to him so that a bad streak would rise inside of him, he said. That evil in him was there for a reason.

"I started to think about the bigger picture—what was happening in the world," he continued. "I believe that the world is coming to an end. I felt like I could contribute to that. I decided it was [my purpose] to kill everybody. That's the way it's going to happen. That's the way the world is going to end—by people killing one another. It's [God's] plan. It's his world that's being set in motion. It's what he wants to happen."

The acid trip lasted into the next day. That morning, he took a bus to Oceanside, a town big enough for him to "slip through the cracks" after committing his first murder. Once there, he rented a cheap motel room a couple blocks from the beach. He took two more tabs of LSD and sat around and relaxed until near dusk. Then he walked down to the sand and started hunting for a victim.

"I observed that people seemed to be aware of what I was doing—not consciously, but unconsciously," he said. "Obviously, God understood, and God was inside of them. So some part of them understood. Some of them were scared and avoided me. Some of them were just the opposite. They seemed attracted. They were offering themselves to me. All of the children that I saw seemed like they were offering themselves to me."

He said he passed up one woman because she was too fat.

Then he focused on a seventeen-year-old girl who had walked down to the beach after breaking up with her boyfriend. He hesitated because she was attractive, then thought about whether he should rape her first. Wilson said he thought the girl sensed something, because she abruptly left the immediate area.

He began prowling near a playground near the Oceanside Harbor when he spotted Matthew. The boy's family had traveled from out of town for a family reunion and was staying at a recreational vehicle park near the water. The boy and several of his cousins were playing on the equipment, closely watched by several adult family members. Matthew yelled to his aunt that he was going to the bathroom, then he ran right by Wilson. The aunt followed, but the boy went quickly into the building. She did not see Wilson slip into the bathroom behind him.

When asked about the graphic details of the stabbing, he showed neither regret or sorrow, nor did he attempt to minimize the cruelty of the act.

"I wanted someone who was pure, younger, and more innocent," said Wilson, whose soft voice could barely be heard in the packed but silent courtroom. "When you offer a sacrifice, it's supposed to be a lamb that's pure."

Wilson was eerily matter-of-fact as he recounted his thoughts.

"After I'd done it, there was a surge of energy—power," he testified. "I interpreted it as a gift from God . . . that I had done what I was meant to do."

Wilson then hurried out of the bathroom, bumping into the boy's aunt as he left. He yelled, "I can do the same to you!" Then he ran as she turned to look for the child.

Because he was out in the open, Wilson decided against killing the boy's aunt, instead turning his focus toward his escape. He managed to flee the beach area, and the next morning, he took a bus to Los Angeles and made his way to Hollywood. Early the following morning, with a "voracious appetite to kill again," he went out hunting for a second victim.

He spotted a woman walking to work. He struck up a conversation with her, and when her guard was down, he attacked her with the knife, stabbing her in the chest thirteen times. Three of her co-workers heard her scream for help, and they managed to scare Wilson off her and surround him until police arrived.

While detectives questioned him about the Hollywood assault, he confessed to the Oceanside slaying.

During his trial, Wilson already had pleaded guilty to a single count of murder with the special circumstance of lying in wait in connection with the slaying. However, he maintained that he was legally insane at the time.

But was he aware of his acts?

In order to prove his client insane, deputy public defender Curt Owen needed to convince the jury by a preponderance of the evidence that, at the time of the crime, Wilson had a mental disease or defect that prevented him from understanding the nature and quality of his acts—or in other words, knowing the difference between right and wrong.

By this definition, no, he was not insane. McDonough asked him if he knew it was wrong to kill, and Wilson's answer was a resounding yes.

He told the Oceanside detective that he had a plan in place that would allow him to commit the crime and avoid capture. That is not insanity. Rather, that is the clearly thought-out and planned homicide of an innocent child.

"He made a conscious choice to escape rather than kill Matthew's aunt," McDonough said. "During his confession, he said he had to kill the aunt, but when it came time to decide, he made the choice to escape instead."

When he took the stand in that San Diego County courtroom, Wilson tried to pass himself off as insane by explaining to a jury that God came to him during an LSD trip and made it clear that the young man's divine purpose was to kill everyone in the world.

It just so happened that Wilson started with nine-year-old Matthew Cecchi.

The fact is that he committed this murder because he needed something to make him feel important. If Wilson were completely truthful with himself, he would say that Matthew wasn't a sacrifice for God. Rather, he was a sacrifice that fed the ego of a small man.

This is one case in which we cannot point to something the victim's family could have done to absolutely prevent this from happening. The perpetrator of this crime was bent on finding and killing an innocent victim.

The only thing that might have saved this boy's life would have been to have a male member of the family accompany Matthew to the bathroom. That would have been the only conceivable risk reducer in this particular case.

Still, what if Wilson would have wanted to use a gun? There is nothing that even an adult male could reasonably do to stop a killer bent on shooting his victim.

In fact, one of the very sad aspects of this case is that, twenty minutes prior to the murder, Matthew's mother pulled him aside to role-play with him in case he encountered a dangerous stranger.

"Unfortunately," McDonough said, "Brandon Wilson was a master manipulator and had the presence of mind to disarm Matthew with a simple smile."

The lesson we learn from this is to be aware—and to a certain point, suspicious—of your surroundings. Teach your children to stay in public view where you can see and hear them. Don't assume that everyone in the area is a good person. Most people are good, but not everybody. If a child has to go into a private setting like a bathroom, then go with that child or send a trusted adult.

Remember, people you don't know are just that: unknown. It has nothing to do with judging them as being good or bad based on their appearances. In fact, judging is the worst thing you can do because it can cause you to let your guard down around dangerous people just because they are clean-cut and well spoken.

When we were talking to him during the research for this book, McDonough made a great point. He said, "Ted Bundy was a great guy until someone got into his car and he locked the doors."

Just like you would learn in a defensive-driving course, teach yourself and your children to expect the unexpected. If you do that, you and your children will be alert when potentially dangerous situations arise.

As an aside, Chris McDonough is one detective we have worked with quite often as we have conducted various law enforcement trainings around the country. He is one of the most respected homicide detectives in Southern California—not just from a law enforcement perspective but also from a victim perspective. One reason he is so well respected is due to the fact that, in each case he worked, he assigned a detective to the victim's family in order to keep them abreast of anything new pertaining to the investigation. That way, family members, already trying to cope with an emotionally taxing situation, wouldn't feel left in the dark about something that they were usually in the middle of. Police departments could learn a lot from that practice and, quite frankly, should be doing more of it.

Earlier in this chapter, we discussed what you can teach your children to help them improve their safety. As far as what you, as a parent, can do to help ensure your child's well-being, here are a few principles:

1. **Monitor your children.** We don't want to delve too far into parenting issues, but as a matter of safety, there is nothing wrong with holding your children accountable for their whereabouts. Knowing where they are and what time they will be there helps you know when something is right with your child and when it is not. For instance, if your teenage son is supposed to be at a friend's house at 9:30 p.m. after going to a seven o'clock movie, and he hasn't checked in with you yet, you know something is wrong, and you can track his possible whereabouts based on the schedule he gave you. As for Internet crimes against children, it doesn't hurt to make it a rule of thumb to have the family computer out in the open so you can take an occasional peek at what your children are browsing and whom they are in contact with.

2. **Be careful in regard to whom you relinquish responsibility for your kids.** It stands to reason that the more you surrender responsibility to your children, the higher the risk level you put

them on the Risk Continuum scale. It also means that it is most important that you check out who is watching your kids. For example, as a general rule, never let a male teenager baby-sit your children. Teenage boys tend to make up a large majority of sex abusers. In addition, always check out your daycare provider for complaints. In general, if you have any misgivings at all, follow your instincts. It's better to err on the side of caution.

3. **If at all possible, avoid sleepovers.** Many child offenses, especially sex assaults, occur during sleepovers. It can be difficult to choose who is safe and who isn't, especially when you know that most assaults occur within family and friendship bonds. Again, the smart thing to do is to avoid taking on the responsibility of being the judge of character. Instead, ask yourself how the activity tips the Risk Continuum scale. Is a sleepover, for example, an activity that puts your child at a much higher risk of victimization? The easy thing is to make a clear rule against sleepovers. Perhaps you could let your children join the party and make arrangements to pick them up at a reasonable hour—9 or 10 p.m., for example.

4. **Stay within seeing and hearing distance of your children.** It takes a lot of effort, and we know it isn't always practical, but if you have to get up a hundred times to check on your kids, then get up a hundred times. Especially at a social gathering or a crowded setting such as a park, it can be difficult and inconvenient to break away from conversations with friends. But if you teach your children to stay within your sight, and you make an effort to keep an eye on them, then you keep their risk level low.

As we have said, the tactics child predators typically use are basically the same today as they were years ago, notwithstanding the offender's motive. But it seems that there are more child offenders than ever.

That is why it is crucial, maybe now more than ever, that we protect our children. They are our innocence, and their innocence is the light of our future. Every time a child is abused or taken from us, another spark of our world's luminance is lost and replaced by darkness. This is truly where the battlefield between darkness and brightness is fought, and the only way to win is by protecting our children.

That means our principles of defense need to be based on risk reduction. Whether it's on the playground or over the Internet, we need to educate ourselves and our children in regard to predatory strategies. Above all, we need to teach them what they should do if a predator tries to utilize these tactics on them.

Remember, child offenders are looking for two things: access and anonymity.

Take even one of those things away from the predators, and you beat them. Even more important, if you teach your child to take just one of those things away from them, then even the smallest child can win.

4

TERRORISM

How could anybody do something so horrible?" asked one of the secretaries standing next to me as we watched the events of the morning unfold on national TV.

"The more important question is who," I answered, neither of us taking our eyes off the monitors. "At least for us it is. I think we're going to be in for a long day."

I was sitting ten tomb lengths below the earth in my office at the FBI Academy when I first got word of the bombing in Oklahoma City. Several questions immediately ran through my mind as images of a decimated Alfred P. Murrah Federal Building flashed across my screen. I wondered just who had committed this despicable act and why.

This wasn't just an attack on federal agents, which would have been heinous in its own right, but it was a massive assault on innocent bystanders, many of them children. If somebody had something against the United States government, why would he target a wing full of harmless kids? Of course, those were the same questions the entire country wanted—or more correctly, demanded—answers to, and it was up to us to come up with them.

And we wouldn't have long to find those answers.

"Greg, I don't need to tell you what we're up against," said Gene O'Leary, the assistant special agent in charge of the FBI's Critical Incident Response Group. Gene was a well-respected veteran of the bureau and had several years' experience in dealing with crises of all magnitudes. "We need to act fast, so we're going to have to call everybody in on this one. Get your people over to the operations center and assign them shifts. We will be doing twenty-four-hour coverage."

"I'm already on it, Gene," I answered from my office in Quantico, Virginia.

It wasn't long before I began to feel the weight of the responsibility of coordinating our unit's role in the Oklahoma City bombing investigation. Not that coordinating an investigation was new to me. For the past several months prior to the bombing, I had been serving as acting unit chief for the Investigative Support Unit, stepping into the position when our former chief—and my good friend—John Douglas was forced to take an extended sick leave.

But, somehow, I sensed this would be different.

Everything we did over the next several days and weeks would be heavily scrutinized. Our work would definitely be under a microscope because not only would it affect a criminal investigation, but it would also have potential repercussions all the way up the ladder throughout the bureau and even to the White House.

Our team quickly gathered in a conference room at the FBI Academy in Quantico, Virginia. Every available criminal profiler in the FBI Investigative Support Unit was in the consultation room watching news footage of the bombing when I arrived.

An overwhelming feeling of shock had penetrated the room. Except for the sound of the TV, not one voice could be heard. It was as if someone had hypnotized every member of the unit.

From the outside looking in, that might seem like a natural reaction, given the circumstances. But such a response was highly unusual for this group because surprise and horror were emotions that we, as profilers, had almost become desensitized to. We dealt with the worst humanity had to offer on a daily basis, and everyone in that room had collectively worked thousands of the most gruesome crimes imaginable. We had dealt with twisted individuals who tortured their victims, seen mutilated bodies, and listened to countless hours of the oppressed begging for mercy at the hands of their tormentors. We had to learn to control our emotions if we were going to last long in this vocation.

But this was, up to that point, the worst act of terrorism ever to occur in the United States, and no one who was in that room that day will soon forget the devastating scene that lay before us. This was, in fact, the first attack of this magnitude waged on continental US soil since the Civil War. I don't think anyone was prepared to see that.

Still, we had a job to do, and every minute was critical if we were going to catch whoever did this. The task at hand was upon us and we quickly shifted into problem-solving mode.

"OK, everybody," I said, interrupting the collective mood. "We have been assigned twenty-four-hour coverage on this case, so each of us will be taking twelve-hour shifts at the Special Investigations Operations Center at FBI headquarters. If anything comes up, I will be available 24/7 until this thing gets resolved."

"What will our assignments be?" asked one team member.

"We will be gathering and assessing data and assisting field agents as they call in," I answered. "We will also be consulting on interview/interrogation techniques and investigative leads of any persons of interest or potential suspects. We will be receiving our shifts and assignments shortly. Let me know if you have any questions."

I paused for a moment to look around the room and make sure everyone had received assignments. I also wanted to gauge the group's demeanor. As they got their assignments, they appeared focused and ready to go.

"OK, let's get to work then," I said. With that, everyone immediately was on task.

As you can imagine, our shifts were extremely long and taxing. Information was pouring into the center, and it was all we could do to keep up with it. I had been up all night, and the center was as pressure packed as I had ever seen it. I didn't think it could get any more hectic.

I would soon find out just how wrong I was.

Shortly after I had finished my second shift, I was on my way out the door and looking forward to getting some much-needed rest when someone from FBI administration stopped me.

"Chief Cooper?" she called out.

"Yes," I replied, glancing down at my watch. It was about 10 a.m.

"Director Freeh wants to meet with you," she said. "He's on his way up right now. He wants you to wait here for him."

I sat down and rubbed my eyes, knowing that whatever he wanted to talk about would be big. Any notion I had of getting some rest was probably lost. The director of the Federal Bureau of Investigation doesn't talk to his unit chiefs—especially during this kind of a crisis—unless he has something important to say. It wasn't long before I found out just exactly what FBI Director Louis Freeh had in mind.

"Chief Cooper," he said, greeting me with a handshake. "How is your team holding up?"

"They're doing a great job, sir," I responded.

"Good," he said. "I have a special assignment for you and your team, Greg."

"Yes, sir?"

"The president is preparing to address the nation in regard to Wednesday's attack," he continued. "He needs to know what we're dealing with and how confident he can be in relaying that information to the country."

"OK. What exactly do you need us to do?" I asked.

"As you know, we already have a suspect in hand," he said, referring to Timothy McVeigh. "We have some strong evidence that suggests that he was the one who parked the Ryder truck in front of the building and planted the explosives. What we don't know is whom he was working with."

"And you want us to profile potential groups he may have been working with?" I asked.

"Yes, in part. What we really need to know is if we are dealing with a paramilitary group—domestic or foreign. If so, we need to know how large that group is and what its level of sophistication is. Above all, we need to know how likely they will be to strike again and, if so, how soon."

The director paused a moment. I could see it had been a long day for him, too. Then he looked up and said, "Greg, I want to know how great a threat these people pose to the country and to the FBI."

As he laid out the assignment, my mind began to churn out different possibilities. I thought about whom to assign each task to. I figured we would have two or three days, when Freeh interrupted my thoughts with one last mandate.

"And I want your report by three o'clock today."

My jaw nearly hit the floor, but I quickly regained my composure before answering, "Yes, sir, we will get on it right away."

"Good. I will look forward to your report then."

With that, we shook hands, and the director exited the building, leaving us five hours to complete a Herculean task.

I quickly called the team in and we began coordinating our assignments.

"Director Freeh has just given us a special assignment," I told the team, which consisted of about a half-dozen profilers. "And we don't have much time to complete it. Our charge is twofold: One, we have to find out who is responsible for Wednesday's attack, meaning the president wants to know if this was done by a paramilitary group, foreign or domestic. If so, he wants to know which group it is, how large it is, and how quickly they will attack again, if at all. The director is expecting a report at three o'clock today."

Immediately after I uttered those words, I heard a collective gasp.

"I know it's a lot," I quickly acknowledged. "But I'm confident we can do this. Let's start by coming up with a game plan, then we'll see from there."

The job we had was complex because of what it represented. We weren't just trying to find the bad guy. This time, we had the weight of the public's perception of safety to consider, as well. People were demanding to know whether this was an act of war committed by terrorist cells, and they weren't going to be denied answers for much longer. But I had confidence in this group that we had the ability to get this accomplished. There was just too much talent and collective experience in the room not to.

Government agencies, schools, restaurants, and even roller rinks had been the targets of hundreds of bomb scares nationwide, as pranksters and vindictive people exploited the anxiety and fear created by the bombing in Oklahoma City. Individual government agencies, even as small as those on the county and city levels, had received as many as three to five telephoned bomb threats in just a matter of hours.

In other instances across the nation, evacuations of thousands of workers from agencies such as Health and Human Services, Welfare, and others had been reported. At one point, the General Services Administration stated that about 130 bomb-related incidents—including bomb threats and suspicious packages—had been reported in federal buildings nationwide within the first few days after the Oklahoma City bombing. Emotions were running high, and it was vital that President Clinton be able to address the nation quickly. All around the country, people were wondering if their city was the next target. If it could happen in our nation's heartland, then it could happen anywhere.

In large part, the president was relying on this information to tell him if this was an act of sophisticated, organized terrorism or the work of a small, isolated group of people. Moreover, he needed to be able to quash the increasing uneasiness without fear of repercussion.

"If we say this was done by a large paramilitary group, then we run the risk of creating a panic," I thought as I analyzed the data. "On the other hand, if we conclude that the attack was carried out by a small, isolated group, and another attack ensues, it could mean mayhem."

I didn't dwell on those thoughts for long, but it was a way for me to center myself on the purpose of our job.

As we devised a general profile of the perpetrator, we went through the signature methods of operation of each type of terrorist group and began to rule each organization out, one by one.

We also called every domestic paramilitary group imaginable. All of them came back with the same general response: "In no way did we have anything to do this bombing. We do not target the innocent."

Their message was consistent with their past actions.

None of these groups was about killing civilians. Domestic paramilitary groups, at least the most organized ones, are about creating a change in the government, which they believe to be corrupt. If anything, they would be more of a threat to usurp power from higher-level government authorities, not to kill lower-level citizens.

After each member of the unit pulled their individual findings together, we gathered together and discussed the probabilities. As usual, every team member had something valuable to contribute, and we were quickly able to narrow a list of probable profiles. We finally came to a consensus on a profile around 2:30 p.m., and we quickly pulled the data together and readied our report. When the time came for us to present to Director Freeh, we were confident that we had made the correct determination.

Freeh and his assistant directors arrived at 3 p.m. sharp.

"First, I just want to tell you all how much I appreciate all your hard work," the director said. "I know that the assignment I gave you to do and the time frame I gave you to do it in was extremely demanding, but I'm looking forward to hearing your findings, so I will turn the time over to Chief Cooper."

"Thank you, Director Freeh," I began. "First, I also want to thank everyone for your hard work. I believe we can be extremely confident in our assessment."

From there, the meeting evolved into a question-and-answer session in which we proceeded to explain that we believed the attack was carried out domestically by a small, isolated group of individuals and that we didn't think they would strike again anytime soon.

"How did you arrive at that conclusion?" Freeh asked.

"Well, sir, first, we ran a database of every known terrorist group, domestic and foreign," one group member explained. "Then, we cross-referenced their corresponding methods of operation with the signature methods used in the attack on the Murrah building. The bombing in Oklahoma City didn't match signature philosophies or methods of any of the terrorist groups. In general, foreign terrorist groups, such as al Qaeda, are looking for trophies."

"Trophies?" the director asked.

"Yes, sir, trophies. They want to hit something symbolic to our nation, such as the Statue of Liberty, the White House, or the World Trade Center, which, as you know, al Qaeda attempted to destroy two years ago. They want the people of this country to suffer emotionally, as well as physically. On the other hand, domestic groups, like the antigovernment paramilitary organizations we constantly monitor, are looking to force change in the government. If they were to attack a government building like this, they would have taken measures to ensure that there were no women or children in the building. At the very least, they would have taken steps to minimize any potential collateral damage. In fact, they abhor our political leaders because they think our government hurts our country's poor and middle class. They view themselves as protectors of the innocent citizens of this nation. Had they carried out an attack like this, they would have done so in a manner that portrayed them, at least in their minds, as heroes trying to save the Constitution from a corrupt government, not as hooligans who kill innocent civilians."

"OK, good, so how do you know they won't strike again?"

"They are too small, probably five or fewer people. The amount of explosives they used had to have depleted most, if not all, of their resources. We know they aren't wealthy because the level of sophistication used in the attack was very low. The explosives were basically homemade and randomly loaded into a Ryder truck. They just parked it in front of the building and waited for it to blow up, hoping it would do as much damage as possible. A more sophisticated operation would have required more training and precision and more sophisticated weaponry."

"Does Timothy McVeigh, who was recently taken into custody, fit this profile?" Freeh asked.

"Yes, sir, he does. Knowing what we know about his training and background, we can say with a high level of confidence that he fits the profile very closely."

The director continued asking questions for several minutes. Every member of the unit provided answers based on their respective areas of expertise, and I truly believe that Freeh was impressed by what each person had to contribute.

"Well, I think that's all we needed to know," the director concluded. "I just want to say again how much I appreciate all of your efforts here today. Keep up the good work."

With that, Freeh and his assistants left, and we went back to our initial assignments. But the sense of pride we all felt in knowing that we could help bring some measure of peace to the nation gave us an extra boost to get through the next few grueling weeks.

Just a few days later, at Michigan State University, President Clinton made a now-famous speech in which he pointed his remarks directly toward paramilitary groups, some of whom had been advocating and encouraging violence against government agencies. In his address, he urged those groups within the nation to use nonviolent methods to create change.

"I would like to say something to the paramilitary groups and to others who believe the greatest threat to America comes not from terrorists from within our country or beyond our borders, but from our own government," he began. "I want to say this to the militias and to others who believe this, to those nearby and those far away: I am well aware that most of you have never violated the law of the land. I welcome the comments that some of you have made recently condemning the bombing in Oklahoma City. I believe you have every right, indeed you have the responsibility, to question our government when you disagree with its policies. And I will do everything in my power to protect your right to do so.

"But I also know there have been lawbreakers among those who espouse your philosophy. I know from painful personal experience as a governor of a state who lived through the cold-blooded killing of a young sheriff and a young African-American state trooper, who were friends of mine, by people who espouse the view that the government was the biggest problem in America and that people had a right to take violence into their own hands. So I ask you to hear me now. It is one thing to believe that the federal government has too much power and to work within the law to reduce it. It is quite another to break the law of the land and threaten to shoot officers of the law if all they do is their duty to uphold it."

Since the Oklahoma City bombing, there has not been one large attack carried out by domestic terrorists. This is also a credit to many paramilitary groups in our country. The majority of them condemned, and still do condemn, the measure of violence that was taken that day to express antigovernment views.

When we finished that assignment, our next focus was to assist in the capture and conviction of anyone involved in conspiring to commit the attack. Once the authorities had apprehended McVeigh, our mission was to provide interrogation strategies for law enforcement personnel interviewing people of interest during the course of the investigation.

For the next several days, someone from our unit was on the phone with investigators from all over the world who inquired about everything from suspect profiles to interrogation strategies. Because the unit was in a state of transition and had been somewhat depleted, I assigned myself and about a half dozen others to take ten-to-twelve-hour shifts on a rotational basis. Over the next few weeks, and especially during those first several days, there was immense stress and pressure on everyone associated with the investigation.

The public demand for a swift resolution to the case was enormous, as well as it should have been, and we felt a great responsibility to the victims to solve it. As if that weren't enough stress, this kind of case could make or break a career. One wrong recommendation or profile could compromise the investigation and make it possible for the perpetrators of this crime to walk. The person responsible for that would be shamed and could expect to have to find another line of work immediately.

Despite those pressures, each member of the team did a fantastic job and, in my opinion, made a significant contribution in building solid cases against Timothy McVeigh and, more especially, Terry Nichols, both of whom would eventually be convicted for their respective roles in the bombing.

It so happened that during one of my shifts, I got a call from an FBI coordinator in Chicago. She told me that bureau investigators had made contact with Nichols's estranged wife and twelve-year-old son. Understandably so, his ex-wife was very hesitant to allow the FBI to interview the boy, concerned about the effect that implicating his father in such a heinous act would have on him.

Still, we needed to know the level of Nichols's participation in the crime, and we had reason to believe that he had taken his son to meetings that he and McVeigh had held to plan the bombing. With the heavy publicity surrounding the crime, Nichols's ex-wife was growing more determined by the minute to do whatever it took to protect her son. The coordinator and her team had to act fast, and they needed to know the best way to get mother and son to cooperate.

I had seen interviews with Nichols in which he vehemently denied that he had any recent dealings with McVeigh and that he had no involvement whatsoever in the bombing. Those of us who watched those interviews came to the quick consensus that he was full of it. He was, as Shakespeare would say, protesting too much—way too much.

As more information confirmed his recent association with McVeigh, we knew for certain he was lying. For one, their relatives knew of recent meetings between the two and had seen them together on several occasions—so that blew a big hole in Nichols's story.

Armed with this information, the coordinator and I quickly began a brief question-and-answer session.

I asked her if she thought Nichols's wife had any knowledge of his involvement in planning the bombing. She couldn't be certain, but she didn't think so.

"Then you'll need to find that out," I told her. "If it turns out she was involved or had any knowledge of his plans, help her see that she'll be saving her own skin if she cooperates."

"What if it turns out she didn't know he was involved?" she asked.

"If she didn't know, then make her sympathize with the victims," I advised. "She needs to put herself in their shoes, feel their pain, if she is going to have any incentive to cooperate at all."

"Yes, I agree. What would be the next line of questioning after that?"

"The next part is the clincher," I replied. "Even though she feels an overwhelming sense of sympathy for the victims and their families, that is only one part of the equation. She will still feel the need to protect her closest family, her son. She probably feels like it will scar him forever to turn on his father. She also most likely wants him to continue to have a relationship with his father. Most mothers do. Also, she might still have feelings for Nichols. Just because they're separated doesn't mean part of her doesn't still love him. That means you'll need to drive a wedge between her and Nichols. By the time you're done, you need to make sure she doesn't feel any allegiance to him at all. She needs to feel sick that, not only is he responsible for the deaths of over a hundred men, women, and children, but also he would stoop so low as to involve his own child—*their* child—in the conspiracy."

"Then, at that point, should I ask for permission to interview the boy?" she asked.

"Yes, once you're certain that she sympathizes with the victims and understands that Nichols is on the opposite side of the fence than she is, then that's when you get the boy involved. If she understands those two things, she will give you permission to talk to her son, though she will still probably be protective."

"All right, then, if we do get permission to talk to the boy, in your opinion, what would be the best way to proceed with him?"

"Well, from what you know, what is the boy's relationship with his father like?"

"As far as we can gather, he really looks up to Nichols. If we do get through the mom, it may be even harder to get the boy to cooperate."

"Yes, it will, but you can do it. He's in a vulnerable position, so he's going to be on the defensive. You'll have to mother him. Take off the professional veneer and be his friend. It's important that he feels like he can trust you. If he admires his father, then there is a strong likelihood that he has adopted some of the same distrust of federal authority that Nichols has. You will have to make the boy believe that you don't want to hurt his dad, but you are there to help him, and you want to show the world that his dad was just a pawn in this crime, not a major player. If you can achieve that level of trust, he will tell you what he knows."

"All right, Greg, you've been very helpful. We'll let you know how it goes. Thank you."

"You bet. Good luck and call if you need anything else."

Something to realize about our interrogation strategy is that we didn't enjoy finishing off someone's relationship and destroying the family, but there was a good chance that Nichols had shared responsibility for the deaths of 168 innocent people. We were forced to play the hand we were dealt. If he did indeed share responsibility for this crime, it was our job to find out the truth and bring closure to the hundreds of friends and loved ones who had suffered great losses that day.

In the end, the investigators were able to talk to Nichols's son. I'm not entirely certain of the nature of their discussions with him, but apparently, they were able to get some information from him.

Another aspect to closing this case was to get Nichols himself to confess, or at least in some part acknowledge, his involvement in the bombing. I received calls from FBI agents assigned to interrogate Nichols. They knew he was lying about the level of his association with McVeigh, and there was some pretty strong circumstantial evidence linking him to the bombing, but a confession is always a prosecutor's best friend, especially in a high-profile case like this one.

The interrogators wanted to know how to get it from him.

"You're going to have to dress down," I told them on a conference call. "I would strongly advise against going into the interrogation room wearing standard FBI attire. He has absolute disdain and distrust for the federal government, and the mere sight of your clothing will be a constant reminder to him that you are Big Brother. Does that make sense?"

"Yes, we got it. How do you suggest we proceed once we get into the room with him?"

"The best thing to do is to go in, talk to him casually, and let him know that you're just a guy doing your job," I advised. "Build a rapport with him. Start off by talking about his hobbies, his military service, anything that he loves that will loosen him up. And talk about yourself as a person. If you build on something you have in common, his perception of you as a threat will significantly be reduced. He still won't completely trust you, but he might let his guard down enough that he will be willing to talk to you."

"What do you think is the best way to approach him once we broach the subject of the bombing?" a voice on the other line asked.

"Once you see he's relaxed and not so defensive, then you can start discussing it, but realize that the first thing you want to do is to minimize his role in the bombing. Tell him that the evidence in the investigation is showing that the whole idea was McVeigh's and that he was just there for support. Above all, tell him that we don't think he knew there were children in the building, that we don't think he is the kind of guy who was willing to see children die. By approaching it that way, you will make him think you have a case, but at the same time, you give him justification to confess by making him see that you don't think he is in the same class as McVeigh. Also, you give him an opportunity to save face and repair his reputation. But keep in mind that this strategy is just the groundwork you are laying to soften him up for the key part of the interview."

"What's that, Greg?"

"His son," I said. "Once you have him thinking he can save face, you need to talk about his son. Ask him what kind of legacy he wants to leave for the boy. 'Do you want your son to remember you as someone who helped slaughter innocent women and children, or do you want him to remember you as someone who was simply fighting for what you believe in?'"

"Are you sure it's a good idea to bring his son into the conversation?" one of the agents asked skeptically.

"Absolutely," I countered. "If the interrogator can get him to think that there is a solid case against him and that he can improve, at least in his son's eyes, the image he has created for himself, then you have a chance of getting a confession out of him."

"I don't know," said another agent. "It sounds kind of risky to me."

"You have to realize that he's never going to believe that we're going to cut him a deal," I asserted. "He is convinced that we are out to get him. But if he thinks that right now his son views him as a child killer, then he will cooperate—at least on some level—because he will want to change the boy's perception of him. You want him to think that, if he cooperates, his son will realize that once he knew that women and children were in the Murrah building, he was opposed to the plan, that he wanted nothing to do with it at that point, and that McVeigh carried it out anyway. I think this gives us the best chance of facilitating a confession."

"I see what you're saying, Cooper, but my concern is that we will alienate him by letting him know we're dragging his son into this mess," the agent on the other line insisted. "If that happens, he will completely clam up, and then we can forget about getting anything out of him."

"I know, but let me explain why I don't think that will happen. McVeigh was the leader, and every leader needs a submissive follower. In profiling Nichols, all the information that we have received on this case is that there is a high probability that he is that guy. He was probably intimidated by McVeigh and, maybe in some cases, even emotionally manipulated and threatened into going along with the attack. Because he was the weaker of the two, he chose to participate despite any misgivings he may have had."

"That doesn't excuse what he did," the agent interjected. "Nor does it explain why he exposed the boy to the bombing plot."

"No, in and of itself, it doesn't," I continued. "But, given his behavioral weaknesses, the reason he brought the boy to the planning rendezvous was to make himself feel like a big man in someone else's eyes, even if that person was merely a child. Think about it. What dad doesn't want his son to think he's a hero? And someone with insecurities, like Nichols, would feel even more compelled to play the hero to his son. That's why we believe that, given his past behaviors with the boy, turning him into a larger-than-life hero in his son's eyes is the most effective interrogation strategy."

"OK, I see what you're saying. Well, we will give it a try and see what we come up with."

"All right," I said. "If you get stuck, give me a call, let me know where you're at with him, and we'll go from there."

With that, we ended the call.

As it turned out, Nichols, who had up to that point utterly refused to speak about McVeigh or the bombing, made two key admissions that led to his convictions. The first was that he knew a lot about building bombs, including the kind used in the Oklahoma City bombing. The second was that he had recent contact with Timothy McVeigh.

As a result of those admissions, coupled with the physical evidence gathered by investigators, Nichols was convicted in 1997 of federal conspiracy and manslaughter charges for the deaths of eight law enforcement agents in the bombing of the Alfred P. Murrah Federal Building. In 2004 he was again convicted, this time of arson, conspiracy to commit arson, and 161 counts of first-degree murder in the Oklahoma state trial. In both cases, Nichols was sentenced to life in prison with no possibility of parole. He avoided the death penalty because jurors at both his federal and state trials could not agree on the punishment.

McVeigh, of course, was convicted of federal murder charges for the bombing and was executed in 2001.

Nichols never testified, but he did apologize during sentencing in the state case. His apology seemed to be the end of the ordeal, and it looked like we would never get the whole story from him. But in summer 2005, FBI agents discovered hundreds of blasting caps and other explosives buried beneath his former house in Herington, Kansas. The findings led investigators to question Nichols again, at which time he made a full disclosure of his part in the bombing. The confession came only after he was convicted in both his state and federal trials and the threat of the death penalty was off the table.

And when he did finally divulge everything, it turned out that our profile of Terry Nichols was dead on.

He told FBI investigators that he first thought McVeigh was going to blow up a monument to avenge those who he felt wrongfully died during the government siege at the Branch Davidian compound in Waco, Texas—exactly two years before the Oklahoma City bombing.

Nichols also said he robbed an Arkansas gun collector just a few months before the bombing, an act he reluctantly committed due to McVeigh's intimidation tactics. That admission was consistent with the prosecutors' theory that weapons, coins, and other valuables stolen from the collector were used to finance the bombing. Again, this information turned out to confirm our initial profile, which was that a small, unsophisticated group of people had committed the act—not a large paramilitary terrorist organization.

In addition to the Arkansas robbery, Nichols said he helped McVeigh steal explosives from a Kansas rock quarry around that same time. The pair bought fertilizer for the bomb from a Kansas farm store and purchased nitromethane racing fuel from a racetrack in Texas. Nichols confessed to being with McVeigh in Oklahoma City three days before the bombing, and he told investigators that McVeigh drove from Kansas to Oklahoma City to park a getaway car, while he followed in a truck.

Nichols also confessed that, the day before the attack, he did help McVeigh build the bomb in the back of the rented Ryder truck next to a Kansas lake, something he denied during the initial rounds of interrogations and throughout the justice process.

This information was also consistent with our initial profile because we concluded that the group had only enough money to strike once. Our conclusion turned out to be true, because the purchases McVeigh and Nichols made in Kansas and Texas definitely sapped their resources, leaving them unable to immediately strike again, even if they had escaped capture.

In terms of the relationship between Nichols and McVeigh, he told the FBI that McVeigh was domineering and very secretive, leading

Nichols to believe that his former army buddy had other accomplices. In published news reports, Nichols's mother indicated that McVeigh threatened her son with a gun on several occasions, and she also thought others were involved in the bombing plot. Other family members have said Nichols has Asperger's syndrome, a developmental disorder that can make a sufferer especially vulnerable to manipulation and peer pressure.

As we profiled potential accomplices, this is the very type of person we came up with, because in any terrorist organization, regardless of the size, two components are absolutely necessary to make the group function—leaders with dominant personality types and followers willing to do anything for those leaders. Once you put those two ingredients together, the results can be downright lethal. Furthermore, if such an organization finds a cause that they are fanatical about, then they will do anything to eradicate what they perceive as a grave injustice.

In the case of McVeigh and Nichols, those ingredients proved to be catastrophic for the people of Oklahoma City on that spring day in 1995.

Six years later, those same components combined to destroy the World Trade Center buildings and a large section of the Pentagon, costing our nation thousands of American lives. Three months after September 11, 2001, Richard Reid tried, though unsuccessfully, to blow a plane out of the sky with a shoe bomb. Again, a fanatic follower was willing to do anything, dying included, for his leader.

People often wonder how terrorists can be so hateful and go to such extremes, even giving up their own lives, to commit such acts of terrible violence. There are several reasons, ranging from social to political to hunger for power.

At the center of those reasons, however, is simple economics.

Since the beginning of humanity, economics has fed into people's perceptions of self-importance. Not everyone, obviously, feels that way, but a lot of people do. As human beings, economics can control our emotions. If we are doing well financially, a level of stress is taken

On the road that I have taken,
one day, walking, I awaken,
amazed to get where I have come,
where I'm going, where I'm from.

This is not the path I thought.
This is not the place I sought.
This is not the dream I bought,
just a fever I've caught.

I'll change highways in a while,
at the crossbacks, one more mile.
My path is like my own fire.
I'll soon be going where my heart desires.

On the road that I have taken,
one day, walking, I awaken.
On the new road I am taking,
on this road, no longer forsaken.

This poem, written by Gerrish, gave King and Cooper valuable insight into the mind of a serial child molester. (Courtesy of Michael King)

Family photo of Oliver Benjamin Gerrish, who confessed to more than five hundred counts of child molestation. The photo includes Gerrish's parents and his younger brother, Stanley. Sadly, one of Gerrish's earliest victims was Stanley, whom Gerrish said he often molested in the bathtub. (Courtesy of Michael King)

Gerrish spoke to a group of law enforcement officials at a conference designed to give investigators more insight into the mind of a serial child molester. (Courtesy of Michael King)

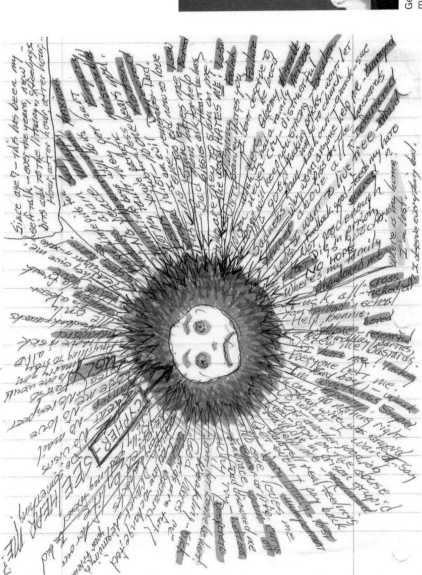

This is an illustration created by Gerrish, which depicts the emotional turmoil he says he felt as he struggled with what he termed "child molestation addiction." Gerrish told King and Cooper that he was at the center of a barrage of conflicting emotions. (Courtesy of Michael King)

IMPACT

What do I leave behind?,
empty skies
barren fields
dead grasses
dandelions, weeds
birds swooping
hands... little hands...
...groping blindly
hands... little hands...
...waving in the mists
faces, faces
...each one, veiled
...each one, mirroring
my passing!

Oliver Gerrish

This note from Gerrish was written shortly before his death. He told King that he had come to the realization that his life's legacy was nothing but the pain he had caused countless children and their families. (Courtesy of Michael King)

My name is Mr. Ken Gerrish. I [?] the ice arena and do some ice dance. Your daughter was here at the arena trying on the skates of a friend (another young lady). No harm there. She seemed to be very interested in ice skating. If your approve (I'll need a note), she'll skate and go around [?] a little time with her, until the gate [?] to it.

One of the most devious ways Gerrish gained access to his victims was by obtaining the trust of their parents. Gerrish wrote this note hoping that the mother of a six-year-old girl would allow him to have time alone with her daughter. Unfortunately, he was successful. However, this victim later came forward, an act that led to Gerrish's conviction. (Courtesy of Michael King)

Rifle Accident at Camp Wood Is Fatal

Ten-Year-Old Stanley Gerrish, of Atchison, Is Victim in Mishap Tuesday Morning.

An accident at the YMCA area camp, Camp Wood, Elmdale, shortly before noon Tuesday, claimed the life of Stanley Gerrish, 10-year-old son of Mr. and Mrs. O. B. Gerrish, of Atchison.

The tragedy occurred on the rifle range when a .22 caliber bullet struck the youngster in the back, punctured a lung and severed an artery leading either to or from the heart. Death was due to internal hemmorhaging.

Immediately following the accident the boy was brought to a local physician by camp staff members. He was rushed from Cottonwood Falls to the Newman Memorial hospital,

Emporia, where blood plasma was administered and he showed signs of rallying for a time. He died about 1:30 o'clock the same afternoon, shortly beofre his parents and his older brother, Ben, arrived at the hospital from Atchison in a chartered plane.

Camp officials said Gerrish went to the target pit to retrieve bullets after the cease fire order had been given, but was not seen. Not seeing Stanley as he kneeled behind the targets, another boy was given permission to fire another round. The first shot struck Stanley as he raised up.

He came to Camp Wood a week ago Sunday and was slated to leave this Wednesday. His father is head chemist at the Midwest Solvents company, Atchison.

BLOOD DONOR RECRUITMENT COMMITTEE MEMBERS NAMED

Cooper and King believe Stanley's death has many unanswered questions, leading them to believe also that there may be more to learn about what was termed an "accidental shooting." The shooting death occurred during a Boy Scout campout. (Courtesy of Michael King)

	DAY	WEEK	MONTH	YEAR	31 YEARS
Depression	2.5	17.5	70	840	31,080
Anger	2.5	17.5	70	840	31,080
Pornography	1.0	7.0	28	336	12,432
Fantasizing	5.0	35.0	140	1,680	62,160
Mast'	2.0	14.0	56	672	24,864
Planning	1.0	7.0	28	336	12,432
Cruising	2.0	14.0	56	672	24,864
A/Out	1.0	7.0	28	336	12,432
			TOTAL DEVIANT HOURS =		211,184

From 13 thru 44 = 31 yrs.   [24 hrs/day = 8,760/year]

31 yrs = 271,560 hours
- 211,184 deviant hours
60,376 deviant-free hours in 31 years!

1. Guilt Trips
2. False friendships
3. Lies
4. Lures
5. Tickle games
6. Playing dumb
7. I need help
8. Me help you
9. Salesman
10. Photo jobs
11. Roots
12. Cruising
13. Want to ...
14. Birthday gifts
15. Are you lost.
16. Poor me.

As part of his prison therapy, Gerrish kept a log accounting for the time and energy he spent in deviant thought and behavior. He estimated that more than half of his life was consumed by his desire to sexually molest children. (Courtesy of Michael King)

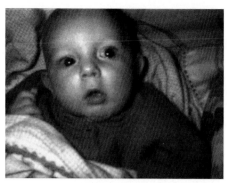

Booking photo of Mark Wing, who confessed to squeezing his seven-week-old son to death. King concluded that, essentially, Wing murdered the child because his idea of a perfect family unit consisted of only two children, not three. *(Courtesy of Utah Department of Corrections)*

Ian Wing, only a few weeks old when this photo was taken, suffered twenty-nine rib fractures and two broken legs at the hands of his father. *(Photo of Ian Wing entered as state's exhibit in the case of the* State of Utah v. Mark Wing*)*

Booking photo of Arvin Shreeve, the man who masterminded the infamous "Zion Society." At the time of his arrest in 1991, Shreeve was at the center of what was then the largest known child sex abuse ring in the nation. *(Courtesy of Utah Department of Corrections)*

The "Zion Society" created its own lingerie line as a way to support itself financially. The Ogden, Utah, neighborhood consisted of well-groomed homes and yards but was a façade for the ring. *(Flyer entered as state's exhibit in the case of the* State of Utah v. Arvin Shreeve, 1991*)*

Shreeve spoke to a large group of police officers about the cult's mentality. In the wake of the Branch Davidian group and other such cults, it is important for everyone involved in the case to understand how such an organization works. *(Courtesy of Michael King)*

Booking and court document photos for Dan *(left)* and Ron Lafferty *(right)*, who made national headlines when they carried out the gruesome slayings of their sister-in-law, Brenda Lafferty, and eighteen-month-old niece, Erica Lafferty. The brothers claimed they were acting in the name of God. *(Courtesy of Utah Department of Corrections)*

Photo of Brenda Lafferty. *(Photo entered as state's exhibit in the case of the* State of Utah v. Dan Lafferty, Ron Lafferty, *1985)*

Photo of Erica Lafferty, taken just months before her death. *(Photo entered as state's exhibit in the case of the* State of Utah v. Dan Lafferty, Ron Lafferty, *1985)*

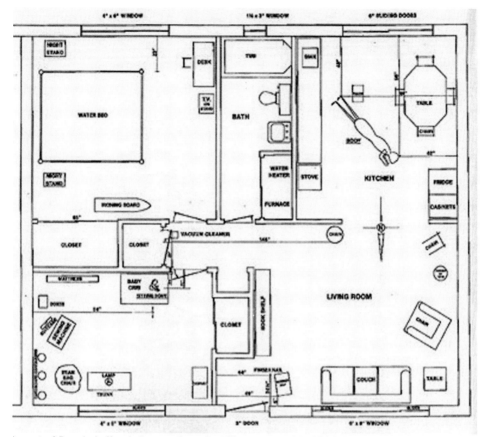

Layout of Brenda Lafferty's home, where the killings occurred in 1984. Dan and Ron barged into the house and killed Brenda in the kitchen. Dan, acting on instruction from his older brother Ron, then went into Erica's room and slashed her throat while she was in her crib. *(Layout entered as state's exhibit in the case of the* State of Utah v. Dan Lafferty, Ron Lafferty, *1985)*

Dan Lafferty speaks to a group of law enforcement officials at a training session designed to help law enforcement understand the psychology of a zealot willing to do anything—including murder—to achieve his objective. *(Courtesy of Michael King)*

THUS SAITH THE LORD UNTO MY SERVENTS
THE PROPHETS. IT IS MY WILL AND
COMMANDMENT THAT YE REMOVE THE
FOLLOWING INDIVIDUALS IN ORDER THAT
MY WORK MIGHT GO FORWARD. FOR THEY
HAVE TRULY BECOME OBSTACLES IN MY
PATH AND I WILL NOT ALLOW MY WORK
TO BE STOPPED. FIRST THY BROTHER'S
WIFE BRENDA AND HER BABY, THEN
CHLOE LOW, AND THEN RICHARD STOWE.
AND IT IS MY WILL THAT THEY BE RE-
MOVED IN RAPID SUCCESSION AND THAT
AN EXAMPLE BE MADE OF THEM IN
ORDER THAT OTHERS MIGHT SEE THE
FATE OF THOSE WHO FIGHT AGAINST
THE TRUE SAINTS OF GOD. AND IT
IS MY WILL THAT THIS MATTER BE
TAKEN CARE OF AS SOON AS POSSIBLE
AND I WILL PREPARE A WAY FOR MY
INSTRUMENT TO BE DELIVERED AND
INSTRUCTION BE GIVEN UNTO MY SER-
VANT TODD. AND IT IS MY WILL THAT
HE SHOW GREAT CARE IN HIS DUTIES
FOR I HAVE RAISED HIM UP AND
PREPARED HIM FOR THIS IMPORTANT
WORK AND IS HE NOT LIKE UNTO MY
SERVANT PORTER ROCKWELL. AND GREAT
BLESSINGS AWAIT HIM IF HE WILL
DO MY WILL, FOR I AM THE LORD THY

GOD AND HAVE CONTROL OVER ALL THINGS.
BE STILL AND KNOW THAT I AM WITH THEE.

EVEN SO AMEN

The infamous "Removal Letter," a document in which Ron and Dan Lafferty say the Lord instructed them to remove Brenda and Erica from the earth. (Letter entered as state's exhibit in the case of the State of Utah v. Dan Lafferty, Ron Lafferty, 1985) off our shoulders. If we are doing poorly economically, that stress can lead to downright desperation.

If we are to combat terrorism, it is important to understand the role economics play in creating terrorist cells.

In the Middle East, for instance, many families have a hard time even putting food on the table. An able-bodied young man can stand on the corner, begging for work, day after day, and still be unable to find gainful employment. As this goes on, his hunger burns, and he becomes frustrated and angry, often looking for someone to blame. It's not long before someone like Osama bin Laden uses that anger to his advantage. He brings the young man into his organization, offers him a purpose in life, and ultimately teaches him that his purpose is to hate and destroy the enemy. By so doing, he creates within that young man an unwavering allegiance to him.

It's nothing more than Brainwashing 101.

And, in many cases, it's easy to do because there are so many desperate people in the world, including in the United States, who are looking to find someone to lead them out of their dire circumstances.

Another aspect of terrorism is the need we all have to feel significant, to leave our mark on the world. That is why terrorism so often is committed in the name of religion or politics. Terrorism needs a cause, and those two emotionally charged topics provide the best causes possible for someone looking to head up a terrorist organization.

That's why we still hear the old saying, "Never discuss religion or politics."

Big fights on those issues occur everywhere, from the national news to around the dinner table. How often have you seen a polite discussion about religion or politics quickly turn from a mild debate to a heated argument?

Of course, the people you have seen argue probably never became terrorists, but it's the people who, given the right set of circumstances, allow the heat to rise within themselves and turn it up within the hearts of others that begins the descent into coercive practices.

For McVeigh and Nichols, the impetus for their violence was

political, but on smaller, more local levels, we see people committing violent acts in the name of religion on a daily basis all over the world.

One such group, albeit very small and local, committed one of the worst terrorist acts imaginable in the name of religion in a small central Utah community in the summer of 1984.

Dan and Ron Lafferty had founded an organization they called "The School of the Prophets," a church they organized because they were dissatisfied with the teachings of their childhood religion, the Church of Jesus Christ of Latter-day Saints. As is the case with Islamic extremists, the pair obviously didn't completely comprehend the standards of their original church, or they never would have spun off into the direction they did.

But, like we have recently seen with Islam, there are people willing to take the positive teachings of a religion and spin them to suit their own desires. In this case, the Laffertys had a need to feel ultra-important in their community, and they created an organization that supported that need.

The need to feel important wasn't their crime. Everyone needs to feel important in his or her respective communities, but not everyone *kills* to do it.

The two brothers had a third brother, Allen, who had joined their sect. But when his wife, Brenda, raised objections, Allen Lafferty disassociated himself from the self-proclaimed prophets. Then Dan and Ron perceived that their religion was being threatened and felt compelled to do something to protect it. That something would turn out to be the brutal slayings of their sister-in-law, Brenda Lafferty, and their fifteen-month-old niece, Erica Lafferty.

Ron refused to speak to us, but in 1999, Mike and I received permission to remove Dan from his Utah prison and fly him out to a conference in New Mexico, where he told his story to a group of about two hundred law enforcement professionals.

"I had a premonition that it was something that needed to be done," he explained to the audience. "And I sold all my weapons at a garage sale. And, incidentally, from that garage sale, my brother [Ron] took some of the money, and he bought some items at the mall, one of which was the knife, which was ultimately used to take the lives of these two individuals. . . . I'm not ashamed of it, I'm not embarrassed by it, and I may speak of it so calmly it might unnerve you a little bit, but to me, there was no emotional involvement in it. . . . It is a phenomenon that I don't understand completely. It raises a lot of interesting questions in my own mind about God and about what this experience we call life is."

Dan then explained how he and Ron had gone to their brother's home on July 24, when they knew that only their sister-in-law and her daughter would be home. When they knocked on the door, Brenda refused to let them inside. They forced their way in, pulled her into the kitchen, then brutally beat her and strangled her unconscious with a cord.

"It got pretty unpleasant," Dan continued. "Blood was spattered, at that point, quite severely, actually. . . . We strangled her until I was satisfied that she wouldn't regain consciousness. Then, I walked back, and I walked right into the child's room. The baby was standing in the bed [crib], and, uh, I really believe that the baby thought that I was her father, because her father and I have identical voices. We both have beards and such. So I talked to her briefly. I said, 'I don't understand this completely. I understand, from what I'm being directed, that you need to go back to Heavenly Father.' Now, I don't think she understood any of this, but it was important that I felt like I had to do this anyway. I told her, 'I don't understand, but maybe we can talk about this sometime in the presence of God. I don't know. But it's imperative, apparently, that you leave this world.' And so I put my left hand on her head, and I raised the knife with my right hand. And I closed my eyes and turned my head as I drew it across her throat. I didn't feel anything. I didn't hear anything, and I didn't turn back. I turned directly to the door and left. In fact, I was worried, as I explained to Mike and Greg. I was a little bit worried, later, thinking, 'I wonder if I did as I was supposed to?' I was worried that I maybe hadn't taken the child's life. But the thing that reassured me was that, as I recall, I walked to the bathroom and washed the knife off. Then, from there, I went into the kitchen and untied the cord from Brenda's neck, and then I took her life. And, then, I turned to Ron and said, 'OK, we can leave now.'"

As if Dan Lafferty's account of those events wasn't chilling enough, to illustrate just how much conviction and commitment terrorists have for their causes, an incident occurred toward the end of Dan's presentation, during the question-and-answer portion, that will show you just how entrenched he was in his beliefs.

When he had finished speaking to the group, the tone of the meeting had taken an intense turn. Despite all the collective law enforcement experience in the conference room that day, it was as if no one had ever seen or heard anything quite so shocking before. Maybe it was the horror of the crime itself, or maybe it was just that no one in the room had ever seen a killer describe his crime in such a calm demeanor before. I don't know. In any case, there was an unusual feeling in the room.

As Dan took questions, one of the attendees, a potbellied sheriff from a small town in West Texas sitting in the front row, asked Dan, "Let me get this straight: you say God told you to do this?"

"Yes, sir, he did," Dan answered matter-of-factly.

In a drawl common to West Texas residents, the sheriff responded, "Boy, I'm telling you right now that I think that's a bunch of B.S."

Dan, with his long hair and long double-pointed beard, looked down at the sheriff and, as unfazed as could be, said, "Well, I respect your opinion, sir, but the fact of the matter is, if God told me to take your life, as sure as I'm standing here, I'd kill you, too."

With that, the sheriff bolted from his chair and started to go after Dan before he was restrained by other officers sitting around him.

I'm sure Dan didn't expect he would be attacked by an officer of the law, but the fact that he was as calm as he was, given those circumstances, indicates that he was absolutely convinced, beyond a shadow of a doubt, that God directed him to commit this crime. Whether he convinced himself or is a victim of brainwashing is subject to debate, but he has had several years to create revisionist history in his own mind, and his beliefs are solidified. In that respect, he is no different from any other terrorist who feels 100 percent justified in committing terrible crimes in the name of his or her cause.

To get a better understanding of just how committed Ron and Dan Lafferty were to their religious designs, we share a note that they wrote just weeks before the murders, in which they claim God had commanded them to kill Brenda and Erica Lafferty:

> Thus saith the Lord unto my servants, the Prophets. It is my will and command that ye remove the following individuals in order that my work might go forward, for they have truly become obstacles in my path and I will not allow my work to be stopped. First, thy brother's wife Brenda and her baby. . . . And it is my will that they be removed in rapid succession and that an example be made of them in order that others might see the fate of those who fight against the true saints of God. And it is my will that this matter be taken care of as soon as possible.

This disturbing script echoes what we said earlier about criminals who try to fill legitimate needs through illegitimate means.

Ron and Dan Lafferty, and their followers, were absolutely convinced that they received continuous direction from the Almighty himself to be leaders of people in the last days. As their congregation grew, they became more and more entrenched in that belief, to the point that they felt they were at the center of the universe. But when one of their own, their brother Allen, disagreed and tried to break away, Ron and Dan had an inability to cope with their brother's decision, viewing it as betrayal. They, of course, will argue differently, but it got to the point that they felt someone had to pay for what they perceived as an act of treachery.

In another passage that they had written, this one just three weeks before the murders as the brothers traveled through Kansas, it is clear that they had created a world for themselves in which they were grandiose.

> Thus saith the Lord unto my servants, The Prophets. It is my will and desire that you move along as rapidly as possible and take the

North route as ye have thought. I promised that ye would have many important experiences in your travels and I have fulfilled those promises and even given the further instructions that I promised here in Wichita. For the thoughts ye have had concerning the regaining of my stolen property are correct. And ye are justified in whatever ye do in my name, for truly ye are my chosen sons and I will go before you and be your rearward!

In reading their notes, it's not hard to see how they went from a state in which they were just regular working guys to a place in their minds in which they were above the law. The last portion of the passage, "And ye are justified in whatever ye do," is typical of the terrorist mind-set, which vehemently declares, "Anything I do is justified because my cause is just!"

You might be wondering why we place Ron and Dan Lafferty in the category of terrorists instead of simply classifying them as murderers.

What makes them terrorists is that, even though their crimes were against a woman and a small child, their mentality was terroristic in nature. Even though they weren't as combative or sophisticated as, say, Osama bin Laden and the al Qaeda network, the Laffertys still felt they were fighting a "holy war" of sorts. Just as the members of al Qaeda believe they are waging a religious battle against the United States, Ron and Dan Lafferty were truly convinced that their sister-in-law, niece, and anybody who strongly opposed their views were ultimately a threat to the progress of their church, which was really nothing more than an organization that housed and supported their delusional vision of themselves as "chosen ones."

The bottom line is that they were and still are convinced that God told them they were so superior to everyone else that they were given special permission from the highest being in the universe to act above the law and commit murder.

As for what we as law-abiding citizens can do to prevent such acts of terrorism from occurring in our country and in our communities, the answer is simple: Help law enforcement by being their eyes and ears.

In other words, watch, listen, and act.

If you see something unusual or suspicious, please don't hesitate to contact the authorities. You have no need to be afraid or embarrassed. Believe me, the best possible scenario is for you to call the police and then have it turn out to be nothing. As long as you're making the call because you truly feel that there is something suspicious going on, then you haven't wasted their time. It's their job to check out those calls, and they would much rather see that than to have you not call and have something terrible happen, like the Oklahoma City bombing.

After I left the FBI and had served as chief of the Provo Police Department, I was asked to join an agency headed up by Tom Ridge that would be known as a key cog in the new war on terror, an agency now known as the Department of Homeland Security. I was assigned to be one of twenty-eight individuals, nationwide, to take the position of Assistant Federal Security Director over Law Enforcement.

My territory included Montana and Utah, which was significant because that territory has a history of being a hideout for some of the nation's most notorious criminals. Look no further than serial killer Ted Bundy; Ted Kaczynski, the Unabomber; or Warren Jeffs, who built a compound in the Four Corners area in Colorado City, Arizona. Jeffs, who spent several months on the FBI's Top 10 Most Wanted on allegations of sex crimes involving underage girls, traveled quite extensively between Arizona, Utah, and Nevada and was extremely elusive, partly because of the wide-open territory he had to roam. He was eventually apprehended near Las Vegas after being pulled over for a traffic violation in August 2006.

One thing I learned during the nearly two years I held that position was that we need, as a society, to learn how to expect the unexpected. We learn that principle in driving courses, but now we need to practice it in our daily lives.

We need to train ourselves to look for potential trouble.

For example, if you see a car parked in an unusual location, alert the authorities. At the very least, the vehicle gets towed for blocking traffic. But what if it was something more, like a car bomb, and you didn't make that call?

Contact police if you spot a suitcase or another unusual object left out in an open public area or positioned next to a building. It might turn out that it was just someone who forgot to take her briefcase onto the subway with her. But, again, what if it's something more?

Learn to look for people whose disposition is unusual for the situation. For instance, if a person has an intense demeanor when he is among those who are celebrating (at a circus or an amusement park, for example), then that person might be planning something devious. You don't have to be the one who stops that person. Simply point that person out to the nearest authority, such as a police officer or a security guard. The authorities will know what to do from there and, at the very least, will keep a close eye on that suspicious person.

There are a lot of unusual people and circumstances to watch out for. The best general guideline we gave to the public when I was with Homeland Security, the FBI, and local law enforcement was to trust your instincts.

If the situation doesn't feel right, let the authorities know so they can check it out.

Ted Kaczynski's brother, David, is a stellar example of someone who followed his intuition. As difficult as it was for him to do, he turned his brother's name over to the authorities. It turned out that Theodore Kaczynski was the Unabomber, a man the FBI had tried to catch for nearly twenty years for killing three people and injuring twenty-nine others with package bombs. In 1978 he unsuccessfully tried to blow up a plane flying from Chicago to Washington, DC. It wasn't until this brave man, David, followed his instincts and contacted the FBI with his suspicions that agents were able to apprehend Ted Kaczynski at a remote cabin in Montana.

You would be amazed at how accurate your instincts can be. But, now more than ever, you need to use them because we are constantly being threatened, both from within and from abroad.

Look at what the people of Israel have gone through.

Since 1948, when Israel was officially declared a nation-state, the Israelites have lived under a constant cloud of terrorism. Nearly every day, they have been bombed or shot at. It has happened so often that it has become a way of life for them.

As citizens of the United States, we have recently gotten a taste of what they go through in the Middle East all the time. Up until the Oklahoma City attack, we had been fortunate. But now that we see we are vulnerable, it is the ordinary citizen who needs to play the critical role as the eyes and ears of law enforcement if we are going to prevent acts of terror from penetrating our free culture.

We also need to understand that terrorism is a much different crime than robbery or rape or even murder. Rapists and murderers commit their crimes in such a way that they try to avoid getting caught. Because they are trying to avoid capture, they are limited in the commission of their crimes. They can't just go out into the open and kill or rape somebody. They rely on the right opportunity to present itself.

Most terrorists don't care if they get caught or killed during the commission of their crimes. In their minds, they are waging a war. That way of thinking opens up a wide variety of opportunities. We learned that unfortunate lesson on September 11, 2001.

We also have learned this lesson through the sad incidents of school shootings. It's alarming that our nation's children are now engaging in domestic terrorism. To combat this problem, we have to intervene at a younger age, which means we must understand the origins of the individual terrorist.

Terrorists often spring from isolation. They are social outcasts, many times as youngsters. We see school shootings perpetrated primarily by kids who have been bullied. If we really want to cut this off at its roots, we need to make sure to befriend. Teach our children to be kind to those who seem lonely and don't have friends. In a country that is known for rooting for the underdog, it's ironic that we don't seem to support the ones who need it most—our children.

Even with adults, the same principles apply. In social circles at the workplace, do what you can to make the shy person feel welcome. Terrorists include the guy who walks into his former workplace and starts shooting. He is born of frustration and animosity toward others. He feels that society has given him a raw deal, and his frustration finally boils over to anger so combative that he takes a "me against the world" mentality. The terrorists' mind-set becomes such that their only design is to accomplish their mission, personal consequences aside.

Even Timothy McVeigh, after he was apprehended, treated his interrogation as if he were a prisoner of war. When the FBI questioned him, he would only repeat his name, rank, and serial number. Dan Lafferty, as you just read, is not ashamed or embarrassed by his crimes. In fact, he doesn't view his acts as criminal at all. He simply insists he is an agent of God. Remember, almost all terrorists at one time or another have lacked a sense of importance, and they try to fill that need somehow.

Because of that psychology, it is imperative that law enforcement includes the public in defending our country from further attacks. No matter how well trained law enforcement agencies are, it is extremely difficult to stop somebody from carrying out a crime that he is willing to die to commit. The only way to stop him is to catch him before he attempts to carry it out.

And that requires your sharp eyes and ears.

5

CRIMES AGAINST THE ELDERLY

J-just stay q-quiet and e-everything will be OK-K," Terrence Adderly whispered to Ida, his stutter becoming more pronounced as it did every time he began to carry out an attack on one of his victims.

Restraining the elderly woman from behind, he had one hand firmly pressed against her mouth, while he used his other arm to pin Ida's arms against her frail body. The kindly old woman had been rendered entirely motionless.

Ida Bloomfield was in shock at the overwhelming sense of helplessness she was feeling.

Just minutes before, she had been thrilled by the prospect of getting a friendly visitor to break the monotony of her otherwise dull existence. Most of her days were spent crocheting or sitting within twelve inches of the television in an attempt to discern what was on. Most days it seemed as if the show wasn't even worth straining to watch. At eighty-four, it was difficult to see or hear much of anything. Sleeping didn't come easily, and her family was rarely able to stop in for a visit, especially on a weekday.

"I understand—you're busy," she would tell her youngest son,

Dalton. "You're just in that time of life when you have to take care of your own family. Maybe you can come over next Saturday."

"Sure, that would be great, Mom," he would tell her noncommittally. "I'll see if we can clear our schedule after Robbie's game."

She didn't mean to bore anybody, especially her family. But anytime she had visitors, she would talk to them for as long as they could stand to stay. She knew she was taking up their precious time, but she just couldn't help herself. Any human contact seemed so few and far between for Ida that she leapt at the slightest chance to talk to anybody who would stay and visit. Since her husband had passed away ten years earlier, she craved the companionship, and it seemed as if all she had left to offer were the stories of her life.

This particular morning, she seemed destined for another ho-hum day until Terrence knocked on her door.

He seemed so well spoken and friendly at the doorstep.

"Hi, ma'am," he said in a typical Alabaman drawl. "I was just passing by, and I couldn't help but notice your yard. I'm trying to earn some extra money for school, and I was wondering if you would give me the privilege of doing some of this here work for you."

"Why, that would be wonderful," Ida told him. "But I don't know that I could afford to pay you. I live on a fixed income, and I don't have very much to offer."

"Oh, no, ma'am," Terrence replied. "It wouldn't be much at all. I would mow, weed, and edge your yard for just ten dollars."

"That hardly seems like enough for all that work," she protested.

"Not at all, ma'am. The way I look at it, we would be doing each other a favor. And like my mother always said, 'You get more when you give more.'"

"It sounds like you have a very wise mother."

"Yes, ma'am, I do," said Terrence with a smile.

Ida knew she shouldn't let strangers in, but this young gentleman was well kept. His hair was trimmed neatly, he was clean-shaven, and above all, he seemed like such a nice young man. He had a bright smile and was so friendly. A young man doing good old-fashioned hard work to put himself through college certainly had to be trust-worthy. Against her better judgment, Ida decided she could use the company and invited Terrence in for a visit.

"I'll tell you what," she said. "I can't afford more than the ten dollars you're asking, but I hardly think that's fair for what you'd be doing for me. So why don't I make you a nice lunch on top of your fee, and we'll call it a deal."

"Oh, I don't know, ma'am. You're too kind," said Terrence, feigning hesitancy. He had done this so many times before that he knew exactly what was coming next.

"Not at all," she said. "A nice young man like you deserves to at least eat a nice meal. Besides, I could use the company. Now, you come on in, and we'll call it a deal."

"OK, it's a deal then," he agreed with an aw-shucks demeanor.

Once Ida let him in, he sat down on the living room sofa and waited for her to go into the kitchen.

The front room was adorned with family pictures, past and present. Some, like her wedding photo, went back more than fifty years, and others had been taken just last Christmas. Against one wall sat a piano and against the adjacent wall leaned a small end table that served as a television stand. The carpet was dark brown, the kind that was typical during the early 1970s, and the furniture appeared to have been purchased around the same time.

When Terrence heard Ida open the refrigerator, he quickly got up and locked the door. When she reentered the living room, the young man's countenance had changed entirely. His pleasant smile disappeared, and he was extremely nervous. He began to stutter, and his demeanor was ridged.

"I thought I heard something at the door," Ida said. "Did you lock the door?"

Before she could utter another word, Terrence had restrained her and began to take off her day gown.

Ida was physically limited and could barely move, much less try to fight off her attacker. She did as he told her and didn't make a sound. Paralyzed with fear, the elderly woman didn't even try to resist as Terrence unclothed her. She couldn't even speak. Her thoughts raced so fast that she couldn't even complete any of them.

"Am I being raped?" she asked herself. "What would a good-looking young man like this want with a shriveled old woman like me? Surely, he could have his pick of any young beautiful woman his age."

Ida thought about how she had forgotten to take her heart medication that morning, and all of the sudden, the elderly woman grew frightened.

"Oh, my, he's going to kill me," she thought.

As she processed what was happening to her and the grim possibilities darted through her mind, she felt her heart palpitate.

"W-what's wrong w-with you?" the young man asked, beginning to panic.

As Ida slumped to the floor, she could barely mouth the words "heart attack" to Terrence before she clutched her chest and died at his feet.

Her attacker didn't know what to do. He had raped more than a dozen elderly women, but nothing like this had ever happened before. For an instant, Terrence was angry with the old woman.

He grabbed her by the face and yelled, "Y-y-you can't d-die! I-I t-told you t-to do w-what I s-say."

Then he realized that he was yelling and feared that someone might hear him and come to check on the old woman.

"I'd better get out of here," Terrence thought. For an instant, he thought about putting her clothes back on and placing her in bed so it would look like she died of natural causes, but he thought he heard someone at the front porch, so he decided to flee through the back door.

In the backyard, he looked around to make sure nobody saw him then calmly but quickly made his way to the sidewalk and around the corner before he started running to where he had parked his car several blocks away.

I was out shopping when I got a call from police investigators in Alabama who had picked up Terrence Adderly and were trying to question him.

Several witnesses had seen an individual matching his description around Ida Bloomfield's neighborhood. One alert resident thought he was acting so suspicious that he even wrote down Adderly's license plate number and called it in.

Just hours after a neighbor found Ida, police used the witness descriptions and plate number to find the suspect and bring him into custody.

But as alarmed as Adderly was when he watched his victim die, he was even more terrified after police picked him up. He completely clammed up and wouldn't say a word. He couldn't even speak to ask for a lawyer. The detectives tried everything. They presented him with witness accounts, physical evidence, and threats of prison time. They tried to befriend him and be helpful to him. No matter what they did, the suspect wouldn't budge.

I was with the FBI Investigative Support Unit at the time, so they called me, hoping to get a profile of the killer and work up an interrogation strategy for him.

In addition, for more than a year, investigators in that area had been trying to catch a serial rapist—one who targeted elderly women. Though he hadn't actually raped Ida Bloomfield, they suspected that because he had attempted to sexually assault her, this might be the guy they were looking for.

But they needed him to at least admit to something in this case before they could question him about the other rapes.

"Let me start by asking you about the victim," I told them. "What is her background?"

"She was eighty-four years old, lived by herself, took medication for heart problems, just typical stuff for a woman her age," the detective answered.

"OK, did she have family nearby or neighbors who looked after her?"

"Well, it was a neighbor lady who found her, and I think the officer who took the report said she checked in on her about once or twice a week. And she does have some family in the area, a son and grandchildren, I think. One of our detectives went to tell him the bad news.

But from what I gather, she was pretty self-sufficient and didn't need too much looking after."

"Did the neighbor say how often the family visited?"

"About once every couple weeks."

"How mobile was she?"

"From what I understand, she used a cane or sometimes a walker to get around, but she was able to get from here to there pretty well."

At that point, I knew the killer had an experienced hand at attacking elderly women. He had done an effective job of identifying an easy target, and from what the police reports showed, there was no evidence of forced entry or theft, so he had conned his way into her home for a purpose other than money or drugs.

What gave me even more reason to suspect that the perpetrator was experienced was the victim's lifestyle.

She was still predominantly self-sufficient and wasn't entirely ignored by family and neighbors, which means that, although she was still wanting for company, she wasn't so desperate for it that she would let just anybody into the house. The perpetrator had to be a good con artist, which meant he had definitely pulled this routine before.

I just needed to know one more thing before I could ascertain whether he intentionally killed her or was just looking to assault her.

"Detective, how was the victim's body displayed?"

"She was down on the floor, completely naked."

"Was she on her stomach or on her back?"

"Her back."

"Were there signs of violent beating or any indication that he had thrown her forcefully to the floor?"

"No, just the opposite. There wasn't a scratch on her. It looked like she had lay down peacefully on the floor by herself. In fact, if her day gown and underwear hadn't been lying on the floor beside her, it probably would have looked like a simple heart attack, and nobody would have known any different."

"I think I know who did this," I told the lieutenant. "Your perpetrator didn't intentionally kill the victim, that's for sure."

"How do you know that?"

"Because everything you're telling me points to an attempted rape with no intent to kill. He was probably just as surprised as she was when she had her heart attack. When he entered that house, he was looking to have sex with that woman and then leave as quickly as possible. If he had wanted to kill her there would have been signs of brutality, such as ligature marks, cuts, deep bruises, that kind of thing. But there weren't. This guy is what we call a 'gentleman rapist.'"

"A 'gentleman rapist'? Sounds like a contradiction in terms to me."

"That's exactly what it is, and for very good reason. In the perpetrator's mind, he is just out for sex. He's not hurting anybody. He's merely satisfying a need. In fact, a lot of times, he will ask the victim how he performed because he needs the validation. But your perpetrator has an added dimension."

"What's that?"

"Not only is he a rapist, but his target suggests he is extremely immature socially. Not only does he have an inability to interact with women of his own age, but he doesn't have the maturity or self-esteem to target someone his own age for rape. He has to go after someone ultravulnerable."

"Then why isn't he a child molester? Why go after an old lady?"

"Because, in his mind, he is a child. In essence, he is a child in a man's body with the same sexual desires of a man. He just doesn't know what to do, so he's acting on those needs the only way he knows how. That's probably why the victim let him into her home. No one can melt the heart of a grandparent more than a grandchild. To get into the house, he probably manipulated the situation just like a child would manipulate his grandma into giving him a cookie."

"That's sick," the detective said, sounding utterly disgusted at the comparison.

"Yes, it is, but at least now you know what you're working with."

"So how do we get him to talk to us?"

"Well, since you're dealing with somebody who's in his early twenties but still has the mind of a child, you'll need to treat him as if he's your son. Treat him with the same kind of understanding that you would your kid if he got in trouble."

"Yeah, well, my kid ain't no rapist."

"No, I'm sure he's not, but remember, in the perpetrator's mind, he has done nothing more than the equivalent of breaking his mom's favorite vase. That's why you'll have to show compassion toward him, but at the same time explain to him that he has done something wrong and that there are consequences for his actions. Just like you would your ten-year-old son, tell him that it's not good to lie and that the right thing to do would be to tell the truth. Tell him he will feel better for being truthful."

"All right," the lieutenant said skeptically. "I'm not so sure about this, but we're not getting anywhere with him anyway, so we'll give it a try."

A few hours later, I was leaving a movie theater when I received another call from the lieutenant. They were close, but they still couldn't quite get him to confess.

"We've tried everything you said," he told me. "We were real nice to him and made him comfortable. Then, we just started talking some football, and after a few minutes, he started to join in on the conversation. We got him relaxed, but when we started talking about the old lady, he wouldn't talk about it. We didn't press too much, but we told him if he told the truth, he would feel better. That's where we're at now, and we're stuck."

"It sounds like you've done great so far," I replied. Then, out of nowhere, a thought occurred to me. "Why don't you offer him a candy bar?"

"Excuse me, but did you just say, offer him a candy bar?" said the puzzled voice.

"Yes. I know it sounds strange, but I just got the sudden notion that this guy probably has the mentality of a five- or six-year-old. If you have made him comfortable enough to talk to you, and he truly is the assailant, then he is listening when you say he will feel better if he confesses. Now, just like you would with a young child, you have to show him some evidence that will make him believe that. What better way than to offer him a treat?"

"You know what?" the lieutenant asked rhetorically in a tone that suggested he was shaking his head. "As crazy as that sounds, we'll give it a try. Even crazier, I'm starting to believe it just might work."

It wasn't ten minutes later before I got one last call from this lieutenant.

"Mr. Cooper," he said with a chuckle. "I don't know what they're teaching you over there in the FBI, but I'm about ready to eat my hat. He just confessed to everything. That crazy candy bar idea of yours worked!"

When I hung up the phone, I just shook my head, somewhat surprised and somewhat amused. As a result of that candy bar, not only did Adderly confess to the Bloomfield attack, but he admitted to several other sexual assaults against elderly women, some the department had been investigating, a few that had occurred outside of their jurisdiction.

I had never even heard of a candy bar being used as bait to elicit a confession, but I had been doing criminal profiling long enough that I had developed an instinct for that kind of thing.

I am a firm believer in instinct, or the sixth sense, as some people call it. Anyone in law enforcement can probably tell some kind of a story involving an event in which intuition helped him solve a case or save a life, maybe even his own.

That's what we're hoping you will learn from this chapter.

We are hoping not only that you will utilize proper safety tools and guidelines to protect yourself and your loved ones but, just as important, that you will train yourself to use that sixth sense. If it doesn't feel right, act on those feelings and do what it takes to protect yourself, even if it means that you have to create a socially awkward situation, such as not being as polite as you would normally be.

We want you—whether for yourself or a loved one—to use this information to reduce the risks of one of our nation's precious assets, our senior citizens.

As we discussed in our chapter involving crimes against children, today's youth are our most precious asset because they represent the future. That being the case, the elderly are our second-most precious asset. They carry the resource of experience, and without their wisdom, we are doomed to repeat the mistakes of the past.

Unfortunately, our nation's senior citizens are also among the most criminally targeted demographic. They are victimized for several reasons, most predominantly for their money (much of which they have spent a lifetime saving for the purpose of enjoying retirement), their pharmaceuticals, or, as you have just read, other selfish purposes, such as sex and murder.

From a behavioral-profiling perspective, the people who commit these offenses are similar in psychological makeup to those who attack children. The point of difference is that those who commit crimes against children—though they, too, are seeking out the most vulnerable victims due to their own low self-esteem—still have the ability to fit in socially with adults. In fact, they often get away with their crimes because, like Oliver Gerrish, they know how to win the trust of adults to gain private access to their children.

People who target senior citizens, on the other hand, have such minimal social skills that they are almost childlike and thus have no desire to harm children because they relate to them so closely. Their low self-esteem drives them to prey on one of society's most vulnerable segments, but their social immaturity prevents them from attacking someone who is on par with them psychologically.

Adderly, for example, had adult sexual needs but didn't have the mature social skills to fill those needs. That's why he conned his victims like a child would. He used the child in him to manipulate his way into situations where he could use his adult physical strength to overpower his victims for the purpose of sexual gratification.

Others who commit these atrocious crimes do so for a variety of reasons but still have that one behavioral flaw in common. They don't know how to reconcile their adult needs on an acceptable adult level.

Several years ago, Mike and I interviewed inmates as part of our criminal-tracking project who had commited crimes against elderly citizens. As a result of our work, we were invited by Ann Burgess, a renowned forensic nurse and author from Boston College, to participate in a study funded by the National Institute of Justice on this type of crime. One inmate, Terry Donnelly, who confessed to killing five elderly women over a nine-year period, explained why he preyed on senior citizens.

"I think part of the thing about why people, like myself, attack the elderly is because the elderly are abandoned in our society," he said. "There's nobody to come around, nobody to come to visit because, [as adult kids], we're busy with our own lives. We don't have time to go to Mom's house every day. So somebody who's their son's age comes up to them and wants to talk to them about anything. Well, they're lonely. They will talk to anybody about anything."

Donnelly was very forthcoming when Mike and I talked to him. Sentenced to life in prison, he had already served about ten years and readily admitted that he would probably kill again if he were let out into society without any structure to his life.

We asked him how he determined which senior citizens he would attack next.

"Money," he said. "I needed the money, and I knew they were the easiest ones to get it from. My first victim was about revenge. I went there knowing I was going to kill her. I wasn't worried about getting the money until after I killed her. After that first homicide, I [eventually] discovered that I got off on it. After that, it was nothing more than taking their money and getting my own murderous satisfaction, doing the animal thing, feeling the animal emotions, feeling the animal euphoria. . . . I'm a hunter walking around the woods, and the woods happen to be a neighborhood. I'm looking for Bambi because Bambi was willing to come up to me. That's all it was. . . . Control was the other thing. If you take someone else's life, what do you have? Control. Total control. You are a god, at least here [on earth] you are."

When we asked him why he didn't target people his own age for financial gain, his answer was very telling in regard to himself and others who violently attack senior citizens.

"I don't like confrontation," he said. "I'm not looking for a fight. I don't want a struggle. I just wanted to get what I came for and get it the easiest way possible. An older woman is so feeble, she can hardly move, much less fight back."

Donnelly told us that he was extremely angry when he started murdering. He had been in jail previously on a sexual assault charge (brought against him by a sixty-five-year-old woman who had refused to buy alcohol for him). While in prison, he had been raped. Shortly before his release, he concocted a plan to kill his first victim—his former cell mate's seventy-year-old mother.

He felt he needed to get revenge for his cell mate's trespass against him, and taking it out on the innocent made him feel empowered. Even the method he used to murder his victims indicates he was looking for a way to find some control over life. In each of the five murders, Donnelly strangled his victims from behind using only his forearm. The reason he chose this method was simply that is was the path of least resistance. It was the quickest and easiest way to fill his need for total domination.

"When I raped [the sexual assault victim], I was happy," he told us. "I felt happy because I had total control. Nobody was going to push me around anymore. That night, I became a predator. I became a predator for the weaker prey, and when I got out of prison, it just escalated into murder."

Finally, we asked him what made him think he could get away with these murders. Why was he so confident?

"I wasn't a planned killer," he explained. "I didn't plan or organize a murder before I did it. Afterwards, I would try to organize things, clean it up. But before and during, there was no plan of attack. . . . In fact, on two of the homicides, I didn't even want to waste my time talking my way in. I just forced my way in. I only talked my way in on three of them. . . . [The reason I was so confident] is that, after I killed, a couple of months go by, a couple of years go by, and nobody says anything. Nobody worries about it. Not like they do with a younger person. . . . I was a serial killer in the same city, and there was hardly any media coverage on it until I confessed to the murders."

Donnelly's last answer is the saddest of all because there is some semblance of truth. Sometimes we focus so much time and attention on protecting the younger members of our society that we don't put enough focus on the safety of our senior citizens.

We're not saying that nobody cares about the elderly. People do. But as a society, we need to place a higher priority on their safety, show more concern, and pay closer attention. We need to educate, not only ourselves, but the seniors we care about in regard to their personal security.

One question we asked Donnelly is what would have kept him from going through with an attack on all or any one of his victims once he had targeted them.

He had to take a moment to think about it, but then he said, "What they could have done, or what any elderly person should do, is take it outside. When a stranger approaches an elderly female, or even a male, the first thing they should do is take it to the street [or sidewalk]. Look for other people. If other people notice somebody like me talking to you, and I'm focused on you becoming my victim, and you take me over here, and there's a guy standing over there, and I notice this guy, you're no longer a victim, because he noticed me. And if I noticed him, then he noticed me, and I don't want anybody noticing that I was around you.

"Don't ever let anybody come in, even if it's cold outside. Just tell them, 'Wait a minute,' lock the door, then go get a coat and go outside. Even if it's cold, somebody is going to be walking [or driving] by. If you can, call a neighbor just so they know someone's watching. You know most everyone in the neighborhood, so make sure they are aware of me talking to you. . . . Anything like that would have turned [the switch] off for me."

Notice how Donnelly said he would have abandoned his plans if a passerby would have seen him with one of his intended victims. Just as potential victims take steps to reduce their risks, it is equally important to realize that potential predators also take steps to reduce their risk levels.

For Donnelly, as strong as his desire was to feel the rush of the primitive animal kill, the power of that attraction was still superseded by his need for self-preservation. No matter how hungry the wolf is, it still won't pounce on its prey if it senses danger nearby. That's why hunters are taught to stay close to fire after dark if wolves are in the area. As much as the wolf yearns to attack, it won't go near fire. As much as the predatory criminal thirsts for blood, he fears the loss of his freedom more. Anything you can do to increase the risk of him getting caught reduces your risk of being victimized.

And that principle doesn't just apply on a face-to-face level.

Telephone fraud is big criminal business among those looking to take advantage of senior citizens. Illegal scam organizations know that retirees have large nest eggs, and these despicable people look to gain access to their savings through trickery and deceit, whether it's in person, over the phone, through the mail, or over the Internet.

One typical example of how these groups can victimize seniors involves a case in which a young lady called an elderly gentleman in Arizona claiming that she was screening candidates to see if they qualified for low-cost health insurance for senior citizens. She was extremely friendly and quickly gained his trust by asking him a number of legitimate questions in regard to his health.

"I'm not sure if I can qualify for any benefits at all," he told her. "I'm seventy-five, and I've got quite a few health problems. Medicaid is probably all I can get."

"That's exactly why I'm calling," she replied in a friendly, all-American-girl-next-door tone. "We have found a way to get a lot of people in your situation better health coverage at a lower cost."

"How do you do that?" he asked. "I've never heard of such a thing. I was under the impression that the only way to get affordable insurance was to be in tip-top shape. And at my age, I'm certainly not the poster boy for tip-top shape, I'll tell you that much."

"You're so funny," she giggled. "You remind me of my grandpa. The great thing about this program is that we have investors who subsidize the program because they feel very strongly that everyone should have quality healthcare available to them, especially those people like you who have worked a lifetime to earn it. I got my grandpa on this program. Even though he has diabetes, he still has all his prescriptions paid for, as well as all of his doctor visits. He's only required to pay a ten-dollar co-pay for anything, even surgical procedures."

"Well, that sounds pretty good."

"It is and he loves it. It makes things so much easier on him. The only thing we require is that we verify that you are sixty-five or older, and we do need to make sure that your financial history is sound. Unfortunately, there are dishonest people out there who try to take advantage of the system and take what's not rightfully theirs."

"I'll tell you, that makes my blood boil," he said. "It's a shame that people do that. You just can't trust people these days."

"No, unfortunately, you can't," the young lady slyly agreed. "I know it's kind of a pain, but that's why I will need to get your social security number and your credit card or checking account information to make sure you do meet the criteria for the program."

"Well, young lady, all you'd need to do is take one look at me, and you'd see that I meet your criteria."

"Oh, don't be so hard on yourself," she mused. "You sound like a sweetheart to me, and I'm sure you're as handsome as ever."

"That may be, but I'm a sweetheart who has trouble getting out of his chair. Now, what did you say you needed, my social security number and my checking account number?"

"Yes sir, that's all."

"Great. You hold on, and I'll be right back with them."

Unfortunately, for this gentleman, it wasn't a week before his entire savings was wiped out and his identity stolen. He was completely devastated and humiliated. His family was left to care for him, and maybe worst of all, he was stripped of his dignity and independence as a result of the scam.

This is exactly what we hope to help you avoid.

But because there are a variety of ways of preying on the elderly, there is no one list of do's and don'ts. We can, however, offer some suggestions in terms of principles or questions you can ask yourself when it comes to your protection.

Because predators who predominantly target the elderly are cognizant of what seniors feel comfortable with, it is important to keep in mind that the vast majority of these criminals are going to look and act clean-cut in order to gain access to their intended victims. Therefore, it is vital that seniors understand that the person standing on their porch with the squeaky-clean image is the one they should exercise the most caution with. According to Donnelly, the creepy Christopher Walken look isn't going to cut it, and serial predators know this. That is why it is so important for you to use your instincts. As we said earlier, if you are a family member or you care for an elderly citizen, please use your sixth sense in regard to that person's care. If you don't feel like they would use good judgment in a potentially dangerous situation, then perhaps it's not a good idea to keep your loved ones isolated, thus making them vulnerable to these predators.

The other thing to keep in mind is that these offenders don't want to be seen with their intended victims. Their purpose is to secure the easy, undetectable strike. They are counting on the apathy of their victims and those within the victim's community. They are hoping that nobody is paying attention to the senior citizen whom they have targeted. The best thing seniors can do when confronted is to somehow garner attention. If Ida Bloomfield, or any of Adderly's victims, would have kept her visitor outside, where neighbors or anyone passing by could have seen them, she would have greatly reduced her risk of victimization.

Finally, consistently train yourself or your loved ones to avoid sharing information that will make them even more vulnerable. Information is power, and that is exactly what this offender is looking for— power and control. If you are afraid that your parents or grandparents, for example, are vulnerable to this predator, then offer to assist them with their finances so that someone whom they trust has access, not a predator who will use that information to leave them destitute.

In short, if senior citizens can learn to cut off private access to themselves and their personal information, they will swing quickly from high to low on the Risk Continuum scale and be able to preserve the life that they have worked so hard to earn.

6

SEXUAL ASSAULT

Kathryn Evans couldn't grasp that what was happening to her was real.

She was on her knees in front of a man who had just forced her to perform oral sex on him. For just a few seconds, he had her by the back of the head, clutching a fistful of her hair and pushing her head down to his crotch.

Finally, he let her up.

"Please don't do that again," she pleaded, nearly out of breath and tears welling up in her eyes. "I told you, I've never done that. I don't like it."

"Oh, come on. It wasn't that bad, honey," he chuckled.

"No. I'm serious. I don't like it," she responded. "Please don't make me do that again."

"Well, I've never had any complaints before, but I guess there's a first time for everything," he said wryly, shrugging his shoulders and clearly amused by his own wit.

Then, without another word, he zipped up his pants and left Kathryn alone in the walk-in closet of the master bedroom. She wasn't tied up or restrained in any way, but still, she couldn't find the strength to get off her knees. Kathryn sat there for a few minutes, hoping he wouldn't return.

Finally, she heard his truck start and drive away.

As she sat there, Kathryn felt strange—a sense of relief, disbelief, and shame all rolled into one, not to mention the overwhelming realization that her life had just been changed permanently. She would never again look in the mirror and see the same person. To her, she had been forever damaged.

Kathryn gazed at her surroundings in a dazed stupor when she noticed the flowered patterns that adorned the closet door, shades of pink and light-blue sponge-based designs that seemed to flutter their way up to the ceiling. She couldn't help but compare them to her life as she thought back to the fascination she'd had with flowers as a young girl. Katie, as she was called back then, would pick fully bloomed roses and smash them between her hands for good luck. Later, she would fold her favorites in between the pages of her journal as keepsakes, each one marking a momentous occasion for that day.

How ironic, she thought, that the flowers she brutalized as a child were so metaphoric to what had just happened to her. The attack didn't take much longer than the time it took her to pick a flower and flatten it in her hands. Yet, like the flowers, something inside of her had died, and the effects would last a lifetime. She wondered if the man who assaulted her kept a journal of his victims like she did her flowers.

Or was she the first one?

It was so hard to grasp that this had really happened to her, that someone had really done this to her. She had heard about other women being sexually assaulted, but like the many others who preceded her, she never imagined that she would actually be victimized.

"What did I do to deserve this?" she asked herself tearfully. "Am I that bad of a person that I had this coming to me?"

She sat and stared blankly at the bedroom walls for a few more moments then suddenly looked at her watch. It was almost four. Her son's baseball game was supposed to start in half an hour. If she hurried, she could make it in time.

"How could I?" she thought, slumping against the closet wall. "How could I even show my face at a baseball game after what just happened? How can I face my son? Or my husband? Or anyone?"

She buried her face in her hands and sobbed.

Just a few hours earlier, the most pressing thing on Kathryn's mind was getting her work done in time to see Jason's ball game. How interesting it was, she thought, that she had talked to her husband, Steve, just a few minutes before this man arrived at her office, to make sure that Jason had a ride to his game in case she had to work late.

Now, none of that seemed to matter. The only thing on her mind was . . . nothing.

"Nothing seems to matter now," she thought. "I just feel so numb. How can I go on living a normal life, knowing what's happened? How can I even look at my husband or my kids again?"

She wondered what would happen if Steve found out.

"Would he believe me?" she asked herself. "Would he be angry with me or even be able to look at me again? Or touch me? Do I even want to be touched again?"

Again, she buried her face in her hands and began to cry some more.

Those questions—and others like them—overwhelmed her as she contemplated what her life would hold for her and her family after this horrible experience.

"How can something that lasted just a few minutes turn my life upside down so badly?" she thought. "How could things have turned so quickly?"

After all, just three hours before, she was actually excited to see Michael Carson.

Kathryn, a beautiful blonde in her late thirties, was a successful real estate agent, and she felt confident that she was going to find Carson the house he was looking for. He had called the day before hoping to find a nice house in a somewhat rural neighborhood, and best of all, he seemed anxious to buy.

Carson, a burly man in his mid-thirties, was a typical rugged Wyoming cowboy. Like many men from that area, he had dark, bushy facial hair, a well-groomed goatee. As they talked, he had a gentle-manlike quality that was typical to the area.

"It don't need to be nothin' fancy," he told her over the phone. "I'm just looking for something nice for me and my lady to live in. But I do need something with enough land that I can keep my horses on. Do you know what I'm saying?"

"Oh, yes," Kathryn told him. "There are plenty of areas around here where you can find enough acreage to keep horses. Do you have an idea of a specific part of the valley you want to live in?"

"Yeah, actually, I was hoping to find something down south, near the river bottoms," Carson replied. "Do you know what part of town I'm talking about?"

"I know the general area, but I'm not as familiar with it as I am with some of the other areas around the valley," she said. "But what I can do is look up some listings for the area, and maybe we can set up a time when I can show you some houses. How does that sound?"

"That sounds good to me," he said. "But I'm gonna have to be going out of town here in a few days. Do you think we would be able to see some houses in the next day or two? If I see one I like, maybe I could even make an offer."

"Oh, definitely. I can have the listings by the end of the day today. In fact, maybe we can meet tomorrow, just outside my office?"

"Yeah. Great. Would, say, eleven o'clock work for you?"

"Yes, that would work just fine. Do you know where the office is here?"

"Yeah, I can find it all right."

"OK, then I'll see you tomorrow right in front of the office, and we can go look around at some houses."

"Sounds good. See you then."

The next day, Carson pulled up to Kathryn's office complex in his truck, a dark-blue three-quarter-ton Ford he had purchased just months before. It was great for pulling a horse trailer, something he did regularly to and from rodeos. For Carson, there was nothing like the thrill of a rodeo. Only one thing even came close, he would often say, jokingly, to his buddies, "And it don't have nothin' to do with riding horses!"

He saw Kathryn waiting out in front for him. As in her ad, she was striking, wearing a blue blazer, a white blouse, and a dark-blue skirt that ended just above the knee. She had her briefcase in hand and greeted Carson with a warm smile.

"How are you, Mr. Carson?" she said, extending her hand and giving him a firm, businesslike handshake. "It's good to meet you."

"Likewise," he said, amused by the professionalism that women in her industry always seemed to put forth. He always thought that they were just dirty, sex-starved women trying to be something they weren't. To him, the real estate garb and phony smile were just disguises they used to appear cleaner than they were, and this lady was no different.

"Well, I've got some listings here with me," she began. "Some of them look really attractive. Are you ready to see them?"

"You bet. Should we take your car or mine?" he asked, already knowing what her response would be.

"You know, you seem to be more familiar with the area than I am, so why don't we take yours."

Like so many women before her, she gave him the answer he wanted. In selecting a victim, Carson was thorough in his research. He knew which houses were listed and which ones were located in isolated areas. He also knew which neighborhoods composed the hot markets, and those typically weren't the isolated homes. Finally, he made sure his intended victims hadn't had much exposure to the areas he expressed interest in. That way, more often than not, he would be the one doing the driving, which meant he would also be the one assuming control over the situation.

"Sounds good to me," he answered. "Let me get the door for you."

Without knowing it, Kathryn had given him just the opportunity he was looking for. "We're going to have a fun time today," he thought.

"Thank you, Mr. Carson."

"Oh, you don't have to call me that. Why don't you just call me Mike?"

"Well, OK, Mike. Which one of these houses would you like to see first?"

"Why don't we start furthest south and work our way up?"

"Sounds good."

As they began the drive, Kathryn was still hoping she could finish showing him the houses as quickly as possible. She had already missed two of Jason's games, and she didn't want to miss another if she didn't have to. As rewarding as her career was, she sometimes felt her work schedule was taking a toll on her family. She felt especially guilty that her relationship with Jason wasn't what it used to be. He was growing up so fast.

Carson, meanwhile, was plotting his strategy.

"I can't wait to get the skirt off this hottie," he thought. Then, he looked over and smiled at her. "Are you comfortable? Do you need me to turn up the air-conditioning?"

"No, I'm just fine, thank you."

"OK, just let me know if there is anything I can do to make you more comfortable."

During the next hour, the pair walked through two houses, and Carson, who had been very cordial, hadn't seemed very interested in either. Still, Kathryn had been in the business long enough to know that it just took one house to catch a person's eye in order for him to make an offer. Once people fell in love with a house, she did everything she could to get them into it.

As they went to each home, Carson was the perfect gentleman. He insisted on opening the door for Kathryn at every turn.

"After all, that's the way my mom raised me to treat a lady," he told her.

At each stop, he would help her out of the truck and even seemed conscious of shielding her from seeing his tobacco chewing habit. He made it a point to spit only when he was out of her view, usually behind the truck. She wasn't particularly fond of the habit, but she thought it was sweet that he would be considerate enough to avoid spitting in front of her, and as a result, she began to feel more comfortable around him as the day wore on.

Kathryn had tried to make it a point of not putting herself in compromising positions when she showed men different real estate properties, but Carson had been so friendly that she felt safe with him.

Finally, they parked in front of an old converted farmhouse that Carson seemed to like.

"This looks like my kind of place," he commented as he again helped Kathryn out of the truck.

"Well, good," she said. "Let's go see what it looks like on the inside, shall we?"

"You bet."

As they walked around, they were both impressed at how well the home had been restored. The plumbing had been upgraded, as had the wood floors. They walked through the kitchen and family room then headed upstairs into the bedrooms.

"I don't know how much need you would have for an office, but this room would be great for an office space," Kathryn suggested. "Or, if you have visitors stay over, it could make for a great guest room."

"Yeah, I have friends come in from out of town every once in a while," he replied. "I think they would feel pretty comfortable here. It would do anyway."

"There's room for a couple of beds and a chest of drawers," she observed.

"Well, there is, but to be honest with you, most of my friends aren't exactly what you would call the Ritz type," he joked. "I don't even know if they would use the drawers."

As the tour made its way to the master bedroom, Carson began to question her about the pipes in the master bathroom.

"These look like they're broken here, under the sink," he commented.

"Oh, let me take a look," she said.

As she got down on the floor and stretched her head under the sink for a better look, Carson suggested she take her blazer off.

"You don't want to get that dirty," he said.

"Oh, thank you," she said as he helped her with the jacket.

As she checked the pipes, Carson began to gawk at the contours of Kathryn's body. For a few seconds, he began to fantasize about what she would look like and how she would feel. She seemed like a nice lady, someone nice enough to spare, but the operative word for Carson was "seemed." They all seemed sweet, but underneath it all, they were all the same, he thought. They were just dirty whores whose lot in life should be to please him. He squatted down beside her and began to lightly caress her from behind. She didn't say anything at first but then asked, "What are you doing?"

"What? Oh, I'm sorry. I was just having a hard time hearing, and I was trying to listen to what you were saying. I guess I wasn't paying attention."

"Oh. I was just saying I could see some cracks in these bottom pipes," she replied, feeling a little embarrassed that she had even asked Carson about the touching. "If you put an offer on the house, we will definitely bring that to the attention of the seller."

As they continued to make their way around the master bedroom, Carson asked about the walk-in closet.

"What would you say the measurements are in this closet?" he asked, opening the door for her and politely making way for her to pass into the closet ahead of him. He had her trapped, and she didn't even realize it.

"I don't know the exact dimensions," she answered. "But it looks like they're maybe about six by eight feet."

"Yeah, that's about what I was thinking," he said. "You know, I was wondering if I could expand a little and add some shelves back in here. Do you see what I'm talking about?"

"I'm not sure. What size shelves were you thinking?"

"Well, here, let me show you," he said, taking a hold of her shoulders and positioning her toward the back of the closet.

As he went through the possibilities for expansion, he raised up her hands to "give her an idea of the shelf size he was talking about." Then, before she knew what was happening, his hands made their way down Kathryn's arms, and he began to fondle her breasts.

"What are you doing? Don't do that," she snapped, clearly startled by his sudden advances.

"Oh, I'm sorry," he responded. "My bad. I just thought you were sending out signals, you know?"

"I think it's time for us to go," Kathryn said curtly.

"OK," Carson said. "Here, let me help you with the door."

But as he held the closet door open, Carson gave her just enough room to pass in front of him then slammed the door shut in front of her and pinned her up against it from behind.

"What are you doing?" she demanded nervously.

"Oh, come on," he said as he began to fondle. "You know."

"Stop it!" she ordered. "Please don't. My husband will be mad if he finds out about this."

"Well, then don't let him find out," Carson replied, amused by his own wit. He unzipped his pants and exposed himself, then wrestled Kathryn to her knees, took her by the back of the head, and grabbed a handful of her hair. Then he pushed her head down and forced her to perform oral sex on him.

An hour after the assault, she was still sitting in the closet, recounting the day's events. Somehow the decor of the room, with its light-blue carpet, white walls, and pink trim, had lost its charm.

"What happened?" she mumbled to herself. "This seemed like such a quaint, cozy little home. Now I just hate it. How could I have let this happen?"

She tried to figure out, not only how she had let it all happen but also how she was going to go back to her life, the way it was before.

"What am I still doing here?" she thought. "I've got to get out of here."

She wondered what she would tell her husband and her son. Jason would certainly be disappointed that she missed yet another game. It would be tough to come up with an excuse for this one, she thought.

As for her husband, who knew? It seemed as if telling him could only bring about endless consequences, all of them bad. But if she didn't tell him—or anyone, for that matter—then maybe she could just go on with her life and pretend it never happened.

And that's what she chose to do—make-believe it never happened.

It was clearly the more simple solution. As time went on, she surmised, the memory would certainly be buried deep enough that it would seem like a figment of her imagination. Then she could just move on. It would just take time.

"After all," she thought, "they say time does heal all wounds."

Having made her decision, Kathryn finally found the resolve to pick herself up off the floor. She cleaned herself up in the master bathroom and went home as if it was just another day that she had to work late.

Unfortunately, that is what all but two of Michael Justin Carson's victims—more than a hundred, by his own estimation—decided to do. Sadly, that is also the choice that the vast majority of sexual assault victims in this country make.

It's a horrible thing to have to live through once, let alone again and again, which is what many victims feel will happen when they report the assault to police and prosecutors. Because sexual assault is such a difficult crime to prove, oftentimes, women feel like they will be the ones on trial if they do report the incident. They worry about having to go through the grueling process of evidence collection, testimony, and cross-examination. Then, as if that's not enough, if the process gets to a courtroom trial, they worry that their assailants are going to be found not guilty and set free.

It can be a scary ordeal.

And that is exactly what Carson counted on as he continued on his long trail of sexual assaults.

"I had a whole herd of them," Carson told Mike King and me during an interview just four years after he was convicted of his last rape. "And, you know what, Mike? Only one of them ever reported, and she only reported inappropriate touching because she didn't want to be in the news. She didn't want people to see that she had been humiliated."

Carson, who is serving life in prison for his crimes, probably represents the majority of rapists in terms of how and why he chose to commit the assaults.

Typically, he chose real estate agents because he could preview them first, and he knew he could get them alone in order to more freely execute his crimes. He counted on there being no witnesses because he was convinced that if it was his word versus hers, he would win. He says he never punched or slapped his victims, and he never used a knife or a gun in committing his crimes.

"Most of the time, all we did was wrestle," he told us. "Sometimes I tied them up or handcuffed them, but most of the time, they just rolled over, and let me have my way."

As is the case with date rape or any kind of rape, he selected women he felt he could control using little or no effort.

"Anytime you pick a victim, of any crime, I think you probably pick someone who is vulnerable," he said. "Someone you can control, not just physically, but mentally and emotionally too. . . . I knew pretty quick if she was someone I could have my way with. If I thought she would put up a fight, a real fight, then I wouldn't go through with it."

Carson was finally brought to justice because one victim came forward within a couple of hours of the crime. As difficult as it was for her, she went through the process of evidence collection, told her husband, and saw this through the legal process. She was very brave for doing so and is a great example of someone who used the system properly. The woman has had to endure a lot of heartache, but she has returned to the real estate industry and has championed several changes in the way realtors do business, no doubt ensuring the safety of many in her profession.

"I wish and hope that this had never happened to me," she told a group of law enforcement officials attending a conference in 1999, just two years after she was raped. "But, unfortunately, we cannot go back and change it. . . . I love this profession. The good that has come out of this is that the whole real estate industry knows what happened, and they are making changes. I see agents trying to do business differently. I see agents screening their potential clients, asking them more questions. The awareness is there. I do my business differently. I do a lot of open houses. I would say 80 percent of my clients come from open houses, and since this has happened to me, my husband is with me at my open houses most of the time."

In this book, we talk about what to do to reduce your risks of becoming a predatory victim.

In terms of sexual assaults, this woman's story illustrates what to do if you are unable to avoid an attack and do have to endure a sexual assault. Remember, our purpose is to minimize risk. But we are not so unrealistic that we think that every crime can absolutely, positively be prevented, especially crimes of this nature. In this crime, this woman's circumstances were similar to those of her colleagues. The only difference is what she chose to do afterward, knowing that there would be challenges ahead yet still finding the strength to go forward.

"When I came back to the office, I think I was in shock. The receptionist was there, and my first words were, 'Call the police.' She asked me what happened, and I said, 'Just, please, call the police.'"

At that moment, she decided to take an extreme negative in her life and turn it into something positive for a lot of people, both in and out of her industry.

By so doing, her choice has made her recovery from this ordeal about as smooth as it could be, given the circumstances. She now has the confidence derived from confronting her attacker. In fact, many women who decide to report sexual assaults, regardless of the outcome, often feel as if a weight has been lifted off their shoulders. Even if the result doesn't turn out to be what they wanted, more often than not they say that at least they found closure from confronting the men who assaulted them and feel like they can start healing.

Not that it was easy, but taking the path she chose helped this woman lift herself from the bottom to where she was eventually able to return to the profession she loved.

"The list of how this affected my life is long," she continued. "It not only affected my life, but my family's life—my husband, my son, my co-workers. The physical abuse healed very quickly. The emotional took a long time. I remember having nightmares every night, sometimes ten or fifteen a night. I was getting very little sleep, and my energy level was almost nothing. The first thing I wanted to do was just to stay home and stay in the closet and never see anybody. I was horribly angry with myself, and I constantly asked myself where my judgment was that day. I was horribly ashamed. I felt like, 'What have I done to cause this?'"

The answer, of course, is nothing. No victim ever causes or asks to be victimized. But what she can do to reduce her risks is an entirely different question altogether.

Rape, or any kind of sexual assault, is not as much about sex as it is about power and control.

Remember, Carson said that he, like most rapists, looked for a person and an opportunity that he thought he could take advantage of. The words he used were "vulnerable" and "control."

So how does knowing how a rapist thinks help you reduce your risks of being sexually assaulted?

Make sure that you are someone a rapist cannot control.

That doesn't necessarily mean that you need to go out and take martial arts classes so that you can't be overcome physically, although some type of self-defense course is always recommended. What we mean is that you maintain control of your environment and circumstances. You create a pattern of thinking that seldom, if ever, allows you to put yourself in a situation where you would be vulnerable to an attacker.

An assailant is going to be able to fill his need for control only if the person he accosts is controllable. And rapists will only attack someone over whom they feel they can exercise their will. They actually look for women they can absolutely dominate.

Brad Morrison, whom we introduced in chapter 2 as the man who raped seventy-five women in eleven states, said women can keep themselves safer just by giving the appearance that they—or their environment—will be difficult to control.

"If I had the slightest inkling that a woman wasn't someone I could easily handle," Morrison told us during an interview for this book, "then I would pass right on by. Or if I thought I couldn't control the situation, then I wouldn't even mess with the house, much less attempt a rape there."

Some things Morrison shared with us in terms of giving a defensible appearance are very telling.

"There were all kinds of things that would make me say, 'This isn't the right place,'" he said. "Like, if they had a dog, then forget it. Even a small one makes too much noise. If I saw a pair of construction boots, for example, out on the porch or on the landing, I walked right on by. In fact, I think if women who live alone put a pair of old construction boots—or something that makes it look like a physically fit manly-man type of guy lives with them—out in front of their door, most rapists or even burglars wouldn't even think about trying to get into the home. The last thing we want is a fight. That's not what we're looking for. We're just looking for an easy target. We just want to get in and get out. I just wanted the sex."

Of course, the behavior of some women actually encourages sexual assailants and makes it that much more difficult for future potential victims.

Morrison, for example, had an experience during the course of his third rape attempt that did nothing but spur him on to more confidence by reinforcing the idea that his victims really wanted it.

Because Morrison had been burglarizing homes for years before he began his series of rapes, he was very aware of the police and had an almost paranoid view of where the police might be next. It was almost to the point where he thought they might jump out of the bushes at any second.

One night, he broke into a house and began burglarizing it when he noticed a woman sleeping on her bed alone, nude and completely uncovered. As was his usual method of operation, he proceeded to put his hand over her mouth and startled her awake.

"Don't scream. If you do what I say, then you won't get hurt," he warned her. "Now, I'm going to take my hand off your mouth. Do you promise not to scream?"

When the woman nodded, he slowly uncovered her mouth, upon which she said, "I just want to tell you that you are the man of my dreams."

"What?" he responded, taken totally off guard.

"You have no idea," she continued. "This is my biggest sexual fantasy ever. It's why I sleep naked and leave my doors unlocked."

At that point, Morrison thought, "Wow, the police are getting good. This has got to be the best sting operation I've ever seen. But I've only done this twice. How do they know already?"

"What's the matter?" she asked him, as if she were disappointed that he wasn't being more aggressive.

"OK," he said. "Are you working with the cops?"

"What?"

"Look, I know it sounds strange, but I just don't want to take any chances," he continued. "If you really want to do this, and you're not working with the cops, I will be on the east side of that park across the street. Meet me there in ten minutes. OK?"

"OK, whatever."

With that, Morrison took off and hid in the bushes, still convinced that this woman was part of some sort of ploy to catch him.

Much to his surprise, however, it wasn't ten minutes before the woman approached him, dressed in lingerie and carrying a blanket and two beers.

"I couldn't believe it," Morrison said, shaking his head. "It was the wackiest thing that ever happened to me."

He referred to that experience often to justify subsequent rapes, thinking that, deep down, every woman secretly fantasized about having a spontaneous sexual experience with a strange man in the middle of the night.

"After a while, after each rape, I would tell myself, 'This is the last one,'" he told us. "But I would always find a justification for doing it again. It had control over me."

As strange an experience as that was for Morrison, we relate this story for one reason. We know that some women out there think like this woman did, and we know that this story seems like it is straight out of a movie. But, the bottom line is, she got lucky—he wasn't homicidal. She was lucky that, at the time he struck, Morrison was nonviolent and that sex was all he wanted.

Romanticizing this kind of thing is only going to put you at the extreme high end of the risk scale. There is no such thing as a "Kissing Bandit," and keeping your doors and windows unlocked in hopes of one coming into your bedroom and whisking you away for a night of romance is extremely unwise, to say the least. If it's romance you are looking for, find it some other way— or instead of finding yourself in a romantic comedy, you may find yourself in the middle of a horror story. Moreover, keep in mind that Morrison raped seventy-five women. That means that he was so encouraged by his third experience that the seventy-two other women had to suffer for this lady's negligence, and some of them suffered badly.

"He definitely got more vicious toward the end," said Chris Zimmerman, the detective who arrested Morrison and ultimately elicited his confession. Chris is now the deputy chief for the Weber County Sheriff's Office in Utah. "He would demand oral sex, and if he got it, then he would go home. But if he didn't get it, then he would want intercourse. If a woman refused to have intercourse with him, then he would knock her around pretty bad. He may not know this or want to admit to it, but he was headed down the path of homicide."

Again, this underscores just how fortunate this woman was that, when she encountered Morrison, he was still in the mold of the less violent rapist. And this is an important distinction to make.

Because there are different types of sexual predators, the strategies to combat them vary somewhat, as well. For example, investigators can tell how much experience an attacker has based on the amount of time he spends with his victim. The longer he stays, the more experience he has, which means he has done it to someone else and will almost certainly prey on another victim. It's important that you learn to recognize the different kinds of sexual assailants so that you can take the appropriate steps to protect yourself.

To categorize them, there are four types of sexual predators to watch out for, all of whom vary in their methods, strategies, needs, and degrees of violence.

We have provided the following outline—one that Mike and I have used to train criminal investigators from all over the world—so that you can better understand the thought process of a potential attacker. These rape typologies, which were originated by Dr. A. Nicholas Groth, include psychological descriptions of each kind of rapist and interview techniques used for questioning the victims of each type of sexual assault.

This is important information for you to have because thinking like a predator and those who investigate predators can help you evaluate your life (as a potential victim) and determine what changes you can make to minimize your risks. That said, the following outlines the rapist's purpose, method of operation, and criminal profile.

1. POWER REASSURANCE (WANNABE)

A. Purpose

This assailant rapes to reassure himself of his masculinity through exercising power over women. We use the term "wannabe" because he lacks the confidence to develop and maintain a social and sexual relationship with women, so he resorts to rape to prove to himself that he truly is a "man."

B. Method of Operation

- Verbally unselfish. His fantasy is that the victim wants him. He may even instruct her to tell him so.

- Sexually unselfish.

- The level of force he uses is most often minimal to moderate. He will usually use only as much force as necessary to control the victim. This type is frequently referred to as the "gentleman" rapist. That is not to say this type of rapist will not kill, given the right set of circumstances.

- Surprise attack—he lacks the confidence to use any other approach.

- He will rely on the threat of a weapon, but most often he will not have one. If he uses a weapon, it is often unintentional. He will sometimes advise the victim he has an accomplice.

- He will normally commit his crimes in close proximity to where he lives or works. It is an area he is comfortable with.

- Victim selection will be made in advance of the attack, normally through surveillance or peeping. He has likely selected many targets, and if one is unavailable, he will move on to the next one on the list. This explains why you might have an attempted rape followed by another attack in the same neighborhood.

- The time of attack will usually be between the hours of midnight and 5 a.m.

- The victim will usually be alone or in the company of small children.

- He will often have the victim undress herself and may have the victim undress him. To do so fuels his fantasy of a consenting sexual relationship.

- He strikes every seven to fifteen days. Gaps are explainable. The cycle may accelerate if he is unsuccessful.

- This rapist generally spends a short time with his victims since he does not have the confidence or social skills to spend more time. However, if he happens to have a compliant victim, he may spend a considerable time acting out his fantasies and may even tell the victim his life story.

- Erectile insufficiency and premature ejaculation are the most common dysfunctions with this type of rapist. (Both are signs of performance anxiety.)

- He will normally select victims within three to four years of his own age.

- He may recontact his victims to relive the fantasy, return to apologize, or return to a victim with whom he was successful following an unsuccessful event.

- He may take a souvenir to use at a later time to relive the event.

- He may keep records in the form of a diary, charts, or possibly computer records.

C. Profile

- Low self-esteem permeated his life.

- Described by those who know him as gentle, quiet, and passive.

- Underachiever—may be capable of doing better but does not try.

- Nonathletic.

- Solitary pastimes—reads, watches television, etc.

- Nocturnal—he is more comfortable in hours of darkness.

- Single.

- Dates significantly younger girls if he dates at all.

- He may take little pride in his personal appearance.

- Prior arrest for nuisance sexual offenses—peeping, panty thefts, etc.

- Often lives alone or with a parent.

- Possibly referred to a counselor in school because of an inability to interact and/or because he is an underachiever.

- Loner.

- Lives, works, or visits within walking distance of assaults.

- Sees himself as a "loser" and is probably seen by others as a "loser."

- Menial work—usually night work—that involves little or no contact with the public.

Brad Morrison is a typical example of the Power Reassurance rapist. This rapist utilizes a quiet, sneaky method. He looks for an easy target, someone who is not going to fight him. He finds a victim who has left her doors and/or windows unlocked then quietly sneaks up. He attacks her when she is at her most vulnerable—asleep, for example—because he doesn't want a violent confrontation. He just wants to get sex and then get out without being caught.

Because this type of rape requires only a moderate amount of planning, the rapist can carry out his attack in a relatively short period of time, as was the case with Morrison. He would often preselect a neighborhood, usually lower-income-level housing, then prowl around until he found a residence that he was confident he could take advantage of. That is why it is so important to cut off opportunities and access into your home. The majority of these rapists are burglars as well. Incidentally, these rapes are most often reported because the victim has no prior relationship with her attacker and feels the least amount of responsibility for the rape.

When he began his criminal career, Morrison told us that his only aim was self-gratification. He had been married and actually had three daughters during that marriage, but the relationship with his wife dissolved because of his drug abuse, and he looked for illegitimate avenues in which to fill that void. He didn't want to hurt anybody, and for the first three years he committed rapes, he didn't hit any of his victims. He was just out to live a sexual fantasy, and in his mind, he wasn't hurting anybody.

Because of an experience he had in prison, however, he now knows that his actions were extremely harmful to his victims.

A few years into his sentence, which began in 1988, Morrison received a visit from one of his daughters. She asked him if he knew one of the other inmates, a man who was to be transferred in just a few days to another facility to serve the remaining two years of his sentence for child molestation.

"I've heard of him, but I don't really know him," Morrison told his daughter. "Why do you ask?"

Her response hit him like a bullet right between the eyes.

"I was one of his victims, Dad."

After his daughter's visit, Morrison sought out this man and confronted him.

"At first, he tried to act like he didn't know who I was," Morrison told us. "But he knew, and once I cornered him, he admitted it. I looked him in the eye and said, 'God knows I'm not someone who has a right to judge, and I believe everyone deserves a second chance. But when you get out, you make sure you make the most of your chance, because if you end up back in here, I'll personally make sure you don't ever get out again.'"

One reason we thought Morrison's point of view would be valuable to this section is because of this very experience. He is one of the few sexual assailants who carries this perspective, and he wants to do his part to help others avoid victimization.

Now, how does knowing Brad Morrison's personality help you reduce your risks of becoming a victim of sexual assault? We'll let him answer that question.

"I think the main thing women need to know about me, or anyone out there like me, is that we don't want a fight," he said. "We're just looking for the easiest way possible to get sex or money or whatever it is we're looking to get by breaking into your house. . . . The best thing you can do is to make yourself not look easy. Make it look like you will put up a fight. . . . And, if you're attacked and already single, have a man's name already in mind to yell out. Because, even if I'm 90 percent positive that there is no man in the house, a woman yelling down the hall to a man, even if there really is no man there, puts enough doubt in my mind that I'm probably going to stop what I'm doing and get out of there."

2. POWER ASSERTIVE (MACHO MAN)

A. *Purpose*

This type of rapist is out to prove his virility. He sees himself as a man's man. Many date rapists are included in this category.

B. *Method of Operation*

- Sexual behavior—selfish. The rapist has no concern for his victim.

- Verbal behavior—selfish.

- Level of force—moderate. There is no need to harm his victims, but he will use enough force to get what he wants.

- Approach—con. He has the confidence to use a good con.

- Attacks the same age range (give or take four years).

- Often meets his victims on the same evening as the assault—meets them in bars, dance clubs, etc.

- Assaults during early evening hours when he can meet women.

- Victims are those of opportunity.

- Assaults away from his work and residence since he has the confidence to leave his immediate area.

- Tears off victim's clothing since he has no doubts about the victim wanting him.

- Multiple assaults during the same evening. What better way to prove his masculinity?

- Most often his sexual dysfunction is retarded ejaculation (hostility and anger).

- Relies on his fist as a weapon—no preplanning, so he will not have a weapon unless he usually carries one.

C. Profile

- He has a macho image, and the most important thing to him is to have others see him as a "man."

- Athletic.

- Drinks a masculine drink. There will never be a little umbrella in his drink.

- Exercises regularly—jogs, possibly a body builder. He wants to look good and takes pride in his appearance.

- Very self-centered. Does not like to be under the control of or work for others.

- Often has numerous relationships. It is very difficult for a woman to stay with him, but his ego dictates that he remarry.

- History of conflict with women because of his selfish behavior.

- Hangs out at dance clubs and bars, where he finds his victims.

- Dresses according to his macho image.

- Drives a macho vehicle.

- Works at a macho job—heavy equipment operator, lumberjack, police, etc.

One of the most classic examples of this assault category that I can think of is a rape that occurred when I was a young police chief in a small Utah town, just a couple years before I went into the FBI.

A man, one of hundreds of temporary laborers at a nearby power plant, had met a woman at a bar in town. They hit it off, and she agreed to go for a ride with him in his truck. One thing led to another, and when he began to make unwanted sexual advances, she refused him and demanded that he drive her back to the bar. He flew into a rage and pulled over into an isolated off-road area.

He beat her viciously and brutally raped her, leaving her for dead on the side of the road. Somehow, through amazing perseverance, she managed to get to the road and flag down a car for help. Unfortunately, however, after she had recovered, several weeks after the attack, she was back at the same bar picking up strange men.

Obviously, this woman's behavior goes completely against what we are trying to teach, but her assailant's actions typify the Power Assertive rapist's behavior.

This rapist uses the "con approach," commonly known as date rape. Once this assailant gets his victim alone, where she has no one to yell to for help, he turns on her and executes his attack. These rapists have little need to plan in advance because the perpetrator usually relies on his victim accompanying him to an isolated area. He needs only time to scout such a setting, but from that point, he needs only to find a woman he can persuade to go with him to such a location. The attacker is usually someone the victim knows casually or very little at all. The degree of violence varies from bondage to homicidal. These rapes are the least reported because, in this situation, the victim feels most responsible for the crime.

Anyone who has teenage daughters worries about this rapist. The best thing to do to reduce the risks is to avoid being isolated with someone you are on a first date with or whom you are just getting to know. If you're not sure but still want to get to know the person, then double-date or arrange to meet your date in a public setting and keep the date to locations that are heavily populated.

3. ANGER RETALIATORY ("RAMBO")

A. Purpose

This rapist's aim is to get even, punish, and degrade women. Anger may be directed at a specific woman or women in general.

B. *Method of Operation*

- Sexual behavior—selfish since his purpose is to punish.

- Verbal behavior—selfish, abusive, and demeaning.

- Force—excessive. Force exceeds that necessary to control the victim.

- Approach—blitz (ambushes his victims, usually in isolated areas).

- Attacks anytime, day or night.

- Attacks spontaneously and out of anger.

- Spends a short time with the victim.

- Victims in own age range or older but not elderly.

- Symbolic victims representing victims he wants to get even with.

- Rips or tears clothing.

- No set timing—precipitated by events in his life.

- No preplanning. Since it is a spontaneous attack, the weapon will be one of opportunity.

- Retarded ejaculation (anger).

- Drinks to release his inhibitions.

C. Profile

- Acquaintances report a "dark side" to the offender.

- Abuses alcohol.

- Minimal use of pornography, if any (no fantasy).

- Married more than once—physical conflict with wife and domestic calls to police.

- High school dropout.

- Explosive personality that may have resulted in arrest for assault.

- Acts impulsively.

- Lone wolf as opposed to a loner. He is capable of socializing but prefers to be alone.

- Relationships are superficial. Nobody really knows him.

- Action-oriented job allowing him to work off some of his aggression.

Michael Carson fits into this category. His anger was directed at a woman who had an affair with his then-wife. He caught them having sex in his bedroom one day. He attributes that experience to the reason he began sexually assaulting women, usually selecting victims who resembled the other woman.

This rapist sometimes uses the "blitz" approach, meaning he will either lie in wait in an isolated location, such as a park or an alley late at night, and spring on his victim, or he tends to scout the victim for an extensive period until he can attack her in her own home. The blitz rapist is usually a very angry man with an ax to grind against women.

In addition to the blitz tactic, Carson used the "con" approach, which, as we mentioned, is common to date rapes. His method was to gain the woman's trust in order to get her to an isolated location before pouncing on her. During their interview, when Mike asked Carson what his most successful method of assault was, he answered, "Just being nice. That's all I had to do, Mike, was just be nice."

4. ANGER EXCITATION (SEXUAL SADIST—DEVIL)

A. Purpose

Sexual gratification comes from inflicting pain and observing the results. This is the least common offender.

B. Method of Operation

- Premeditated. The most premeditated sexual crime. The crime is practiced in his mind before it is ever attempted.

- Sexual behavior—selfish.

- Verbal behavior—selfish.

- Approach—con.

- Victims are strangers.

- He keeps his victims over a period—hours to days (even longer).

- Uses instruments and devices.

- Practices bondage.

- Takes victims to a secluded area (so screams will not be heard).

- Often will videotape acts.

- Favorite weapon is a knife (the most threatening weapon to a woman).

- Voice is nonemotional—instructional—practiced.

- Cuts clothing off the victim.

- Age of victim does not matter.

- No pattern of attacks. Attacks when he wants to.

- Retarded ejaculation—hostility, anger.

C. Profile

- White male.

- Typically has no history of mental healthcare.

- Outgoing, well liked.

- High IQ (above average).

- White-collar job or white-collar criminal.

- Bondage pornography.

- At least some college education.

- Reads soldier-of-fortune or detective magazines.

- Outdoors man, survivalist.

- If he owns a dog, it is typically an aggressive, large dog, such as a German Shepherd or a Doberman.

- No arrest record.

- Does not abuse drugs. He might use but does not want to lose control.

- Compulsive.

- Can be "happily" married.

- Wife will be under his control—a slave. His girlfriend is not under his total control, and he will not act out against her.

- Fixated on anal sex (degrading).

- He drives a family-type vehicle.

- Would do well in the military.

These types of rapists, while garnering huge amounts of media attention because of their sensational nature, are by far the least common of the four categories, and their acts quite often end in homicide.

One of the most notorious examples of the Anger Excitation rapist is the serial killer Ben Rhoades. In early 1990, Rhoades, a long-haul truck driver, was captured when a highway patrol trooper in Arizona stopped in the middle of the night to check out his rig. When the trooper opened the door to the sleeper cab, he found Rhoades with a nude woman he had chained and handcuffed in the back.

They arrested Rhoades for the rape and torture of that victim and, through other evidence discovered at his apartment in Houston, were able to tie him to three homicides. Evidence showed that every one of those murders occurred after the victims were raped and tortured for an extended period. (We will go into more detail regarding Ben Rhoades in chapter 9.)

Now that you have read through the list of different types of rapists, ask yourself what type of attacker would come after you, based on your personality or lifestyle. In what ways are you most vulnerable and how would you react to a rape attempt?

Keep in mind, your personality and lifestyle say a lot about you in terms of the way in which you would be targeted. Again, we're not going for paranoia or blame here, just common sense. If you're the type of person who is outgoing, open, and likeable, that's great. There is no reason you can't continue to be that kind of person. Just use common sense and realize that, while openness is your primary personality trait, it doesn't mean you have to defy good judgment and accept rides from complete strangers you just met at a bar.

Another type of sex offender seems to be surfacing with more frequency—the female sexual predator. We see more and more cases on the news of female junior high or high school teachers sexually assaulting their male students.

This first hit American consciousness in 1997, when a Washington schoolteacher, Mary Kay Letourneau, was convicted of having sex with a twelve-year-old student. She ultimately had two children by this young man, and when she was finally released from prison, the two were married. Since the late 1990s, dozens of similar cases have come to light. It seems that our society is still unsure how to handle it, which is why we thought it was important to address the situation and its effect on the victims.

This criminal trend is breaking all the stereotypes. Everything we thought we knew about women's attitude toward sex and the effect sex has on teenage boys is challenged whenever a crime like this is committed.

From judges to police to parents, and everyone in between, it seems that there is a clash between the stereotypes our society has held for years and how this kind of sexual relationship really affects male adolescents.

One of the most telling examples of how we look at this crime drew national headlines in 2005 when Debbie Lafave, a twenty-three-year-old middle school teacher from Florida, was arrested for having sex with a fourteen-year-old male student.

But what garnered this attention wasn't the crime itself. It was Lafave, a gorgeous blond-haired, blue-eyed beauty who could turn heads walking down any street in the country. Americans were at once appalled and fascinated by the crime. One of the most telling aspects of this case, however, was that even though she had admitted to having sexual intercourse with the boy, a great deal of public sentiment seemed to be on her side.

"To place Debbie into a Florida state women's penitentiary," her attorney told a gathering of national media, "to place an attractive young woman in that kind of hellhole, is like putting a piece of raw meat in with the lions."

In the end, Lafave accepted a plea bargain that gave her no jail time and ten years' probation.

Because neither Mike nor I have had much, if any, experience with these types of cases, we asked a good friend, Harvard Professor Harold J. Bursztajn, MD, to help us sort through the minds of both the female offenders and their male victims. Dr. Bursztajn is the co-founder of the Program in Psychiatry and the Law of the Psychiatry Department of Harvard Medical School and a world-renowned expert in criminal behavior.

Given society's traditional views on sexual relationships, the challenge is to break through the age-old stereotypes, understand the effects this crime has on teenage boys, and find ways to educate and help them so they can avoid victimization, if at all possible.

We have been taught that all teenage boys, at one time or another, sexually fantasize about a teacher. So when a fourteen-year-old boy is victimized by a gorgeous twenty-three-year-old teacher like Debbie

Lafave, society invariably asks two questions.

One, why would an attractive adult woman seduce a teenage boy? And, two, because he got to seemingly live out every teenager's fantasy, is the teenage boy really a victim?

In answer to the first question, Dr. Bursztajn told us that the reason female predators engage in sexual assault is a need for power and control.

"In these instances, a woman feels like she has a great deal of power," he said. "She gets a powerful feeling by engaging in a power-dependency relationship with the victim. It is a way of saying to herself, 'I can do anything I want to do. I am above any standards of morality or law.'"

Unlike a male sexual assailant, who uses brute physical sex to assert his dominance, the female sexual predator seeks to control her victim through emotional manipulation. This happens primarily because female predators generally exhibit a fear of abandonment, which manifests itself by a need to dominate relationships. If the teenage boy begins to have second thoughts or attempts to back out of the relationship, she will employ emotional scare tactics to regain control over him, even using her authority (as a teacher, for example) as a weapon.

"She tells the boy, 'I can do things to you if you don't have sex with me,'" Dr. Bursztajn told us. "Threatening him is a way for her to show that she can control him."

As for the answer to the second question, Dr. Bursztajn says the teenage boy is not only a victim, but he is every bit as much a victim as a teenage female, having had his ability to engage in future meaningful adult relationships seriously compromised.

"These young men who are victimized in this way think to themselves, 'This person who did this to me has power and control over my life,'" he said. "Psychologically, he never develops. He never matures. He virtually winds up frozen in time."

As we talked to him about the subject and society's perspective of this crime, Dr. Bursztajn told us that members of any community where a teenage boy is victimized should be extra careful to define the line between fantasy and reality.

"What happens in these situations is the teacher takes away the mind's ability to be a safe place to fantasize," he said. "Yes, every boy fantasizes about his teacher, but you wouldn't want something like this to be a reality."

No, you certainly wouldn't, which is the point of this section of the chapter. No one deserves to be victimized, physically or psychologically. The difference between sexual male and female predators is that men tend to focus their attacks on the physical aspect of an assault, while women focus on the emotional. In the end, the results are basically the same. The victims wind up damaged in the long run—mentally and emotionally—and the work to repair that damage is seemingly endless.

We opened this chapter using the example of a woman in a sales field, obviously very friendly and intelligent. Unfortunately, she didn't put safeguards in place to protect her from the aspects of her personality and lifestyle that made her vulnerable. And make no mistake, we all have them. It's just recognizing those areas of vulnerability and doing something about them that allows us to strengthen our ability to protect ourselves, especially from a crime as damaging as sexual assault.

That includes our financial circumstances. One thing we, as law enforcement officials, recognize is that economics play a huge role in a potential victim's ability to do the things necessary to reduce her risks.

Having said that, please be aware that, even if your financial situation is tight, you can still make lifestyle changes that will at least reduce your risks of being a rape victim. While these changes won't completely guarantee your safety, anything you can do to minimize the likelihood of this happening to you is a step that could prevent victimization. Keep in mind that rapists actually target low-income housing. They recognize that lower-income residents often don't have the means to beef up their security.

They also feel that women in low-income housing make easier targets.

"I always looked for women who had low self-esteem," Brad Morrison told us. "Because I knew that women with low self-confidence weren't going to put up a fight. . . . I could always tell by the way the house or apartment or the car looked if they would be the type to fight me. If the house was run-down, and things were cluttered, and it was easy to see that it hadn't been cleaned for a while, then I knew I had one that was probably depressed and wouldn't have it in her to make a fuss. If she had kids, then that was even better, because most women will do anything to protect their kids. It's amazing what a woman is willing to do for her children."

Remember, regardless of the type of rapist, the key to taking control from a would-be sexual predator is to avoid situations, inasmuch as possible, in which you become vulnerable and hand control of yourself over to another person. Whether you are in your home or out and about, you should habitually ask yourself a number of questions in regard to keeping yourself as safe as possible. Some examples include:

- Do I keep my doors and windows locked?

- Do I have a dog, an alarm, or something that would make noise should an intruder attempt to enter my house or apartment?

- Do I keep a cell phone on my person at all times? If I can't afford one, is my phone easily accessible and/or nearby my bed?

- If I live alone, do I give the appearance that someone who could protect me stays with me?

- If I live alone with my children, do I disguise the fact that I am taking care of them on my own?

- Is my vehicle arranged in a way that would make it difficult for a would-be attacker to determine if I am a single female who lives alone?

- Do I rearrange my schedule to make it difficult for a potential attacker to scout me? Do the people in my household do the same?

- When I go out, do I allow complete strangers to take me places?

- Do I avoid being in isolated locations with a man I don't know, on a first or second date, for example?

- Do I avoid walking alone at night or in dark places?

- Do I travel in groups and in public places as much as possible?

We mentioned earlier in the book that you might be riding high in life right now and feel as if you would never be in a situation when you wouldn't fight off an attacker. Most of Morrison's victims probably felt that way at some point in their lives as well. But things happen, and we hit low points when we don't feel so on top of the world. We all go through that. If you do happen to be at that point in life, please don't think that you're not worth protecting. No one deserves to be assaulted in such a personal and demeaning manner.

Don't feel as if it doesn't matter if you are attacked. It does. Not only for you but also for the other victims who will most certainly follow if you don't do something to improve your safety. Remember, with each successful rape, the rapist becomes that much more confident and will almost certainly attack again.

Cut off his confidence and you cut off the rapes. The more opportunities you erase, the fewer the victims there will be. It really is the only way to stop these guys or at least slow them down.

Keep in mind also that the questions posed above are not meant to make you feel as if you have either passed or failed. This is not a test, at least not in the sense that you should feel like a failure if you can't answer the questions in the affirmative. The point is to get you thinking in the right direction. We want to get you thinking about cutting off the opportunities of a would-be rapist. The point is to make a potential assailant feel as if he couldn't easily gain the control he craves if he attacked you. If you make the proper adjustments to your lifestyle, there should seldom, if ever, be an instance in which a rapist would feel like you would be an opportune target.

If you discover that there are areas in your life in which you could make changes, then make those changes now. Don't fall into the trap of thinking it won't happen to you. Please do not become complacent. Even if you could answer in the affirmative to all the questions above, try to think of more things you could be doing to minimize your risks. Think of more questions you could ask yourself. As our lives change, so do our areas of vulnerability. That means the questions we need to be asking ourselves change, as well.

Look at your residence, for example, and ask yourself, "If I were a rapist, where could I gain entry into my home and how would I do it? If I were an Anger Retaliatory type of rapist, for example, what would be the best way to scout me?"

During the course of my day, where are the points in my schedule where I am most vulnerable? How could I change my schedule to eliminate or at least bolster that area of vulnerability that a Power Reassurance rapist looks for?

What are some of my habits that a stalker could scout and find a point when he could get me alone and control me? What changes do I need to make to eliminate that opportunity?

If I am confronted by an attacker, what is my immediate plan of action? Have I practiced what I will do if I do find myself in that situation?

At this point, one thing we need to clarify is that we are talking about sexual assailants who aren't looking to kill. You might be wondering if screaming or fighting will get you killed. The answer is probably not. The vast majority of rapists are not looking to murder. They are just looking to fill a need to control. That is why they prey on the vulnerable.

If the sexual predator is also a killer, then he is almost always going to kill anyway, so no matter what you do, if you are alone with this individual, then he is going to try to murder you. If rape is involved, then it is most likely his secondary motive, which means the only way to save yourself is by doing whatever you have to do to get a third party's attention, whether it means screaming or whatever.

Now, there are situations when a rapist has gotten so violent that, in his anger, he has killed his victim. If you find that he has a gun or that he continues to hit you after you have screamed and fought off his initial attack, then you might have to start thinking about just saving your life. But the overwhelming majority of the time, creating a ruckus is going to send him looking for something else.

"It's all about the easy target," said one convicted serial rapist whom Mike interviewed. "I had one woman who, as soon as I opened the door, she screamed. She screamed so loud, it rattled me right to my bones—and I ran."

This offender, incidentally, was relating a story in which he had spent several weeks surveilling this woman. She lived in a duplex, and he waited until the man upstairs had left for work early one morning before he broke into her house. Even after all his work and planning, all it took was the threat of someone hearing her to run him off.

"Screaming, fighting, anything you can do to draw attention to me, that will make it so it's not worth my time," Morrison told us when we asked him what advice he had for women who are confronted by a would-be assailant. "See, I didn't want to get caught. I didn't want problems."

And that's the best defense.

If you can create problems for a sexual predator and put doubt in his mind, then you are more than likely going to stop him from getting to you at all.

7

DOMESTIC VIOLENCE

re you sure you still want to stay?" Jeffrey whispered to his younger brother, Tony, being extra careful to make sure his mother couldn't hear him.

The brothers were sharing a room just across the hall from her. It was clear that Jeffrey wanted his brother to go back to California with him, but Tony was having second thoughts.

"Yeah, I think it will help Mom," answered Tony, who had just turned twelve that summer. "She looked really sad when we were talking about the plane tickets. Maybe if I stay just a little longer, it will help her feel better."

Things had been difficult for the two boys since their parents' divorce a year earlier, but this particular visit made them realize the even greater toll the separation had taken on their mother.

Now, as the pair lay awake that night, neither was sure how their mother would cope after they left. It was just two days before they were scheduled to depart for California, where they lived with their father and stepmother.

At times, it seemed as if the boys' visit injected Margaret Jefferson with new life. She actually smiled once in a while and seemed to find the happiness that had eluded her since the troubles in her marriage began three years earlier. But, at other times, it seemed as if the boys only reminded Margaret of how her life had fallen apart. She felt like a failure as a wife, and her constant outbursts at her children over the tiniest things seemed to reinforce the notion that it was just a matter of time before the relationship with her sons would also meet its demise.

"Why did you even bother coming?" she would scream. On a few occasions, she shattered a glass or a vase or some other breakable object against the wall, narrowly missing one or both of the boys. Once, she nearly hit Jeffrey in the head with a picture frame.

"I know you don't really want to be here!" she would rant. "What? I'm not good enough for you? You think your father and that hussy, Sarah, are better than me, don't you? Then why don't you just stay with them and leave me alone? You made your choice. Why don't you just live with it? If you don't want to be here, just go back to them and get out of my house!"

When she flew into a rage, her sons could only take cover and wait for her to tire out. It was just best to weather the storm. Anything the boys would try to say to reassure their mother just seemed to fuel her anger that much more.

The striped scars on Jeffrey's right arm—the result of her pulling him up by the hand and taking her fingernails to him—were a stark reminder of that. The fourteen-year-old seemed to get the worst of it. Maybe Margaret felt he was the stronger of the two and could take more punishment. Or maybe, in her mind, he just did more to deserve it. Either way, no logic could explain the sudden violent outbursts. Nor was there anything that could explain why she would target one son more than the other.

Eventually, Margaret would run out of steam, and her anger would subside, turning into grave remorse. The screaming would be followed by tears, profuse apologies, and ramblings.

"I'm so sorry," she would sob. "Please don't go. I don't want you to go. I love you two so much. Please stay. You two boys are my life, the only life I have. Please forgive me. Oh, why do I do this? Please, come here and give me a hug."

The boys didn't dare refuse her. If they did, she would either fly into a renewed rage or curl up into a ball and threaten suicide.

It was the ultimate emotional blackmail.

"It's OK, Mom," they would say. "We love you, too. We're sorry we made you mad."

"Oh, no, sweetheart," she would cry, wiping away Tony's tears. "You didn't do anything wrong. You either, Jeffrey. It's all my fault. I don't know why I get so mad. It's just the divorce. I will be fine. I promise. It won't happen again."

"I just want to make it better," Tony would say. He always took it the hardest, believing that, if he could just learn to behave, his mom wouldn't have a reason to get so mad. "I wish I could make it better for you, Mom. I wish I could live with you and not Dad."

The truth is the decision wasn't his, Jeffrey's, or his mother's. It was the court's ruling on the matter. It was clear that abuse—mental, emotional, and some physical—had occurred in the Jefferson home for quite some time before the divorce.

Robert, the boys' father, seemed to be powerless. He had seemingly tried everything, but he couldn't figure out how to handle Margaret's outbursts any better than his sons could. He was raised to keep family problems privately guarded, which made him reluctant to seek outside help. He once confided in an old college friend who knew the pair back when they were dating, but the only advice he could give Robert was to get counseling.

He actually considered that option, but the mere mention of it threw Margaret into a rage, and he never broached the subject again.

It wasn't long after that last futile attempt to solve the problem when Robert met Sarah, a woman who worked with him at his insurance company. She was much different from Margaret. Seven years his junior, Sarah was pleasant and never seemed to get flustered, no matter what kind of stress was thrown her way. She seemed to be able to handle any project with the utmost composure. Robert eventually divorced Margaret and struck up an office romance with Sarah.

He had more than enough evidence to show that she was unfit to take Jeffrey and Tony, and the court awarded him full custody of the boys. They, too, were drawn to Sarah but didn't dare display any affection they had for her in front of their mother.

Devastated, Margaret moved to Utah, where she had family to help her get on her feet. She found a job and eventually bought a house with her share of the divorce settlement. She managed to exhibit enough self-control to win unsupervised visitation rights with her boys.

Once she obtained those visitations, however, she soon fell back into a dark depression. At first, she could pretend all was well when the boys came to visit, but it wasn't long before Margaret reverted to her same destructive habits.

This visit had been especially volatile for Tony and Jeffrey.

They had an open-ended plane ticket for their return, but when they had mentioned that they wanted to go home a couple of days earlier than Margaret had in mind, she flew off the handle and into another tirade. She finally settled down when Tony told her he would stay another few days, but she still went to bed very depressed and despondent.

It was then that Jeffrey decided to talk to his little brother. He worried that, without him there to take the brunt of her anger, Tony would have a hard time surviving one of her outbursts on his own.

Unfortunately, the eldest brother's fears would prove to be more accurate than even he could imagine.

Yet, as the two spoke, Jeffrey seemed unable to persuade his younger brother to come home with him.

"I don't know if there's anything you can do," Jeffrey whispered. "Mom needs more help than you can give her. I think she needs to see a psychiatrist."

"You think Mom's crazy?" Tony asked in a surprised tone.

Tony's surprise caught Jeffrey off guard for a moment.

"No, not crazy, just depressed," he tried to explain, still keeping his voice down in case she was listening at the door. "Mom has been through a tough time with the divorce and all. I think she just needs someone to talk to, someone who can help her get over the depression."

"I can help her get over it," Tony countered. "Remember when we were a family, and we would go to the beach? Mom always says that was the happiest time of her life. Why couldn't we make her happy again? Why couldn't I make her happy now?"

"We do," Jeffrey said. "I just think there's a lot more to it than Mom just having a good time with us being here. She needs to find other things that make her happy, too."

"Like what?"

"Like, I don't know—like, a job she likes or a hobby or even a boyfriend. But she's not going to find that without some help from another adult."

"Why does she need another adult? Why can't we help her find those things?"

"Because we can't," Jeffrey said, somewhat worn out by his little brother's constant debating. "That's just how it is."

"Well, I think I can, so I'm staying," Tony said firmly. "I can't help her find a job or a boyfriend, but I can at least help Mom find a hobby."

"Look, you do what you've got to do," Jeffrey finally said in an exasperated tone that suggested he was out of ideas. "But I don't want you to get hurt. If you see any sign of trouble, you get some help, OK?"

"OK."

"No, I mean it, Tony," said Jeffrey, crawling down from the top bunk so he could look his little brother in the eye. "I'm serious. You get someone, anyone, who can call Dad and get you to the airport—even if you have to leave your stuff here, OK?"

"OK, I promise."

Jeffrey, still not entirely convinced, gave Tony a discerning look. It was as if he could sense what would happen if he left his little brother behind.

"I will," Tony emphasized.

"I will what?" Jeffrey insisted.

"I will get somebody if Mom gets too out of control," the youngest confirmed.

"All right," Jeffrey said, giving his younger brother a hug. "I'm not trying to boss you around. I just want you to be safe, OK?"

"I know," said Tony, flashing his charming little crooked smile.

"OK, let's get some sleep then."

Two days later, Jeffrey flew back to California. At first, Tony felt a little lost without his big brother, but time alone with his mother went very well the first day. Margaret took him out for dinner, and they had a pleasant time, talking about basketball, school, and good times they had back home on the beaches of California. She didn't seem the least bit edgy, and Tony was glad that he had decided to stay the extra few days.

But the next day was a bad one.

"You don't have to pretend you like it, Tony!" Margaret snapped at the boy. "You boys and your father never did like my cooking, did you?"

"Yeah, Mom, we liked it. I-I like it," the boy stuttered.

"Don't lie to me!" she shouted, snatching the plate full of spaghetti in front of him and hurling it across the kitchen. The sound of the plate shattering against the wall made Tony cringe. "Don't make that face! If all you wanted was a sandwich for lunch, you should have just said so! You wasted my time, making me cook. What was I thinking? I thought you would be happy if I went to the trouble to make you a nice lunch. I should have known better. You're so ungrateful!"

"Mom, I'm sorry," Tony cried. "I liked it. I did, really."

"No, you didn't! I can see it by the look on your face. I know that look—it's just like your father's!" she screamed before slapping him across the face. "Wipe those tears off your face before I really give you something to cry about!"

Unfortunately for her son, Margaret didn't stop there. One smack led to another. Finally, she snatched him out of the chair he was sitting in, knocking his head against the table leg as she dragged him across the floor to the dog's dish.

"There! That's what you deserve!" she yelled, shoving his face into the dog kibble. "That's all you're getting. When I come back in, you'd better have eaten every last bit of it!"

Ten minutes later, Margaret rushed back into the kitchen, sobbing.

"I'm so sorry, Tony," she said, as she picked him up from the floor and wrapped her arms around him. "I don't know what got into me. I can't believe I did this to you, to my baby."

"It's OK, Mom. I know you didn't mean it. I know you love me."

"I do love you, son. Oh, look at your face. What did I do? Can you ever forgive me?"

"Yes, Mom, I forgive you. It's OK."

"You probably want to go back to your father now," Margaret cried. "Please don't go. I will make up for this, I promise."

"No, Mom. I want to stay. I'm going to stay."

"You are? Oh, thank you, sweetheart. You were always the sweet one. You know your mom doesn't mean it when she gets like this, right?"

"I know."

"I'll tell you what," she continued, wiping the tears from her face. "Tomorrow, I'll take you out for breakfast, my treat. How does that sound?"

"That sounds great, Mom," he said, forcing a smile and wondering if he should ask a neighbor to take him to the airport, as Jeffrey had told him to do. But he knew he couldn't. It would be the biggest form of betrayal, one that would completely devastate his mother. In that instant, he decided he would stay, no matter how bad things got.

"OK, then, it's all settled. Now, why don't you go out and play, and I'll get started on cleaning up this mess."

It may have been all settled in Margaret's mind, but her psychiatric counselor thought things with his patient were far from stable. Margaret had skipped their last three appointments and hadn't returned any of his phone calls over the past three weeks. Fearing the worst, he called the authorities and requested that we check up on her. He wanted one of our officers to persuade her to contact him.

It wasn't long before Sgt. J. R. McElroy knocked on her door.

It was about three in the afternoon, and when Margaret answered the door, she was still dressed in her bathrobe.

"Mrs. Jefferson?"

"Yeah, who wants to know?"

"Mrs. Jefferson, I'm Sergeant McElroy with the Provo Police Department," he began. "We got a call from your therapist. He says you've missed a few appointments, and he's concerned."

"So I missed a few appointments," she snapped. "Since when is that a crime?"

"Well, it's not a crime. We're just concerned. May I come in and talk?"

"No, you may not."

"Mrs. Jefferson—"

"Don't call me that!" she interrupted, looking up at him. "I haven't been Mrs. Jefferson for over a year."

McElroy noticed that the more aggravated she became, the more she began to twitch. She stared at the ground during the vast majority of their conversation, and he hoped to diffuse the situation and somehow gain enough of her trust that she would allow him to come in and have a look around.

"OK, I won't call you that. But will you let me come in so we can talk, for just a minute?"

"What are we going to talk about? I don't have anything to say to you."

"Well, your counselor is very concerned about you, and he just wanted me to come over here and make sure you're all right."

"Well, now you've seen I'm all right. You can go now."

As McElroy and Margaret were talking, Tony came around the corner and toward the house.

"Tony, come on inside," Margaret called out to him.

"What's going on? Why are the police here?" Tony asked.

"Don't you worry about that. Just come on inside."

"Hi, Tony, I'm Sergeant McElroy. Is everything OK here?"

"Yeah, sure," Tony answered, keeping one eye on his mother.

"Are you sure? Someone said they heard some yelling and screaming coming from your house earlier."

"I just had the TV on loud, that's all."

"Get inside now, son," Margaret demanded, clearly becoming more agitated. Tony quickly did as he was ordered.

"Are you sure I can't just come inside and talk to you?" he tried once more, knowing that if he could find some shred of evidence of abuse, he would have grounds for getting the boy to a safer place. "I just want to make sure everything is OK so I can call your therapist back and let him know you're doing all right."

"I told you, everything is great," she insisted, still twitching. "Now, I know I don't have to let you come inside, and I'm not going to, so why don't you just go and do whatever it is you were doing and leave us alone."

With that, she closed the door on the police sergeant.

He sensed that something was terribly wrong, but he was powerless to do anything about it, so he radioed in his report, talked to a couple neighbors in an effort to get somebody to keep watch over Margaret and her son, then finally left.

Margaret's perceived victory over the police put her in better spirits that night as she watched TV with her son.

"Did you see how I handled that cop?" she gloated to Tony.

"Yeah, Mom, you were great," he said, smiling his crooked smile. "He couldn't get anywhere with you."

"No, he sure couldn't," answered Margaret, in a somewhat subdued tone. "That's how you've got to be with those guys. Firm. You can't let them push you around."

For the next hour, she sat on the couch as her son watched TV. She didn't say a word and seemed to be deep in thought. When it was time for bed, the twitching had subsided, and the twelve-year-old noticed that his mother appeared to be more at peace with herself than she had been at anytime he could remember over the past three years.

"Maybe putting that cop in his place gave her the boost she needed," he thought as he pulled the covers over himself.

The next day, Tony and his mother went out for a nice breakfast. When they returned home, Margaret suggested that he go to the local park to play basketball.

"I'll tell you what," she said. "You go shoot some hoops, and that will give me time to get some work done in the house, then we'll go have a nice lunch and maybe even see a movie. How does that sound?"

"Sounds great, Mom," Tony answered, noticing something different about his mother but not quite sure what it was. On his way out, as he turned to close the door, he told Margaret, "I'm glad I stayed, Mom. I've had a good time being here with you."

Tears welled up in the pleased mother's eyes as she hugged her son. "There couldn't be a more perfect way for me to leave this world," she thought.

"I have too, baby," she replied. "I have, too."

Then, Tony smiled at her one last time before turning to leave for the park.

As soon as her son left, Margaret began to set her plan in motion. She spread towels out over her bedroom floor, removed a handwritten suicide note from the side-table drawer, and placed it on the bed. She pulled a handgun from the drawer, knelt down on the towels, and began to say one last prayer for her children.

But, as she started, she heard a sound that completely unnerved her.

"Mom," Tony hollered from the front room. "Do we have a needle and a pump? My ball is kind of flat."

Margaret was immediately enraged.

This wasn't supposed to happen. But before she could rise to her feet, Tony opened the door to her bedroom.

"Mom—" he started to call, before seeing what lay before him. "What are you doing, Mom?" he asked weakly, his voice cracking.

"What does it look like I'm doing?" she snapped. "Get in here!" Margaret grabbed him by the arm and jerked him into the room. Then, she slapped him, not once, but several times.

"How many times do I have to tell you and your stupid brother not to barge into my room? This is my space! How dare you invade my space!"

"I-I'm sorry, Mom," Tony whimpered. "But what are you doing?"

"Are you that stupid? I always thought you were the smart one. I guess I was wrong. You're just as stupid as your father. What does it look like I'm doing? I'm going to shoot myself! At least, I was, until you decided to come in and screw it all up. You just had to screw it all up, didn't you? I had it all planned out. Things were going perfect. We were going to end on a good note. Finally, something was going to go the way I wanted it to. For once, I finally had control over something in my life. But, no, you just couldn't let that happen, could you? You had to mess it all up!"

At the height of her rage, Margaret pointed the gun at Tony and shot her son point-blank in the head. She didn't want to pull the trigger, but it was as if she were powerless to stop herself, as if somebody else was holding her hand to the gun and forcing her to squeeze the trigger. That's the way it always seemed whenever she flew into an uncontrollable rage.

The whole sordid scene seemed so surreal to Margaret. It was as if she were watching, in slow motion, someone else commit this unspeakable act.

But it wasn't someone else. It was her.

She was the one who had pulled the trigger. She was the one who caused the death of this beautiful twelve-year-old boy who called her "Mom." She had finally gone too far.

Her heart stopped as the realization of what she had just done began to sink in.

"Oh, God," she muttered. "Dear, God, what have I done? What kind of a mother am I? I shot my baby."

The sight of her youngest child lying on her bedroom floor in a pool of blood was too much for Margaret. She couldn't bring herself to even kneel down and try to help him. She couldn't move at all.

All she could do was hold the gun to her head and squeeze the trigger.

That summer evening, I was supposed to be at the wedding of a close friend's daughter. Instead, I found myself in the master bedroom of a two-bedroom house, kneeling over the lifeless bodies of a woman and her twelve-year-old son.

As I studied the situation, all I could think was, "I'm at the scene of another senseless loss of life."

At the time, my oldest son was about the same age as the boy, and to me, his death was the real tragedy. It's always tragic when innocence is taken from us. I could only imagine how terrified the young man must have been when he realized what his mother had in mind. I could envision the look of disbelief on his face. My guess is that the exchange that took place between the two lasted only a few moments, but however short the time frame, it must have seemed like an eternity to him.

As I began to learn more about the circumstances surrounding the case, I realized that there were so many ironic twists. A what-if here or a what-if there might have made the difference in saving their lives or at least the boy's life.

J. R. McElroy, the sergeant who had visited them the day before, was one of my closest friends. We had started our careers around the same time, and we actually started a small private investigation business together back in the early days. Having been pulled into Margaret Jefferson's topsy-turvy world, he took it especially hard when he found out what happened. I waited as long as I could to tell him because it was his daughter's wedding that I had been attending when I got the call. I don't think there would have been a good time to tell him, and I certainly didn't want to spoil the occasion, but unfortunately I was the chief of police, and it was my job to tell him so he could finish his report in time. When I returned from the crime scene, I finally pulled J. R. aside just after his daughter's wedding reception and told him what had happened.

It was difficult for me to do because, in addition to the heart-wrenching circumstances of the case, J. R. is an emotional guy who has had his share of life's tragedies to deal with. Just four years before this case, he had to testify against his sister on domestic violence charges, and his testimony led to her conviction. The next day, she committed suicide, an incident that J. R. obviously took very hard. From that time forth, he was extremely sensitive to domestic violence issues. Of course, he was always a good officer of the law, but I think

J. R. possessed an added element of sensitivity whenever he was called to a domestic dispute, as he did in the case of Margaret and Tony Jefferson. He tried everything he could to help this woman and her son, but she wouldn't budge. He did all that he could legally do, but somehow, I don't think he felt it was enough.

Such is the case with us as a society.

Domestic violence is such a huge problem that it's obvious we aren't doing enough. We are doing a lot, but there are several fronts in which we are still sorely lacking. And I'm not talking about just the authorities—I mean everyone. Family, friends, neighbors, clergy, teachers, other authorities, and anyone else you can think of need to combine to take an active role in stopping this widespread problem. Above all, individuals need to start taking responsibility for their actions. Police get more domestic dispute calls than anything else, and they hear repeatedly that the abuse is not entirely the abuser's fault.

I remember one man telling me, "My dad used to beat me when I was a child. That's why it's so hard for me to control myself. That's just how I was taught."

My response: "Guess what, pal. You're an adult now. You have the power to stop yourself and put an end to this problem in your family, so do it."

During our careers, Mike and I have heard every excuse from depression to alcohol to past abuse to "She pushed me too far." And, yes, they are *excuses*. No matter what's happening in your life, your loved ones do not deserve to be abused—physically, mentally, verbally, or in any other way, period.

Of all the predatory crimes we cover in this book, this one cannot be prevented by locking your doors and windows because it occurs from within. It can be completely prevented only if the abuser, or potential abuser, takes responsibility for his or her behavior and makes a conscious choice to stop.

If he or she fails to do so, then it's up to those next closest to the situation to jump in and help. And we're not talking about one or two people. We're talking about a whole group of people. Abusers are considered predators because they prey on the most vulnerable members of society—the ones who love them. As such, the best way to fend off any predator is to get as many people as it takes to stop him.

A single wolf is tough to handle for one or two individuals, but when a dozen or so people get involved, the wolf is rendered powerless.

Tom McHoes learned that lesson when he was a newspaper reporter. He attended a program called Citizens Academy in Orem, Utah. The class, which ran for about ten consecutive weeks, was designed to give residents a taste of what police do.

Officials who run this academy train these residents through role-playing. On one occasion, the group was role-playing the proper procedures for domestic violence responses. Tom had the misfortune of meeting face-to-face with one of Orem's lieutenants, Mike Larsen, now the department director. Tom is about five-foot-nine. Mike is about six-foot-five. Tom didn't have a chance, and Mike wasn't about to let him off the hook. As a lot of domestic violence suspects do, Mike challenged Tom to a fight. The poor guy had no idea what to do and could only look pleadingly at the class instructor, Karl Hirst, who mercifully ended the role-playing session.

Tom learned that night that even police, upon finding themselves in such a vulnerable situation, will call as many officers as they need to control the situation.

Most of the time, family, friends, clergy, and others don't take action because, like Tom, they don't understand that principle. They are afraid. Of damaging the relationship. Of alienating their loved ones. Of what will happen if they call the authorities.

The key here is the lack of knowledge.

Granted, sometimes situations can be extremely complicated, but when you know how to garner support for the abused, then most of the time the predatory abuser will cut his losses and look elsewhere for someone to victimize. If we all do our part, he won't have anywhere to go and will change his ways. But the only way that can ever happen is one person at a time.

If you are a concerned friend or family member and you're not sure if you should get involved, call your nearest domestic abuse hotline. They will help you assess the situation and find other organizations that can walk you through the appropriate steps.

With so many different domestic violence situations, there is no way we could even hope to advise you otherwise. Every situation has its own solutions. But what we hope to do here is to educate you in regard to a predatory abuser's characteristics and the situations he or she feels most comfortable working in so that you can recognize the red flags when they come up.

The best way to understand an abuser is to understand the victim.

Victims of domestic violence tend to be the most vulnerable members of our society. That is why so many of them are children.

Adult victims tend to be people who rely on the abuser. They are so uncertain of themselves that it's not hard for the abuser to convince them that they couldn't survive without him. When I use the word *uncertain*, I don't mean in every way. There are people who are incredibly sure of themselves in their careers, for example, who you would never think were being abused at home. But, like all of us, they have deep-rooted insecurities that make them feel inadequate and apprehensive about leaving their abusive partners.

They often become victims to predatory abusers who are looking to fill legitimate emotional needs. As is the case with almost all domestic offenders, a sense of emotional desperation causes them to commit the crimes they do.

For men, the abuse usually indicates a need for power and control. That's why their abuse of children is often sexual and physical. When a man feels a need for power, he sometimes tries to illegitimately fill that need by abusing his family.

While female abusers are also looking for control, they are usually looking for a different kind—mastery over their own lives. Typically, female child abusers commit cruel acts because they are trying to fill a need for control over romantic relationships, appearances, finances, and so on.

In Margaret Jefferson's case, she was desperate to pull her closest relationships together. She had recently seen her marriage fall apart and was in the middle of a bitter custody dispute. Margaret initially took her turmoil out on her sons, abusing them as a means of trying to manipulate them into unconditionally loving her. She had been abandoned by her husband and feared she would ultimately meet the same fate with her children. With each incidence of abuse toward Tony and Jeffrey, she felt she was undermining her relationship with them, thus losing their loyalty to her. Eventually, she felt it all slipping away, and in the end, rather than embrace her therapy in an effort to correct the problem, she decided to commit suicide. Unfortunately, her son Tony was a casualty of bad timing and fell victim to her pain as well.

This perfectly illustrates what a group of neighbors could have done. They must have heard the commotion coming from that home during the course of Tony and Jeffrey's visit. But until Margaret's counselor phoned us, we never received a call. Yet the abuse was allowed to continue until it escalated into a tragedy.

In other instances, when abusive women can't define themselves as individuals, they tend to blame their children for their loss of identity. The kids become the enemy, sometimes to a point where the mother feels that the only way to attain happiness is to eliminate them.

In the case of Susan Smith, the woman who drowned her two children in a South Carolina lake, she clearly chose the path of self-preservation. She decided to trade her children's lives in exchange for a declining romance she saw slipping through her fingers.

On the night of October 25, 1994, Smith strapped her three-year-old son Michael and fourteen-month-old son Alex into their car seats and rolled her 1990 Mazda Protégé into the John D. Long Lake in Union, South Carolina, with the helpless children trapped inside. Then, in order to cover up her actions, she ran to a nearby house and claimed her kids had been kidnapped by a black man in his early forties.

For several days, Susan and her estranged husband, David Smith, went on every national TV news show imaginable, pleading for their sons' kidnapper to return them safely. But as Union County Sheriff Howard Wells and FBI investigators delved further, they found several inconsistencies in Susan's kidnapping story.

They began to suspect Susan of foul play, and they asked us to help them by developing a profile of a homicidal mother. I was in my office at the FBI Investigative Support Unit in Quantico, Virginia, and it was late afternoon when Wells contacted us with the request.

"We need to get a profile of typical characteristics of a mother who would kill her children," Wells said.

"OK. Are you looking for something in particular?" asked one of our agents.

"No," he answered. "We just need a general profile. How soon would you be able to get it to me?"

"We can have it for you in a few hours."

"That will be great, thank you. We will talk then."

When we met as a unit, we had, like most people in the country, seen news footage of Susan and David Smith pleading for their sons' safe return. Other than what we saw on the news, we didn't know much more. And we wanted to keep it that way.

Sheriff Wells struck me as a sincere man who was struggling with his investigation. He suspected that Susan may have had something to do with her sons' disappearance, but something about his demeanor told me he didn't want to be right.

As it turned out, my instincts were correct.

He was a friend of Susan's family, which put him in an awkward position, to say the least. If he acted too quickly on his suspicions, he could permanently damage the friendship, but he was a good investigator, and he had a duty—both as an officer of the law and as a family friend—to see the case through, regardless of the outcome. Wells needed to cover his bases from every angle.

As we worked up the profile, we made it a point to leave anything we knew about Susan Smith completely out of the equation.

We asked Wells and the FBI investigators working the case to withhold any background on Smith or any other findings from us. We didn't want the analysis to be compromised. This way, we could provide a composite background of general characteristics derived from previous homicide cases involving mothers and their children.

When we finished, we were confident that we had developed a thorough and accurate profile.

Our analysis described a woman in her twenties who grew up or lived in poverty and was undereducated. She would have a history of physical or sexual abuse or both, remain isolated from social supports, and have depressive and suicidal tendencies.

We told investigators at the scene that a homicidal mother is usually experiencing rejection by a male lover when she commits the murders.

We also described how she might find herself enmeshed with her children and show an inability to define herself separately from them. Basically, this person loses her identity as an individual and has trouble reconciling this loss with her identity as a mother. Depression in the mother is often correlated with a blurring of boundaries. The mother's biological ties, her strong role expectations to be a mother, her significantly greater caregiving responsibilities, her isolation in carrying out those responsibilities, and her greater tendency toward depression and self-destruction are likely to result in her being trapped in enmeshment with her children.

Finally, we told Wells that during the homicidal act, a mother may view a child as a mere extension of herself rather than as a separate being. Her suicidal inclination may often be transformed into filial homicide. In short, the homicidal mother would see herself as sacrificing one part of herself (her children) for another (her individual identity).

As it turned out, the profile we provided fit Susan Smith almost perfectly, and her background was consistent with our findings.

Smith's parents had divorced when she was six, and her father committed suicide a month later. As a child and young teen, she was sexually molested by her stepfather, Beverly Russell, a relationship that would later turn into an adult affair. In a guilt-ridden effort to save Smith from the death penalty, Russell himself actually took the stand at her trial, saying he deserved some of the blame for what happened to Michael and Alex. During one telling moment, he told Smith that he had let her down as a father. He also read from a letter he had sent to her in prison, which read, in part, "You don't have all the guilt in this tragedy."

In addition to her past victimization, Susan Smith and her husband, David Smith, were in the middle of a divorce, and on a number of occasions, she had attempted suicide.

But she was depressed about another romantic relationship gone sour, which would turn out to be the key cog in her decision to take the lives of her children. The man with whom she had had an affair, local business owner Tom Findlay, took the stand at Smith's trial and read a letter he had written to Smith in an attempt to end their relationship. Findlay read, "But like I told you before, there are some things about you that aren't suited to me, and yes, I am speaking about your children."

Those words were her focus as she got out of her car that October night, shifted the Mazda into neutral, and let the vehicle slowly roll down the boat ramp. Michael, her oldest son, had just celebrated his third birthday two weeks earlier. He and his fourteen-month-old brother, Alex, were asleep in the backseat as the car drifted into the lake. The headlights were on as the Mazda slowly entered the water and did not submerge immediately. Instead, it remained on the surface, bobbing peacefully, while slowly filling with water. (To illustrate the horror of the crime, prosecutors later showed the jury a reenactment of Smith's vehicle sinking into John D. Long Lake. A camera was mounted on the backseat so jurors could visualize what the boys saw for the last six minutes of their lives as the car submerged.)

Smith watched the car drift underwater then ran to a nearby house, about one-quarter mile from the lake. Seemingly delirious, Smith banged on the door in a panic. When the homeowner answered the door, she found an inconsolable woman who told her that her sons had just been kidnapped in an apparent carjacking.

"Please help me!" Smith sobbed. "He's got my kids, and he's got my car."

The kind lady and her husband let Smith into their home and calmed her down somewhat. Then Smith uttered these now-infamous words: "A black man has got my kids and my car."

The woman's husband immediately called 911. It was shortly after 9 p.m.

Once Sheriff Wells arrived at the scene, Smith gave him the following account of the evening's events:

> I was stopped at the red light at Monarch Mills, and a black man jumped in and told me to drive. I asked him why he was doing this, and he said, "Shut up and drive, or I'll kill you!" He made me drive northeast of Union until we got right past the sign [for the lake]. Then he made me stop, and he told me to get out. He made me stop in the middle of the road. Nobody was coming, not a single car. I asked him, "Why can't I take my kids?" He said, "I don't have time." Then he pushed me out of the car while he was pointing the gun at me. When he finally got me out, he said, "Don't worry, I'm not going to hurt your kids." Then he had me lay on the ground, and he drove away with my kids. . . . After a while, when I knew it was safe, I got up, and I started running a little ways 'til I saw this house.

After she told Wells her version of events, a police sketch artist met with Smith and, using the description she provided, composed a sketch of a black man, around forty years of age, wearing a dark knit cap, a dark shirt, jeans, and a plaid jacket.

The sketch artist was skeptical of Smith's story because the details she provided weren't typical of someone's description of a man who had just victimized her. The artist's main source of suspicion was that the suspect's countenance in the sketch was too peaceful. As the police artist, the FBI agents, and Wells began to put the pieces of the puzzle together, they found too many holes in her story to find it credible.

A couple of days after we had sent our profile to Sheriff Wells, he confronted Smith about her story of the carjacking.

"Susan, I know you're lying about the carjacker," Wells told her.

"What do you mean?" she asked, clearly caught off guard.

"I mean, it's impossible to stop at the red light at the Monarch intersection if there are no other cars on the road. The light won't turn red unless a vehicle is coming from the other direction. Not only did you lie about that the first time, but you lied about it when you revised your statement."

"I was just confused," she replied. "Everything happened so fast that I couldn't remember every detail."

"That's more than a detail, Susan."

"What are saying? You think I lied about this man who kidnapped my boys?"

"Your story just doesn't add up."

"I can't believe this. Why would you think I would lie about something like that?"

"The evidence is stacked against your story. We had undercover officers at the Carlisle intersection working on a drug investigation that night, Susan. They didn't see the man you described. In fact, they didn't see anybody that even comes close to fitting that description."

For a few moments, Smith sat in stunned silence trying to collect her thoughts.

Finally, the sheriff, knowing that Smith had been overwhelmed by all the intense media coverage, played his strongest interrogative hand. He told her that he would have to tell the press that her story about the alleged black carjacker was not true.

"Your accusations have caused too much tension in the town's black community," he said. "I have no choice but to go public with this information. It's not fair to the black citizens of this community to hide the truth."

Upon hearing those words, Smith asked the sheriff to pray with her.

At the close of the prayer, Wells said, "Lord, we know that all things will be revealed to us in time."

He then looked at Smith and said, "Susan, it is time."

The sheriff's interrogation strategy paid off. Smith hung her head and wailed, "I am so ashamed! I am so ashamed!"

In a moment of desperation, she asked Wells for his gun so that she could kill herself. When he asked her why she wanted to take her own life, Smith answered, "You don't understand—my children are not all right."

Finally, she confessed everything. The sense of guilt Smith had been carrying for nearly two weeks poured out.

In an effort to gain his sympathy, she told Wells about the crushing isolation she had felt while driving along Highway 49 on the night in question. She related to him the overwhelming thoughts she had had about committing suicide. Smith said she had planned to drive her sons to her mother's house but felt so much despair that she believed that even her mother wouldn't be able to help her. She told the sheriff that her whole life had felt wrong, and she couldn't escape the loneliness, isolation, and failure.

Smith then told him about her troubled marriage to David Smith and the affair she had with Tom Findlay, which he had broken off earlier that day.

In a wise interrogative move, Wells never interrupted Smith's ramblings. He simply listened as she continued to pour her heart out, knowing that she would eventually come around to telling him what happened to the children. Had he interrupted her, she might have gathered her thoughts and stopped talking altogether.

Finally, Smith—at this point an emotionally exhausted suspect— told Wells how she parked the Mazda on an incline on the boat ramp, got out of the car, and put the vehicle in neutral with her sons helplessly trapped inside.

With a heavy heart, Wells booked Smith into jail, where she was charged with the murders of her two children.

Susan Smith was tried and convicted for her crimes and sentenced to life in prison, though she will be eligible for parole in thirty years—a scenario highly unlikely to unfold, given the grisly nature of her crimes.

Her actions not only devastated her family and community but also redefined how we, as a nation, perceive domestic violence. Because of the national attention this case received, no longer did society think of domestic violence as simply the man of the house beating his wife and kids in an angry tirade. All of the sudden, we discovered that women could do the unthinkable as well.

Because the story that Smith told captured the nation's sympathy, her version of the events of that night would also cause a community to question some of its own residents, based solely on their race. Smith committed an unthinkable act when she broke society's most sacred trust, the love of a mother for her children.

After her confession went public, many would try to imagine the thoughts that must have been running through her head the night she drowned her children. To this day, people ask how she could have done something so horrible. They wonder, given her life's circumstances, if there is any measure of excuse for what she did.

The abuse and horrible incidents she faced as a child certainly contributed to her state of mind, but as difficult as things may have been for Susan Smith, she still consciously chose to end her sons' lives, and for that there is no excuse. She was simply a predator who killed her own children to feed her selfish desires. Yes, the need to feel loved is legitimate, but she tried to fill it through the most illegitimate means of all—sacrificing her children.

In that sense, male abusers are no different. They also try to fill emotional voids. Only rather than rid themselves of perceived obstacles to their happiness, like their female counterparts do, abusive men seek to fill their needs through the power and domination of a spouse or a girlfriend and/or their children.

Events are set in motion when a man courts a woman he senses is emotionally insecure, then he manipulates her into his trap and keeps her in a cycle of abuse, physical and/or mental.

With every predatory domestic abuser, the cycle is almost always the same, though the steps vary depending on the situation. But, generally speaking, the predator will begin by courting his victim through a series of tender manipulations until he commits her to a long-term relationship. Once he traps her in the net of such a commitment, he usually begins to isolate her from family and friends—anyone she could count on for support other than him. The isolation then empowers him to verbally, psychologically, and physically abuse his victim.

As is the case with all the predatory criminals we have discussed so far, his aim is to manipulate, trap, and control in an effort to fulfill his desires.

One of the more horrific examples of this abuse cycle is a case that Mike King helped resolve while he was a lieutenant with the Utah Attorney General's Office.

Law enforcement officials were having a difficult time solving the mysterious death of a child named Ian Wing, a seven-week-old who died from what the medical examiner declared "unknown circumstances."

The local police department and the county sheriff's office felt that the case had suspicious overtones, particularly surrounding at least six potential suspects in the case, each of whom had solitary access to the child. Those potential suspects included the child's inner circle, specifically the boy's parents, a grandmother, a sibling, an aunt, and a babysitter. The case was nearly three years old, and, at the time, police were getting nowhere. As time passed, the case grew "cold."

Fortunately, the state's Child Fatality Review Board continued to ask the local police about the case. The police chief, Morton Sparks, contacted the Utah Attorney General's Office and requested the help of the Utah Criminal Tracking and Analysis Project (UTAP), and specifically the investigative support of Mike. The city felt that the most probable suspect was the child's father, Mark Wing. Wing had gotten to the point where he was completely unwilling to cooperate with the local authorities and may have even felt that he had the upper hand, thinking that the only way he would be convicted was if he confessed.

Unfortunately, he was right, and in his mind, he was never going to do that.

The crime Mark Wing committed was nothing short of deplorable. He was a suspect in the brutal torture and murder of his infant son, Ian; a series of violent acts against the child had occurred over the seven-week period of the baby's life, from December 28, 1995, to February 23, 1996.

But its roots took hold long before the actual commission of the crime. Wing was on his third marriage. Lt. Mike King, well versed in the principles of victimology, knew that if one victim couldn't talk, probably two or three others would be willing to.

"I need to talk to Mark's ex-wives," Mike told the team of investigators who had handed the case over to him. "If he abused the child, then odds are he was abusive to his wives, too."

"How is that going to help in this case?" asked one detective. "The crime only involves the child, not the mother."

"True, but his ex-wives might know something that we can use to throw Mark off guard when I interrogate him. The key to getting him to confess is in getting him to let his guard down."

Getting Mark Wing to let his guard down wouldn't be easy.

He was confident that he had escaped consequence. It had been almost three years since Ian had been found dead in his crib, and although autopsy results showed a pattern of horrific abuse—twenty-nine rib fractures, two broken legs (femurs), and a disjointed elbow—there wasn't enough evidence to show beyond a reasonable doubt that Wing was the one who had caused those injuries.

By questioning Wing's ex-wives, Mike was hoping to find a common thread—a pattern—in Wing's history of abuse.

"Then, I'll try to find out if there is anything in his history that will rattle him," he told the investigators. "Something he thinks no one but him knows, something that only an ex-wife would know but would never confront him with."

As Mike questioned Wing's three ex-wives, he found one unwilling to cooperate but two very willing participants, and ultimately, they uncovered the commonalities Mike was looking for.

The victim's mother had clearly been unable to accept even the slightest suggestion that Mark Wing might have been involved in her baby's death. Her way of coping was to build a world for herself in which Mark was a very caring, gentle man who never lifted a finger against her or their children. Mike had hit a dead end with her and was hoping he would have more success with the others.

He decided to start with Wing's first wife.

It was a bright summer day when Mike arrived at her home in Salt Lake City. She lived in an old red-brick house, typical of the others in the neighborhood. He wasn't sure exactly how much information she would be willing to divulge. Abused spouses, even if estranged, sometimes fear repercussion for perceived betrayals. But Mike hoped to at least glean something useful from their conversation.

What he found was a more-than-willing participant.

"Yeah, I'll tell you anything you want to know about that man," she blurted.

"OK," Mike started, somewhat surprised by her reaction. "Why don't you give me a rundown on your history with Mark. When did you start dating, and how did he treat you during your courtship?"

"Oh, he was great to me when we were dating. He was smooth. I got flowers and candy and cards, all the good stuff. But that all changed the minute we got married."

"How so?"

"Oh, I'd say about a week after our wedding, he started to act funny. He got real weird and moody. He started playing mind games and just talking about weird stuff."

"What kind of things did he talk about?"

"Just—things he would say, like, how he wanted to see the look in somebody's eyes when they died, stuff like that. And he talked about just some horrible things he did to animals. At first, I thought he was kidding, but when I realized he was serious, I got real worried."

"What kinds of things did he tell you that he did to animals?"

"Well, like taking kittens and putting them into a bag and throwing them in the river. And once he talked about how he took his mom's dog, put the poor thing in a pillowcase, and set it the middle of Hill Field Road, where he watched it get run over by cars, stuff like that. The scary part, though, was the look on his face when he'd talk about it. When Mark talked about killing animals, he would smile and get a distant look in his eyes."

"Did he ever physically harm you or your pets?"

"Are you kidding? That's why I left him. I couldn't take it anymore. After he moved us out to the country, there were some nights he beat me senseless. He was awful to me."

"About how long after you were married did you move out to the house in the country?"

"I'd say about a month or so. It didn't take me long to figure out that the reason he moved us out there was so he could keep me away from my parents. It got to the point where he actually disassembled my car and cut the phone lines so I couldn't go anywhere or talk to anybody while he was at work."

"You mentioned that he had been abusive to you. What kinds of things did he do to you?"

"What did he do to me? What didn't he do to me, short of killing me?"

She paused for a moment and became very reflective, as if she were trying to catch her breath. When she finally did, all the things she suffered at Wing's hands came pouring out. It was as if she had been waiting for the day when she could tell the authorities about what had happened to her, something she had never gotten a chance to do and never thought she would.

"Well, there was this one time that he was irritated about his coffee cup being dirty, and he wanted me to wash it," she began. "I was sick of him bossing me around, you know, so I told him to wash it himself. Well, he gets up, pours scalding hot coffee into the cup and throws it on me. Then, he grabbed me and threw me down to the floor, picked me up and dragged me around the house by my hair, slamming my head into the walls and into the furniture. I was pretty dazed after that. Then, there was another time that he wanted me to iron this poster for him, but I couldn't because I didn't want to be late for work. So I told him no, and I went off to work. Well, we had these pet rats, and while I was at work, he killed them and sprinkled the poster pieces all over my dead pets for me to see. He made sure that was the first thing I saw when I got home that day. That's the kind of person he was. That's what he did to me. If I ticked him off, he would either beat me, or he'd take his gun out and shoot our pets. Sometimes, he would even threaten me with the gun."

"Did he ever actually point a weapon at you?"

"Oh, yeah. Once, he locked me in a room for about three hours. When he opened the door, I was hoping he had cooled off a little. But, instead, he took his shotgun, put the barrel to my head, and said, 'If you ever leave me, I will kill you.' I'll tell you, it's a good thing we never had kids, that's for sure."

"Did he ever mention wanting to have kids?"

"Oh, yeah, all the time. He would always say he wanted two kids—no more, no less. That was his favorite saying."

"Why two kids? Did he ever say?"

"No, he never did. I guess that was just his dream family. I'm just glad I didn't have to be a part of it."

"So, according to my records, you were only married for six months. How were you finally able to leave him?"

"It wasn't easy. The first few times I tried, he either threatened to kill me, or he got real suicidal."

"What do you mean by suicidal? What did he do?"

"Oh, he'd put the barrel of the shotgun in his mouth and say, 'The last thing I do will be to say your name as I pull the trigger, and then you can always remember what you made me do.'"

"So how did you finally get out of the relationship?"

"I finally got a hold of my family, and they got me out of there one day when Mark was gone to work. He didn't bother me too much when I had my family around. I wish I would have done that sooner."

"The important thing is you did it, and you're safe now," Mike said, trying to bring her a measure of comfort.

Mike paused and looked down at his notes for a minute, then said, "Well, I don't have any more questions, but can you think of anything else that might help? Is there anybody from Mark's life you think would be helpful for me to talk to?"

"I'm not sure if this will help, but there is one guy Mark used to see a lot."

"What's his name?"

"Earl. Earl Pagel. After we got married, Mark hung out with him all the time." She paused, and then alluded, "I think they might have been more than friends," but she had no real firsthand knowledge of any relationship between them.

"Why do you think that?"

"Because, after we got married, we weren't exactly what you would call a very intimate couple. I mean, don't get me wrong. Mark definitely liked women. In fact, our sex life was great before we got married. But after we were married, he sure spent an awful lot of time with Earl."

"OK, I'll make a note of that," Mike said as he got up and began to make his way to the front-room door. "Do you know where I can find Earl?"

"I think he's in jail. That's the last I heard, anyway."

"If he is, that would certainly make it easy to find him. Thank you again for your help. If you think of anything else, please give me a call."

"I will," she said, before pausing a moment to hold the screen door open. "You know, when I heard about Mark's baby on the news, my first thought was, 'Mark probably tortured that baby just so he could see the terror in his eyes as he killed it.' He used to talk all the time about wanting to see what it would be like to kill somebody. I hope you get him for what he did."

"We're working on it."

With that, Mike got into his car and drove away.

A few days later, Mike interviewed Wing's second wife. As he questioned her, he noticed a distinct difference in personality from Wing's first wife. She was more submissive than Wing's first wife, which is probably why their marriage lasted three years while Wing's marriage to his first wife lasted only six months.

As the interview went on, Mike noted some eerie similarities between Wing's behavior with the two women. He had beaten his second wife in much the same way he had abused his first, dragging her by the hair and banging her head into furniture. But the abuse was more intense with the second. Once, he had kicked her in the chest for buying a watermelon without his authorization. As was the case with his first wife, Wing also dismantled his second wife's vehicle and isolated her from friends and family. She wasn't allowed to associate with anyone outside the home without his expressed approval.

"What made you stay with him for so long?" Mike asked.

"I don't know," she answered. "I knew he could get violent, even before I married him, but for some reason I thought I could change him. And, for a while, I thought I was changing him because it wasn't like he was beating me every day. The stress would get to him every so often, and he'd just snap. But he always felt so bad afterward. He would be so sorry, and sometimes, he would even get suicidal over it."

"In what way was he suicidal? Did he actually try to commit suicide, or did he just talk about it?"

"He mostly talked about it, but I remember that after one fight, he put a shotgun in his mouth and told me he was going to pull the trigger. He said he just couldn't take it anymore. It took me a while to talk him out of it."

"Did the violence get worse as you got further into the marriage?"

"Yes and no. With me, the abuse went in cycles, but with the animals, he got more and more cruel as time went on."

"In what way?"

"Well, I had these pet ferrets, and at first, when Mark would get mad, he just kicked them or beat them. But then, one day, he became so angry that he took one of my ferrets, smashed it in the door, and killed it. At first I thought he was hurting the ferrets to get back at me, but I don't think he liked animals very much, period."

"What makes you say that?"

"Well, once Mark caught a stray cat that was running around in our yard, and he chained it in the garage. I thought he was just going to call animal control or something, but he kept it there for three days and just tortured the poor thing. He'd do awful things to that cat, like putting firecrackers up his rear and blowing them up. Then, one day, he just killed the poor thing."

"Did Mark ever talk about having children?"

"Yeah, he was always saying that he wanted to have two children, no more, no less."

"Did he say why?"

"No. He just said that's the way he wanted it. I already had one child, so I thought we would have one together and that would be it, but I was never able to get pregnant. I will say this, though: I thought it was quite the coincidence when he married a woman who already had two children. I guess he got what he wanted, at least until that third baby came along."

"Do you think he killed his son?"

"Let's just say I wouldn't be surprised."

"I just have one last question," Mike said. "Did Mark ever have any friends or associates that you knew of?"

"Not really," she said. "There was this one guy, but I think they were more than just friends."

"What was his name?"

"All I know is that it was a guy named Earl."

Earl—there was that name again.

After Mike finished his interview with Wing's second wife, he returned to his office at the attorney general's office and pored over his notes from his conversations with Wing's ex-wives. He began to compose a psychological profile on Wing and to think of interrogation strategies that might get him to agree to confess.

With Wing, the two things that continually popped up—in addition to the abuse—were his ideal fantasy family of two children and his relationship with Earl Pagel. Mike also knew that Wing's sense of manhood and desire for complete control were extremely important to him. He had above-average height; wore a thick, dark mustache; and was physically fit from his days as a construction worker. Mike would definitely use that aspect of his behavioral profile as an interrogative weapon.

Before he questioned the suspect, however, there was one last key person he needed to talk to—Earl Pagel.

He had already made an appointment to talk to another inmate when he saw that Pagel was indeed still serving time for child molestation.

When the guards brought Pagel out to meet with Mike, it was almost as if he knew exactly why Mike had come to visit. He was a rather large man, about six-foot-three and three hundred pounds, with a square jaw and a rounded bald head. His size was offset somewhat by his all-white prison garb and effeminate nature yet underscored by the small room we met in. The meeting conditions were rather cramped, as they sat in plastic chairs at a small middle table in the ten-foot by ten-foot interrogation room. And despite his effeminate personality traits, one thing Mike learned rather quickly about Earl Pagel was that he was very self-assured.

"Hi, Earl, I'm Lieutenant King with the attorney general's office," Mike began. "I appreciate you taking a few minutes to talk to me."

"Sure. What would you like to talk about?"

"Well, a former acquaintance of yours, Mark Wing, knew we were going to be here, and he wanted us to tell you, 'Hi,'" Mike replied.

A large smile immediately crossed Pagel's face, and he nodded almost as if he had fully expected—and hoped—to hear those words.

"Oh, yes, I remember Mark with fondness," said Pagel, his partially toothless smile still as broad as ever. "I was very fond of him."

"Just how fond of Mark were you?" Mike probed.

"Let's just say that we were very close."

"You mean, close as in you had a sexual relationship?"

"From the time he was about fourteen," Pagel answered, almost bragging about his conquest. "We had a lot of good times together."

"Approximately how long did your relationship with Mark last?"

"I'd say about thirteen or fourteen years. Even when he was married, we managed to see each other quite a bit."

"How would you describe Mark?"

"Oh, he was a tender one," Pagel started.

"I mean, from a personality standpoint," Mike interrupted.

"Well, he was tender in that way, too."

"Would you say he had a short temper?"

"Not as a rule, but he would get upset every once in a while. I'd describe it more as emotional. I remember once, he got huffy with me for something or other. The next thing I knew, he grabbed a rifle, put the barrel in his mouth, and said he was going to pull the trigger."

"What did you do?"

"Oh, I knew he wasn't going to pull no trigger. He didn't have the stones to do that. I just wrestled the gun away from him and called the cops. Like I said, he was being real pissy, and I didn't want to deal with him, so I figured it was best to let the police mess with it. But he came back another day, and we made up real nice, if you know what I mean."

"I think I get the idea," Mike said before quickly changing the subject. "Would you say Mark was a controlling person?"

At that, a serious expression suddenly overtook Pagel's countenance. He leaned forward for emphasis and said, "Let's get something straight here. I was always the one in control when we were together. Mark was never in charge."

That was all Mike needed to hear.

He had exactly what he needed to get Mark Wing to talk. When Mike met with Wing at his office a few days later in Salt Lake City, the suspect was clearly irritated at having to return for yet another round of questions about the death of his son. This was the second time Mike would question Wing.

Before Mike had spoken to Wing's ex-wives, he had conducted a nonconfrontational interview with the suspect. Wing cut the interview short, however, when Mike suggested there was no way Ian's injuries had been caused by any alternative manner other than abuse. Still, after nearly three years of interrogations, Wing was arrogantly confident that police wouldn't be able to throw anything at him that he hadn't already heard.

He would soon find out just how wrong he was.

"Thank you for agreeing to meet with me again," Mike started. "Would you like anything to drink?"

"No, let's just get this over with," Wing said, a strong measure of cockiness in his voice.

"OK. Well, we've been going over some of the injuries Ian sustained previous to his death," Mike continued. "I was wondering if you would explain some things for us."

"I'll do what I can, but I don't think there's anything else I can tell you."

"Well, let's just give it a try," Mike said. "You said that you think that the broken ribs Ian sustained might have been from your former mother-in-law rolling over him in bed, is that right?"

"Yeah, that's what I said."

"OK, and you also said he may have sustained some of his injuries because his older brother grabbed him and picked him up, right?"

"Yeah."

"Do you blame your ex-wife for any of this?"

"Why would I blame her?"

"Well, you know, the woman's role is supposed to be in the home, isn't it? You shouldn't have had to be doing her work for her."

"Yeah, I shouldn't have. But what happened, happened."

"Let's talk about that for a minute. What do you think the man's role should be in the home?"

"Well, he should be the provider. He should protect his family."

"That's right. Things just don't run as efficiently when the roles get mixed up, do they? You shouldn't have had to be changing diapers and feeding Ian. That was your wife's place."

"Yeah, it should have been, but it wasn't."

"No, it sure wasn't. The world's got things backwards, doesn't it? Do you ever wonder why things changed? For hundreds of years, the woman stayed in the home, and the man went out and worked, like a real man. Why do you suppose things are different now?"

"I don't know. It probably started with women's lib."

"I agree with you, Mark. Things have changed a lot since then. Even in bed. Women don't seem satisfied like they used to be. Sex just isn't enough anymore. How about you? Could you satisfy your wife's needs in bed?"

"Believe me, she was always satisfied."

"You must have had the touch, then. Was it the same with all the women you've been with?"

"Yeah, all of them."

Mike was right in the middle of this chest-pounding when he threw Wing the bait.

"Uh, you've never had a homosexual relationship, have you?"

"No, man! Don't even go there!"

"I was just checking," Mike said, toying with Wing at this point. "You know, sometimes when a guy has to take on the woman's role, other things change, too."

"Yeah, well, not me. I know what a woman wants, and I give it to her straight, whether she thinks she wants it or not."

"You don't think women know what they want?"

"Oh, come on, man. Half the time they say one thing when they really mean totally the opposite."

"I hear you," Mike agreed. "So in a perfect world, what should you have been doing?"

By this time, Wing was so indignant that he was ready to say almost anything to boost his sense of manhood.

"Just going to work and going to school. That's all I should have had to do. I shouldn't have been doing no women's work."

"Women shouldn't be out of the home at all, should they?"

"No way."

Then Mike decided to drop the bomb on Wing.

"You know what, Mark?" Mike said.

"What?"

"For some reason, and I can't understand why, the attorney general's office wants me to give you one last chance."

"To do what?" Wing shot back.

"To confess."

"To confess what? Give me a break. We're done here!"

As Wing started to get up, Mike got in his face and confronted him. "Look, Mark, you have two choices here! You can either confess and spend a long time in jail, or you can choose not to cooperate and spend a very, very long time in jail. Now, I know a lot more about you than you think, enough to put you away for a long time. In fact, I know you've already lied to me today!"

Wing leaned toward Mike and shouted, "About what?"

Mike paused just briefly then leaned toward the suspect and said, "Well, I spoke to Earl Pagel the other day."

At that, Wing slumped back into his chair, dropped his head, and remained silent for several seconds. He never said a word about Pagel, or if they'd had a relationship.

Still, it was a real Perry Mason moment for Mike.

"OK, what do you want me to do?" Wing asked.

"Tell me the truth. Tell me how you squeezed the life out of Ian because you really only wanted two kids. Isn't it true that you broke Ian's ribs by squeezing him?"

"Yeah, it's true."

"Isn't it true that's what caused his death?"

"It could be. I don't know."

Before Mike could ask another question, Wing collected himself and asked for an attorney, but the damage had already been done. He had already confessed to abusing the baby, and Wing's lawyer advised him to agree to a videotaped confession in return for a plea agreement of manslaughter, a sentence that carried a maximum of fifteen years in prison.

The parties set up a room at the attorney general's office, where Wing demonstrated on a doll just how he had tortured and killed his infant child.

As a panel of investigators asked him questions, Wing showed how he had wrapped both hands around Ian's chest and abdomen, his fingers touching, and squeezed the baby so hard that he could hear "a popping sound, like his back or spine was cracking."

He then said, "He [Ian] was gasping for air. I wrapped him tightly and put him in his crib. In the morning, he was dead."

When asked why he did such a thing, Wing said, "On several occasions, I just got so stressed and frustrated. Ian would become combative, and I'd just get so frustrated that I would give him a squeeze.

... I was taking fourteen credit hours in school and working full-time. I just got stressed out."

Of course, there was a lot more to it than stress.

Not only was the burden on Wing to provide for his family, but Ian's existence had shattered his fantasy and thrown him into an emotional tailspin. He now had three children when he only wanted two. From the day Wing found out that his wife was pregnant with Ian, he wanted nothing more than to eliminate the child's existence.

He had already successfully persuaded his wife to have one abortion, but when she refused to do so when she was pregnant with Ian, he pressured her to put the child up for adoption. At first, she agreed, and all was well. But as her due date drew near, she informed Mark that she was going to keep the baby, which gave him, in his mind, only one very horrific option.

We selected these three cases to illustrate predatory domestic violence because they represented extremes, which is the best way to highlight principles.

We were also careful to avoid picking stereotypical domestic violence cases, especially those involving men. While it is true that men perpetrate the majority of domestic abuse, we wanted to get away from the stereotype so the principles would stand out. We didn't want you to simply write the abuser off as the typical wife-beating jerk. That's exactly how people miss the principles. They're so busy looking at the trees that they miss the forest, and when a potential abuser does come their way, they don't recognize that individual as such because he or she doesn't fit the stereotype.

We want you to understand the traits a domestic abuser possesses so you can get that person help or cut him off before it's too late. In other words, we want you to look for character traits over the stereotypical picture you may carry.

With that in mind, when you look at the three cases above, Jefferson, Smith, and Wing have several predatory characteristics in common—an insatiable need to control others, an inability to communicate their needs rationally, a need to isolate their victims from others, and an overwhelming need to bring their victims to a lower level than they are, at least as they perceive it.

Depending on the situation, an abuser might exhibit one trait much more strongly than another. Mark Wing, for example, had much more of a need to control others than did Margaret Jefferson or Susan Smith. Wing actually disassembled his wives' vehicles and cut off the phone lines so they couldn't associate with anyone he hadn't preapproved. Worst of all, he killed his infant son because the baby's existence didn't match his fantasy of having only two children. Basically, he lost the control he was seeking.

Jefferson's dominant trait was the need to lower her victims to a level beneath her. She would fly into a rage and verbally assault her sons when they failed to live according to her expectations; she felt it reflected on her as a mother and thus made her a failure as a person. To sum it up, her life was falling apart, and rather than take steps to improve it, she decided to drag others down with her.

Smith exhibited a gross inability to communicate her needs rationally, resulting in her drowning her sons. On top of it, she made up a story as a cover-up, much like a child who broke her mother's favorite lamp would do. Until she was cornered, she didn't acknowledge what she had done to her children because in her mind, she was simply taking care of her need for control and love.

Finally, all three perpetrators isolated their victims from any possible means of support. That is not only a trait but a necessary step in the commission of their crimes—they could abuse their victims but still avoid potential consequences. This signature characteristic makes domestic offenders what they are—predators.

The question then becomes, how do we avoid—or help those we care about avoid—being victimized by the predatory domestic abuser?

There are three general things to look for.

Ask yourself if this person exhibits signs of an abuser before you commit to a relationship. In short, refuse to be controlled, isolated, or insulted. If you are able to do that, then the domestic predator most likely won't spend much time with you anyway because he will sense that you are not what he is looking for. If you are a friend or family member, ask those questions of your loved one. Help that person recognize what's going on in her life by having her verbalize it.

If you do find yourself in such a relationship, ask yourself whom you can involve. In truth, it is recommended that you involve as many people as possible in getting yourself out of it. The reason abusers isolate their victims is they know that they can dominate their prey only if they make them vulnerable. There is strength in numbers. Call whomever you have to—family members, police, domestic violence groups, friends. The more the merrier. Not only will getting all these people on your side get you and your children out of harm's way, it will most likely deter the abuser from coming after you again. Not always, but most likely. If you are a friend or a loved one, get as many people—especially the authorities—to intervene with you. Police have more authority now than ever to determine if domestic violence is occurring in the home.

Stop the cycle of abuse. It is alarming that the more children, especially boys, see violence in the home, the more likely they are to commit violence as adults. Remember, the children we pity today become the adults we despise tomorrow. The more quickly we get kids out of those situations, the more likely we stop them from becoming future perpetrators. We said earlier that there was no excuse, regardless of background, for Susan Smith drowning her sons, and there isn't. But one can't help wondering what would have happened had somebody been able to intervene and cut off the abuse she received at the hands of her stepfather.

In short, there are no easy answers to domestic violence. The best thing to do is to know this kind of offender. It's the hardest predatory crime to stop because it requires going into the predator's den to stop him, and as any police officer who has handled a domestic violence call will tell you, those can be the most dangerous and volatile of all circumstances.

The keys are education, awareness, and action.

Because the victims of these crimes are among society's most vulnerable—children, for example—they are most likely not going to be in a position to get the help they need. That is why we need to understand the characteristics of whom we're dealing with and to know whom we can go to for help.

Above all, we need to have the courage to get the innocent victims the help and support they need.

8

KIDNAPPING

Actually, the scriptures teach us—"

"Arvin, we can't talk to you," interrupted Mike King, then the lead investigator with the Weber County Attorney's Office. "You've already asked for an attorney. We can't violate your rights."

Mike and Dave Lucas, a detective with the Ogden Police Department, had just picked up sixty-one-year-old Arvin Shreeve on suspicion of heading up a ritualistic child sex abuse ring.

Police had conducted a raid on ten homes in an Ogden neighborhood but were unable to locate the group's leader. The search warrants were served simultaneously as more than sixty police officers, SWAT officers, and a small cadre of child custody case workers invaded the compound-style neighborhood where the members of Shreeve's sex abuse ring lived.

Shreeve quickly succumbed to the pressure of a statewide manhunt and surrendered to authorities at the Cedar City Police Department, about five hours south of his home. He was detained there for three days before the two investigators picked him up and began driving him back to Ogden to stand trial.

Knowing that they had just a few hours to try to get their suspect to talk, Mike and Dave implemented a strategy in which they would discuss religious topics in an effort to bait Shreeve into justifying his crimes on the basis of religion. They knew that religious doctrine was a subject that Shreeve, a self-proclaimed agent of God, would have a tough time resisting.

Two hours into the drive, Mike and Dave continued to discuss the topic, and Shreeve continued to try to interject his opinions. But every time he tried, he was quickly cut off and reminded he wasn't allowed to talk to the officers because he had already requested an attorney.

It was like waving a steak in front of a hungry dog, then yanking it away from him every time he tried to take a bite.

Finally, Mike thought he would do something to change things up a little.

"Should we stop and get something to eat?" Mike asked.

"Sure, but what do we do with him?" asked Dave, motioning toward the prisoner in the backseat.

"I think he'll be OK. He won't cause us any trouble."

"OK, then let's do it. There's a place up here at the next exit that should be good."

After they pulled into the restaurant parking lot, Mike helped the prisoner out of the backseat and took out the keys to the handcuffs.

"OK, this is how it's going to work," Mike told Shreeve, looking him square in the eye. "I'm going to take the cuffs off. But, if you try anything, anything at all, I will shoot you. And I will not hesitate to shoot you, because if I do, I will be considered a hero to everyone in this state, because, right now, Arvin, you are the most despised person in Utah. Do you understand?"

Without saying a word, Shreeve nodded in agreement.

He knew Mike was right.

It was 1991, and Arvin Shreeve had just been arrested for masterminding what was, at the time, the largest child sex abuse ring ever busted in the history of the United States. Citizens of the state were upset about this crime, not only because it was such a heinous offense against children, but also because it gave the state's image a black eye.

Utah had long been considered a peculiar place, and its citizens had worked hard to shed that image. The negative publicity that Shreeve had brought to the Beehive State definitely did not help, and most residents resented him for it. He'd committed one of the most disgusting crimes imaginable, and he'd done it in such a way that the national media had descended on the region to spotlight the strange behavior of some Utah residents.

Shreeve had persuaded nearly thirty women to become part of a community that engaged in polygamous relationships, lesbianism, and child molestation, though he did not define the activities as such. He had convinced them that such behavior was tied to their spirituality and personal salvation.

Eventually, he gained so much control over them that the women did everything he told them to—including helping him recruit other members of an organization he called The Zion Society.

In the restaurant, Mike and Dave looked over the menu and waited for the waitress to take their order. When she arrived, the two detectives ordered their food, upon which Mike put his arm around Shreeve and told the waitress, "Please get my father whatever he wants to eat."

At that, the suspect began to tear up and told Mike, "Thank you so much. No one has ever treated me so kindly."

"It's no problem," Mike replied. "Every human being deserves to be treated with respect."

As they resumed their drive back to northern Utah, Mike and Dave continued to discuss religion, and Shreeve continued to try to interject. Seeing that their suspect was bent on joining in, the investigators agreed to let him talk as long as he kept to the topic of general religious discussion. Anything involving the case was strictly off-limits. But as they talked, Shreeve's conscience began to get the best of him.

"I feel like I need to tell you what I've done," he said.

"I'm sorry, Arvin," Mike replied. "We'd love to help, but you've already requested an attorney. As I said before, we can't talk to you until your lawyer is present."

"What if I fire my attorney?"

"Then we can talk to you. But we have to make every effort to contact him first."

"Then let's call him. I'd really like to get this off my chest."

Dave and Mike used the mobile phone to call Shreeve's lawyer, but they weren't able to reach him. About half an hour later, they tried again, but he still wasn't in.

"Do we really have to talk to him first?" the suspect asked. "I'll sign whatever I have to in order to prove that I waived my right to an attorney."

"Well, there's a highway patrol station up ahead," Mike said. "Maybe they will let us use their office and recording equipment. If they do, then you can waive your right and give your confession on videotape. Are you willing to do that?"

"Yes, I am."

"OK, then let's pull in."

The highway patrol station did indeed have the necessary equipment, and over the next couple hours, Shreeve confessed to thirty-two incidents of child molestation, including situations that involved touching, photographing, and having oral and vaginal intercourse with children.

Over time, he detailed rituals that included teaching adults (primarily women) and children how to perform specific sex acts that he claimed would increase their spirituality and closeness to God. In less than ten years, Shreeve had recruited a following that consisted of about a hundred fifty members, mostly women, and eight men and thirty-two children. The group lived in a small neighborhood where they occupied ten homes, all beautifully landscaped, in which there was only one way in and out. For protection from the outside world (predominantly law enforcement), key figures in the sect's leadership occupied "sentry" homes adjacent to the access streets to the community.

The group was taught to strictly follow his doctrines, which included participation in the ritual sex abuse of the children, girls ages three to thirteen. In all, he and his followers were responsible for 757 separate felony counts of child sex abuse.

Following Shreeve's confession, a dozen adult participants were convicted of child sex crimes.

He felt such a need to rid himself of his guilt that, not only did he himself confess, but he actually encouraged his adult followers to confess to the very authorities he had spent years preaching against—a significant admission of wrongdoing because at the height of his ministry, Shreeve's followers considered him to be a prophet of God.

But he didn't start that way.

Nearly ten years before he was arrested, he was a gardener who attended the Church of Jesus Christ of Latter-day Saints. But somewhere along the line, he came to disagree with the religion's teachings, was excommunicated from the church, and began to write his own doctrine, which he ultimately used to organize a religious sect. He claimed that his teachings were sent directly from God.

Many of Shreeve's religious writings were collected during the raid on his home, as well as the other participating houses in the neighborhood. Over the several months following his arrest—and against the advice of his attorney—Shreeve told Mike what went on inside the secret walls of The Zion Society.

We share some main points of his teachings so that you can get a view that few have seen from within this type of cult. This is a society on par with that of Jim Jones and David Koresh, and we hope you can glean some insight into the mind-set of this predator and the thinking of his followers.

To begin, it's important to understand his signature precept, which was: "If you wish to be taught the 'Zion Way,' one important thing should be understood from the beginning: You are here to be taught, not to teach! Zion doesn't need anything you have to make Zion succeed. . . . It's already a success!"

All his other teachings were predicated on that one principle.

As Mike studied Shreeve's writings, an organized method of brainwashing became abundantly clear.

The self-proclaimed prophet was very specific in the way he selected prospective members and in the order in which he indoctri-

nated them. He was a predator in the sense that he knew just whom
to target and how to suck them in. He knew, for instance, that the
most likely candidates, by far, were desperate women with little education and nowhere else to turn. He needed people whom he could
convince, manipulate, and control—people who were so destitute
that they would have to rely on him for emotional, financial, and
spiritual support.

One former member, a woman we will call Katie, was a typical
example of Shreeve's target. Mike invited her to speak to a group of
law enforcement officers at a training conference, and she was kind
enough to answer their questions. According to Katie,

> At the time that I went out there, that I joined, I was in a horribly
> abusive marriage, and I had just found out that I was pregnant in a
> high-risk pregnancy. I had already lost five children, meaning I had
> had five miscarriages prior to that pregnancy, and I was afraid that if
> I stayed with my husband, I was going to lose another. . . . Although
> my whole family was aware of my situation, they were either
> unwilling or unable to offer me any kind of help. . . . Before I went
> into the group, all ties to my friends had been cut by my husband. So
> I really didn't have anybody.

Katie told us that, during that period of her life, she had been approached by two female society members named Becky and Sherrie.
They were patrons at a local gym/beauty salon where Katie worked,
and they regularly used the exercise equipment. After several weeks,
they had befriended her, and as Katie described, "They were always
very friendly and easy to talk to."

Katie explained how they eventually drew her into the society.

> One day Sherrie came up to see me and asked me, "[Katie], I know
> something's wrong. Let's go talk." So I went with her, and I just
> started blurting out everything that I was facing with my husband
> and my pregnancy. So Sherrie invited me over to her house and

asked me to come over for dinner, and maybe she and Becky could discuss some ways that they could help me in my marriage.

I agreed to go up there, and we had a nice dinner, then I met some other people in the neighborhood. Now, up to that point, I didn't know anything about a cult. They had explained to me that they were divorced women who lived next to each other in a community that sought to take care of each other to ensure that everyone was safe and happy.

I was introduced to a number of the people that lived there, and they were very, very nice. Then they sat me down and wanted to talk to me about my marriage, and at that point, they said, "We would really like to help you. We have come from similar situations in our marriages, and we would like to offer you and your daughter to come and stay with us. We realize you can't work, and you're free to stay until you can get on your own feet." Now, after coming from abuse my whole life, I would have responded to anyone who showed any kind of compassion or kindness to me. And that's pretty much what I did. I didn't question it at all. I just said, "OK." So I packed up my daughter and my clothes and moved out there.

It wasn't long after I had been there that I made the observation that the female members, who didn't have family members or friends within the group, that had come from wherever, had also suffered similar abusive backgrounds, either by their husbands or by their parents, or by their husbands keeping them subservient.

Though she didn't realize it at the time, Katie had hit the nail right on the head. Shreeve had expanded his circle of followers and had done it in a calculated fashion.

From the beginning, he set himself up as a sort of deity, someone who could prophesy of earthly doom but also serve as a protector from the "outside world." And he wrote his "scriptures" as if he had received them directly from God. One passage, which we left unedited, demonstrates the doctrine he used to lure his followers into submitting themselves to his control:

My son Arvin. Over the years I have given many Instructions to you.
Some written, others verbal. Never have I delivered into your hand's
more important and far reaching instruction than this one. For this
reason you are to hold it most sacred and refer to it by a special title.
It is to be called the "Salvation Instruction", for it will deal with the
means of your temporal salvation in an era of calamity, bloodshed,
disease, war and starvation. Frequently you have been warned by
your mother and Sisters here in the Spirit World, and by my Holy
Spirit, that unless you undertook with great diligence a massive and
totally complete preparation program your very lives would be
endangered. I here, re-affirm all those instructions and statements. In
the next few years this earth will be rocked and buffeted by the most
fearful destruction in the history of mankind.

Millions shall perish. Suffering beyond human immagination
will occur, and all the prophesied plagues, diseases, earthquakes,
floods, wars and pestilence of every imaginable kind will be
poured out without measure. Men shall wish to die to escape the
horror of it all. I cannot paint in words even a millioneth part of the
death and horror that awaits this generation. . . . So important are
these programs to the success of the Millenial Period that I, the Lord,
decreed not only special blessings, but special protections upon
those valiant ones who would so seek to lay this important foundation for my coming. Even as I accepted the "blood upon the door"
of ancient Isreal as a sign of those who were by their faithfulness to
be delivered, so will I accept plural marriage and Sister Programs as
a sign of those who are to be delivered in modern Isreal.

With this passage, Shreeve had two agendas: The first was to set
himself up as God's mouthpiece and the unquestioned leader of the
group. That became more evident as the sect grew. Ultimately, he created such a mystique around himself that members were allowed to
speak with him only if they cleared it with his assistant first.

Two, he laid the foundation for his true ulterior motive, namely,
the realization of his own sexual fantasies.

In reading the passage, you probably see his motives plainly.
You'll note that the passage contains poor grammar and spelling, not

exactly the most articulate biblical language. The key to Shreeve's influence was not in affluent speech or inspirational charisma but in the audience to whom he delivered his messages.

As Katie told us, "You are probably wondering who in their right mind would agree to follow this man. That's the point. None of us were in our right minds. We were all trying to get out of abusive situations."

Once Shreeve targeted such women, he took them under his wing, providing them—and their children, in many cases—with food, shelter, and an ultrasupportive community that shared everything. He then, along with his carefully selected leadership, laid this foundation and introduced new members to a series of doctrines.

First, he used the "Zion Way" decree to test the devotion of his prospective followers. Anyone who questioned the group's mission statement was shunned and rejected and faced the possibility of being declared "unworthy" of the society. This was a scary prospect for the newer members, because most felt they had nowhere to turn outside the society. But if they bought into the philosophy and exhibited the "humility" he was looking for, then they qualified for advancement in their spiritual education.

He continued to emphasize these teachings, making sure he gradually introduced and implemented them in a way that would eventually seem acceptable to sect members. Finally, he would introduce the signature precept for the sexual portion of his teachings, which simply reads, "The only way to Spirituality is through Sexuality."

But before they were taught Shreeve's doctrine of spiritual sexuality, sect members were prepared by first being indoctrinated with more socially acceptable levels of living, which were referred to as the "Ten Steps of Spiritual Training."

According to the self-proclaimed prophet, this education allowed members to ready themselves for the impending apocalypse.

Shreeve taught his members that he had been assigned to prepare them to meet the day of tribulation. This involved the use of food storage, alarm systems, medical-supply storage, and paramilitary training that included the storage of semi-automatic weapons.

Ironically, though Shreeve emphasized honesty to the members of the sect, he also instructed them to manipulate the government's welfare system and to fake illnesses in order to obtain all manner of prescription drugs they used to stockpile their own pharmacy.

So much for pure honesty.

Other principles of the spiritual training program included techniques for scripture study, spiritual guidance, recognition of righteousness—anything that involved leaving the world behind for a higher level of spirituality.

Once Shreeve determined that members had mastered these teachings, he began indoctrinating them with the principles of sexual spirituality. To prepare his pupils, he prefaced his training with this passage:

> That which follows cannot be understood by the carnal mind nor accepted by the worldly. It is (as are all things from God) understood only by those who place themselves in subjection to the dictates of the Holy Spirit, thus allowing their minds to be expanded and enlightened. Trust these sacred truths only in the hands of those subject to the Holy Spirit—to none other. . . . In mortality, however, the carnal and evil dominate the lives of almost all men and women. Rejection of true principles and the abasement of divine truths is usually the result. Therefore, the tender and joyous association possible among the Sisters of a family unit is seldom ever revealed to those in this world. The proper practice of a plurality of wives is not a fit thing for the carnal world or a telestial level, how much less so is the practice of a Sister Program which is an even higher principle. Therefore, you can understand why these things have been withheld from among men, and why you must guard and hold them sacred. Let this that I have revealed to you serve as a guiding principle of understanding, that even as I will, I may enlarge upon it and increase your understanding and comprehension.

As you can see, his aim was to convince prospective members that living this doctrine would set them above the rest of the world. Next, Shreeve rolled out the final part of his plan, a program called the "Five Arts of Sexual Stimulation," which was presented in the following order:

1. **Creating an Environment.** The person was expected to create a romantic setting as a way to sexually excite a male or female companion. This was done similar to traditional romantic encounters, such as with music, candles, and so forth.

2. **Speaking Up.** This art involved the verbal activity of members. More specifically, it required discussion that could arouse a male or female companion. It included vulgarity, gestures, and the like.

3. **Showing Off.** The person performing this so-called art was required to expose herself in a sexual manner with the purpose of sexually arousing a male or female companion.

4. **Using the Thread.** The person was expected to use seductive clothing, such as lingerie, as a way to sexually arouse the male or female companion. Each "sister" became aware of which "thread" was her specialty.

5. **Enjoying Yourself.** This was the "climactic" art that Shreevites strove for. Children, even as young as three years old, were taught how to masturbate, digitally, with fruits and vegetables and other mechanical tools. Shreeve taught that, once children understood how to please themselves, they could then be taught how to please others.

After presenting the five steps, Shreeve, in an effort to secure an unwavering devotion to the program, concluded his presentation with one final thought:

Sister Programs were commenced in the very first days of the pre-existent state. Valient sisters there were desirous of following the example of our God Father and Mothers who lived and accomplished their work within the organization of a Sister Program. . . . Sexual Association there was a mark of high distinction and denoted those who had emulated the Father and his Wives. It denoted the overcoming of personal pride and ambition and the submission of oneself to the will of the Father. Few, in the beginning, were able to accomplish so grand a feat. Thus, few were permitted to enter into this relationship prior to mortality. To those wives of a family unit living under the law of the Sister Program, I God, grant the joy and far reaching privilege of physical love.

The adult sect members were then instructed to practice these arts with one another—women with men and women with women. Then, they were commanded to teach the female children these practices, as the girls would one day become part of a sister council and need to know the teachings.

It is very telling, however, that along with the sexual portion of the teachings, Shreeve also instructed adults to coach these children how to respond if questioned by the authorities. Sect members even went so far as to dress up in police uniforms while they role-played question-and-answer sessions. This practice tells us that Shreeve knew full well that what he was doing was wrong and most certainly not instruction from God.

At this point, you might wonder how this self-proclaimed prophet persuaded so many adults to believe in teachings that, from the outside, seem so easy to see through. Not only was the doctrine so bizarre and stomach-turning, but in addition, Shreeve set up a system in which the women would work regular jobs and turn over their entire paychecks to him. Meanwhile, the men in the sect were required to pay a minimum of 10 percent of their earnings to the self-proclaimed prophet.

Conventional wisdom dictates that because these teachings were so far removed from any social decency, someone surely would have left the group long before it got to that point and reported it to the authorities.

But Shreeve kept the men at bay by promising them their own sister councils, once they had earned that right, of course. No man ever achieved his own sister council, but the men continued to do their best to live in accordance with Shreeve's teachings so that they would one day qualify.

As for the women, Katie explained how they were persuaded to stay:

Mind games and brainwashing seem to be what keeps those people there. For every situation that would arise that seemed strange or that you might question, they had a logical explanation for what took place so that you wouldn't question anything. For example, one day, I went shopping with Becky and Sherrie, and when I came back, I learned that my aunt had showed up to kidnap my daughter, and the police were called. I was standing there in a stupor, not knowing what had happened.

Apparently my husband had contacted my family and let them know where I was, and they had heard the rumors, and so they all rallied together, and they had showed up. My husband was banging on the door, acting crazy and psychotic, and then my brother showed up, and I'm looking out the window seeing this man, my brother, stomping up and down the street, screaming and yelling. And, all the while, Becky, Arvin, and Sherrie are telling me, "Do you see how your choice was right, how your family has turned on you, and now they are in support of your husband?" And it made sense to me. At that time, I couldn't piece together what was going on.

It didn't take long, though. After I had left the group, and it was a couple of months before I was in association with my family again, the pieces started to fit together, and the lies were revealed, such as, yes, my husband was acting crazy when he showed up, but my aunt was not kidnapping my daughter. She was there, and I was gone, and she asked to take my daughter out for ice cream, while waiting for me to return. My brother was ranting and raving up and down the street because they wouldn't let him talk to me, and they threatened him with the police if he didn't leave. So, you see, with just a twist, the truth is a lie or visa versa. The cult, or the group, became my family, and my family became the enemy.

Still, how did one man have so much control over so many people?

The short answer is that Shreeve psychologically kidnapped not only his victims but his fellow perpetrators as well.

This is not to say that his partners in crime do not bear any responsibility for the abuse the children endured. But it does explain why they agreed to engage in these crimes and assist in recruiting other perpetrators.

Remember, Arvin Shreeve was an expert at picking out women (usually mothers with small girls) who were devoid of self-esteem.

Because he owned multiple houses in the same neighborhood, he would take the ladies in and allow them to live in a home with their children. Once he gained their trust, he would create a dependency-based relationship, while slowly indoctrinating them with his religious teachings.

Like many predators we have covered, he was charismatic and presented the appearance of a trustworthy man. In his case, however, he did not use good looks or charm to lure his victims. In fact, he was quite the contrary—a bespectacled, overweight, balding gardener in his late fifties.

What Shreeve did have going for him, though, was the ability to read people, gain their trust, then manipulate that trust to paint people into a corner. He utilized his grandfatherly friendliness as bait and used guilt and fear as his traps.

Katie explained it this way:

He was very charismatic, absolutely. But I don't know if it was so much that it was his charisma or the others saying, "This is your prophet. You've got to listen to him. He's receiving guidance straight from God." And, in his mind, he was God. That's where a lot of the control came from. He held himself in such a way, almost as if you were in the presence of a president or a god.

I questioned the man one time. My son had to go into the hospital, and I was on my way to see him when Arvin and several of the women said, "No, you can't see him. You have a carnal tie. You need to leave." I went and confronted Arvin, and I said, "This is my child, and I'm going." Well, I have never been so scared in my life. The look on that man's face, I thought he was going to kill me. He got so mad he left the house and slammed the door. Then several of the women came at me and said, "How can you question your god, your master, like that? Now go apologize." And I was thinking one of two things. "This guy's a crackpot, and I need to leave. But where do I go? I'm completely isolated from my family, and I have a child in the hospital." I didn't know what to do or where to go. So I went and apologized.

Katie eventually escaped and reported the group's crimes, which she admitted to taking part in, to the authorities. Her report was a huge break in the case and allowed law enforcement the legal authority to search the homes, which they did on August 2, 1991. Three days later, Arvin Shreeve was in custody.

Now, you might wonder why we would include this case in a chapter on kidnapping and abduction. The answer is that the kind of kidnapping that Shreeve engaged in was entirely psychological. He didn't snatch people off the street or incarcerate them or even tie them up. He simply gained control of their minds.

When you take kidnapping by its most basic definition, namely, the theft and possession of human beings, then it is clear that Shreeve did what all kidnappers do: He isolated his victims from any outside support and set himself up as their sole caretaker.

And true to his M.O., he utilized religious teachings to manipulate his subjects. He compared his doctrine to the teachings of biblical times. For example, he used such biblical parables as the "Wheat and the Tares" and the "Sheep from the Goats," in which the righteous were separated from the wicked.

Then, once he created the dependence, Shreeve encouraged his new followers to discuss their new beliefs with family members. If a family did not agree to join the group (which, of course, they never did), then the sect member was not to have any further contact. This enabled the group to avoid any outside interference as the doctrines became more perverted. In some cases, this separation included mothers giving up their parental rights to children to avoid sharing children with an ex-husband.

The influence Shreeve had over his followers was very similar to the power David Koresh had with the Branch Davidians, but probably more influential because unlike Koresh, who merely took over an existing cult, Shreeve organized his own sect.

In fact, when I was with the FBI Investigative Support Unit, we were asked to assess the threat level of Koresh and the Branch Davidians, who had holed themselves up in a compound near Waco, Texas, in early 1993. It was our opinion that, even though they had stockpiled weapons, they posed very little threat because Koresh was losing his grip on the cult.

One reason was the history of the sect. Some members had told authorities that they felt Koresh had seduced his way to the head of the organization, which had spun off from the Seventh-day Adventist Church in the 1930s. During the early 1980s, he had an affair with the sect's prophetess, Lois Roden, a woman in her late sixties. Koresh, then named Vernon Howell, was in his early twenties. After Roden's death in 1986, her son George took over as cult leader and ousted Koresh from the group. But George Roden soon lost the confidence of his followers, and four years later, Koresh again took over leadership of the sect.

It wasn't long, however, before he began to make radical changes to the religion's doctrine, which angered many cult members.

Koresh implemented polygamy only for himself, declaring himself married to several female residents of the small community. We found out that some former cult members accused Koresh of declaring that they owed him more than a hundred wives. They resented that Koresh felt he could claim any woman in the compound as his, and they subsequently left or were excommunicated from the group. Koresh reportedly fathered at least a dozen children by the harem, and there was deep-rooted resentment on the part of many of his followers.

We also received reports that his harem included girls as young as fourteen. However, authorities in Texas had investigated, but never substantiated, any claims of statutory rape or child abuse. On February 28, 1993, the Bureau of Alcohol, Tobacco and Firearms decided to storm the compound, a decision that cost the lives of four agents and six Davidians. Shortly after the initial raid, the FBI took command of the federal operation and, over the next fifty-one days, tried to negotiate with Koresh, who had been wounded in the initial raid.

As we analyzed the case, it seemed as if the self-proclaimed messiah had control over only the most vulnerable members of the sect. It was clear to us that if the FBI just waited it out, the cult would eventually disassemble, and many stronger members would probably turn on Koresh, rendering him powerless.

We recommended that the FBI pull back its tactical team, leave the Branch Davidians alone, and just closely monitor the compound. We thought the tactical hostage team's aggressive approach would just elevate stress levels to the point that the Davidians would feel justified in using their firepower. We also didn't feel like anyone in the compound was in any imminent danger. Koresh's fight was with outside authorities, not with anyone inside the compound. Our assessment was that Koresh would eventually have to leave the site and that agents could take him then.

Unfortunately, Janet Reno, the US attorney general at the time, chose to listen to other powers that be in the FBI brain trust and authorized the now-infamous deadly raid on the compound, which claimed the lives of seventy-six people, seventeen of them children under twelve. In addition, this tragedy ultimately provoked Timothy McVeigh to mastermind the Oklahoma City bombing in retaliation for the raid.

Nonetheless, Koresh did what all kidnappers do and kept most of the more vulnerable Branch Davidians under his control. He, like Arvin Shreeve, used religious doctrine as a way of manipulating these cult members. Again, we see a form of psychological control.

The biggest part of the battle against kidnapping is on the psychological front.

Even against more traditional abductions, keeping control of one's thoughts and emotions can play a huge role in overcoming a potential abductor. Later in the chapter, we will discuss ways to help our children and ourselves prepare mentally—and physically—to reduce our risks of abduction. But, for now, we want to focus on the psychological because we believe it is the most important element to stress.

First, if you are approached or recruited by someone trying to coax you into an illegal closed society, you need to ask what it is about you that interests such a group.

More than likely, if you are recruited by a closed society, you'll be in a low point in which you feel alone or abandoned. Your sense of self-worth may not be very high, and predators from groups like Koresh's or Shreeve's can sense that.

They prey on your sorrow and depression.

Remember, we discussed this in our chapter on sexual assaults. The most critical time to guard yourself from high-risk individuals is not at your highest point emotionally but at your lowest. No matter how low you might feel right now, please heed the words of Ed Smart, the Salt Lake City man whose daughter Elizabeth was abducted in 2002 in a highly publicized kidnapping case: "No one has the right to do this to you."

This is what Ed has told his children, as well as countless others, in an effort to teach them to be safer. But this message applies to everybody, regardless of age or life situation.

If you are a friend or family member who is concerned that a loved one may already be in the throes of a destructive group like this, the most effective thing you can do is to create public awareness of the group. If proper attention is paid to the organization, its leaders will be under constant pressure to conduct themselves according to the law. You need to understand, however, that there is a right way and a wrong way to generate attention. Here are three main principles for doing it the right way:

1. **Avoid persecution.** Members of these groups are programmed to expect persecution and almost invite it because those who are persecuted the most are considered to be the most righteous. Attacking them will only drive them underground and strengthen their cause. Simply allow the authorities to continue to do their jobs, but do so in a polite manner. Several years after his conviction, Arvin Shreeve told us in a law enforcement training conference, "You will get much further if you treat people in these situations with respect and courtesy." And you will. His confession is a prime example of that.

2. **Don't argue religion with members of the group.** You cannot win. These are frustrated people looking for meaning

to their mundane lives. Many are well educated and articulate and really believe in what their cause stands for. Just let them know you are genuinely concerned about your friend or family member. Most groups consider themselves a family. If you build on that common ground, either as a concerned citizen or as an authority, you will get much further because you will take away their power to create a division between you and the group. Remember Katie's experience with The Zion Society. Her brother became angered and screamed in the middle of the street, and Shreeve used that episode to cut Katie off from her family.

3. **Realize that these groups revere free agency.** Unfortunately, many of these people are comfortable and function quite well in a servant-master environment. As long as there is no coercion or abuse involved, there is nothing you can do except to let them know that you and the community are fully aware of them and that you respect their right to live freely—as long as it is in accordance with the law of the land.

In short, paying a closed society some respect, while still letting the members know that the community is largely aware of them, is the best you can do, given the circumstances. And if you are a friend or family member in this situation, you will probably find it to be one of the most difficult things you do because it requires a lot of patience.

It is not a solution that will generate results overnight, by any means, but if the group is engaging in illegal or harmful activity, the members will eventually slip and be held accountable for their actions by the authorities. We learned through the sad experience of the Branch Davidians that this is generally the best way.

Using patience is also one of the best attributes in regard to reducing the risks of the typical abduction. As we stated earlier in the chapter, one misconception about kidnapping is that it is primarily a physical act.

The fact is all kidnappings—whether the victims are children or adults—are predominantly psychological.

That is why we began the chapter with the Shreeve case instead of a more traditional one. We want to underscore the point that predators of this nature look for the most vulnerable and trusting members of our society.

The case of Elizabeth Smart, the fourteen-year-old Salt Lake City girl who was taken from her bedroom in the middle of the night in June 2002, is a prime example of the stereotypical view of kidnapping versus what it really is as a whole.

In her case, for example, the media focus was on the physical aspect.

Someone had broken into the Smart residence and taken Elizabeth, at knifepoint, from her room. It was a harrowing story, and most people who followed it assumed that her kidnapper had immediately taken her to a faraway location. Surely, the public thought, if she were nearby and conscious, she would have heard someone from among the thousands of volunteers who searched for her. If searchers were close enough, she would have called out for help.

But as we learned when she was found and returned to her home nine months later, during the initial days of the search, she actually heard her uncle calling for her from fairly close by but never responded to him. Why not? Because her kidnappers, Brian David Mitchell and Wanda Barzee, had terrorized and brainwashed her to such an extent that she was convinced that they would kill her family if she tried to leave them.

So she remained silent as her uncle, tantalizingly close to her, passed by.

In the weeks and months that followed, schools and organizations across the nation focused their attention on "Stranger Danger" and "Keep Safe" programs, geared toward telling children not to talk to strangers and to yell out if someone tried to grab them. This is good information, but it's an outdated way of educating ourselves and our children—not nearly proactive enough to keep up with the more savvy predators of today's world.

Most of a kidnapper's work is done between the ears. That's why it is our minds that we have to use if we are going to have any chance of protecting ourselves and our children from the predatory kidnapper.

Since his daughter's return, Ed Smart has been actively promoting more proactive methods of safety education for both parents and children. He was kind enough to contribute his insight to this book as a parent who has had to endure this unimaginable nightmare.

"These kinds of predators feed on the fact that children are taught to be respectful to adults," Ed told us. "When David Mitchell abducted Elizabeth, he had her at knifepoint, and it was very real. Then, when he had her captive, he kept telling her that we didn't care anymore. That is the very kind of thing these people do."

As a result of his family's experience, Ed has championed a number of causes dedicated to preventive education, including Kindervision and RadKids. Both impart vital education in regard to helping parents and schools teach children how to reduce their risks of becoming victims of violent crime.

Ed sees these organizations as providing two key elements to education. Kindervision (www.kindervision.org) offers important information that parents and children can use to assess potential situations in which they could be abducted. Children and their parents are then taught methods they can use to avoid or flee those situations. You can find child-safety quizzes for both younger and older children on the Kindervision Web site.

RadKids (www.radkids.org) uses that information in a setting that provides role-playing activities that allow children to practice the things they learn in simulated situations, either at home or in school. As we mentioned earlier, role-playing is essential in solidifying risk-reduction principles and actions.

As a whole, education comes from the most important principle a parent can embrace—you have to take a proactive approach to safety.

"Parents need to realize that it can happen to them," Ed told us. "They can't sit back like I did and think that it never will. I never thought something like this would happen to our family. I grew up in a day when you could keep the door unlocked, and everything would be fine. But those days are gone. There are more and more ways for predators to get to our kids, and we need to be prepared."

That doesn't mean we have to throw our hands up in the air and give up. As Ed pointed out, we can do things to be more prepared.

One is by educating ourselves and our children in a format that includes simulated role-playing. Schools would be the ideal place for this, and many school districts throughout the country are starting to implement more and more safety education. We applaud those leaders who are taking the steps necessary to keep our children safe.

But it's not enough.

Having investigated several kidnapping cases in our careers, Mike and I see a greater need for proactive education, not just in the classroom but in the home as well. So often, we have seen missing children from good families and well-meaning parents, wondering what more they could have done to protect their kids. I've had despondent parents shake their heads and tell me, "We kept meaning to go over this with our kids but just never got around to it." Others have said, "We went over this with him a hundred times. Why didn't he scream or yell out?"

Honestly, sometimes there was nothing more that could have been done. Sometimes a predator is just so bent on getting to an innocent child that he is able to circumvent every protective roadblock to that child.

But more often than not, things could have been done—some things that would have been very proactive.

"It's important to tell children what to do, but there comes a point when you can talk until you're blue in the face," explained Ed, who, along with his family, has taken the simulated training course. "The simulation just really helps them understand. Every child is different and will respond differently to each situation, but if a child has a rehearsed response, then at least that child has something to draw on if they are confronted with a dangerous situation."

Rehearsed responses give children, at least in a simulated sense, some experience in dealing with a potential attacker. But they can go through hundreds of simulated experiences, and until a real incident occurs, we will never know how they will react. The most important thing you can teach your children is to listen to their feelings—that sixth sense, if you will.

In sharing Elizabeth's experience, Ed Smart told us, "Children have got to follow their gut instincts and use those instincts to determine what will be the safest thing for them to do. When Elizabeth was abducted and had a knife held to her, she was told not to scream, or he would kill our family. She didn't scream out, and who knows? That may have saved our family. No one can ever say she did the wrong thing, nor should anyone ever tell children they did the wrong thing. But the best thing is for them to use their instincts."

In addition to education, another element of reducing your child's risks is to be prepared, both mentally and physically, in case you or a loved one is kidnapped. Remember, sometimes a kidnapper will get to a child no matter what education we implement or how many precautions we take. At that point, the best strategy is to enhance the abductor's risk level. Keep in mind, not only do we have a risk level of victimization, but the perpetrator has a risk level for apprehension—one that he is keenly aware of.

That said, every child should have an individual ID kit at home, just in case. The most important time in recovering an abducted child is within the first few hours. A kit that includes a current photo and fingerprints will speed up the investigative process. Most local hospitals and health or police departments can take a sample of your child's DNA and enter it into the system.

Ed related his agonizing experience in trying to gather Elizabeth's information for the police.

"In the hours after Elizabeth was kidnapped, we had graphite all over the house because the police were trying to get, not only fingerprints of the kidnapper, but also Elizabeth's fingerprints," he said. "A lot of time was spent trying to gather information that, had we known, we could have had readily available. We spent a lot of time going through pictures and trying to get DNA off of hairbrushes and combs. It's something you hope you never have to use, but you want to have that insurance policy, just in case."

Finally, avoid putting yourself or your loved ones in vulnerable situations, remembering that kidnappers look for ways to do their bidding undetected.

For example, if you are traveling, use only main travel routes and keep to heavily peopled places. Don't put your well-being in the hands of someone you don't know.

When you are at work or at home, use high-traffic areas when walking to and from your destinations; avoid allowing people you don't know to come to your residence, at least until you have had a chance to check them out or get to know them; travel or walk in well-lit areas; and change your route from time to time.

Basically, do the same things we have discussed throughout this book. Do what you would instruct your twelve-year-old child to do. Just because you are an adult doesn't mean it is any safer for you to abandon prudent rules of safety.

As an adult, if you do end up being taken by a kidnapper, it is important to attempt to understand your abductor's mind-set. If you, as the victim, can somehow assess your captor's wishes and use your best instincts, then you may be able to take the kidnapper off guard just long enough to make an escape. Sometimes it's a long shot, but often, it's the best chance a victim has of survival.

Elizabeth Smart is a great example of someone who survived by following her instincts. She should be commended not only for listening to her gut feelings but also for having the patience to endure. It takes a lot of courage to survive such an ordeal, but she showed that it can be done.

In order to understand an abductor's frame of mind, realize that the typical kidnapper usually wants one of two things—money or a sexual relationship with the victim, sometimes both. With so many variables in between, there is no one easy answer.

Of the two, money is the most obvious to explain. A kidnapper takes someone and demands a ransom in return for the victim. Sometimes the perpetrator is willing to make the exchange, and, unfortunately, sometimes he is using his victim only as bait.

The sexual relationship is more complicated. Usually, the kidnapper has engaged in some prolonged fantasy about the victim and has planned an encounter and/or abduction. The would-be perpetrator may not even have a specific victim in mind, but a general fantasy motivates him to lie in wait at a familiar location until just the right opportunity comes along.

One example involved a case that Mike and I reviewed as part of our criminal-tracking project. We had done a review of eleven Great Basin murders, and one was the 1988 murder of Lisa Kimmell, an eighteen-year-old Denver woman whose body had been found in the North Platte River outside Casper, Wyoming, just a week after her disappearance. At the time we reviewed the case, it had been more than ten years since her body had been found, and her killer still had not been brought to justice.

As we examined the circumstances surrounding her case, it didn't take us long to figure out that Lisa was a victim of bad timing and situation. This beautiful young lady certainly did very little, if anything, to contribute to her own victimization.

Unfortunately, for the perpetrator, the timing couldn't have been better.

About four years after we looked at the case, the criminal database got a hit on DNA found on Lisa's body. It belonged to one Dale Wayne Eaton. He was convicted on March 20, 2004, and given the death penalty.

Lisa's mother, Sheila Kimmell, asked me to write a chapter in a book she wrote after Eaton's conviction—some sixteen years after her daughter's death. I will share with you some of my observations from that book, titled *The Murder of Lil Miss*, and apply them to show you how to avoid this kind of predator.

First, let me just say that the details of this case are difficult. By all accounts, the girl nicknamed "Lil Miss" lived a very low-risk lifestyle.

She worked full-time at a respectable job, never hitchhiked or accepted rides from strangers, had a strong supportive family, and was what we generally call a productive citizen. She had left work in Denver the day of her abduction and was traveling to Cody, Wyoming, to see her boyfriend before continuing on to Billings, Montana, to visit a sick friend in the hospital.

However, the night of March 25, 1988, Lisa was on a highway in an unfamiliar environment. She never made it to Cody. It was getting late, and she was alone in an isolated area. Minutes before her abduction, she had been pulled over and given a traffic ticket for speeding. About an hour after she pulled back onto the highway, she drove to a rest stop. Whether she had car trouble or just needed a quick break, she became a victim of opportunity.

For Lisa, it truly was the wrong place at the wrong time. For the nearby predator, it became the perfect opportunity.

Eaton either initially abducted Lisa against her will or used a con to lure her into a vulnerable position where he could overpower her. I know that he had the ability to seize Lisa's vehicle after taking control of her because of the one-ton dual-wheeled tow truck he drove. Since he was familiar with the area, he was able to take both Lisa and her car to his property, where he lived in an old, broken-down school bus.

He held her captive for six days and raped her repeatedly before finally killing her with a forceful blow to the back of the head and several stabs to the chest. He then took her to the old Government Bridge and dropped her body into the river. No one knew who had done this to Lisa until fourteen years later, when DNA collected at the scene was finally matched to Eaton, who was serving time in jail for an assault charge. When authorities discovered who their man was, they searched his property and dug up Lisa's car with the personalized license plate that read, "LIL MISS."

Some aspects of this case can help you understand the predatory kidnapper's way of thinking and thus assist you in minimizing his opportunities.

One, Eaton was a thief. It's significant that you know this because kidnapping is nothing more than an attempt to possess someone, not just physically, but in every way. He pillaged and burglarized, selling his stolen goods to pawnshops in order to make a living. Sometimes, he worked odd jobs to sustain himself, but only if he had to. Eventually, his thievery of things turned into the theft of human beings.

As you think about reducing your risks of being kidnapped, think about your prized possessions. Do you leave them out to be picked up by any passerby, or do you lock them up safely? We assume you keep your valuables in a secure location, so you should also take the same care to ensure that you and your loved ones are as protected as possible.

Sometimes I think if we protected ourselves half as well as we do our property, we might see far less violent crime than we do.

Another important aspect is that Eaton towed Lisa's vehicle without concealment on the open highway, suggesting that he was familiar with the area and knew that the possibility of being seen was unlikely. Eaton was comfortable enough to abduct a victim and take her to a predetermined location where he would avoid detection or interruption.

This is one situation when it helps to think like an investigator and a perpetrator. You can raise a potential abductor's risk level on the Risk Continuum by stopping at a location with potential witnesses. Finally, after he took Lisa to his property, he subjected her to numerous sexual assaults. As I think about this portion of the case, I shudder to even imagine the horror that poor girl endured.

Eaton used restraints on her wrists, arms, ankles, and legs, suggesting that he was playing out an extensive fantasy while she was in captivity. I would expect that part of Eaton's fantasy included a legitimate relationship with Lisa that he pretended would last. Perhaps he was beginning to trust her to stay with him. At some point, it appears that he may have removed her restraints, which would have validated in his mind her willingness, and even desire, to remain with him.

Perhaps she tried to escape, which caused him to react violently. If he let his guard down, and she attempted to escape, it would definitely have precipitated a spontaneous reaction of rage. This would explain the amount of blunt force trauma to the back of Lisa's skull.

Again, the point here would be to assess your captor's mind-set, should you ever be kidnapped. If the kidnapper, for instance, removes your restraints, see how much more trust or freedom he will give you if you honor his first sign of confidence. The more trust he has in you, the more information you can gather about the surroundings. It's also more likely he will let his guard down. Then, at the opportune moment, you have a better chance of escape. Again, we are not suggesting that this is the only approach. It is an incredibly difficult circumstance to be in, and every scenario is different. The idea here is to assess the situation so you can do whatever it takes to create an opportunity for escape or a call for help.

We hope that you never find yourself in a situation like this one. Our hearts go out to the Kimmell family. Mike and I consider them friends, and that is why it was an honor for me to have been asked to contribute to Sheila's book.

To conclude this chapter, we would like to address one more issue.

Statistics show that abductions are often the result of domestic relationships gone bad, in which the victim knows her captor well. If you are in a relationship in which your partner becomes ultrapossessive, then that could be a sign that it's time to get some outside help, similar to what we discussed in the chapter on domestic violence.

It's difficult to enforce laws against stalking and harassment because stalking is hard to prove. In domestic disputes, stalking and harassment are often the precursors to abduction. Since kidnapping is the attempt to possess another human being, it stands to reason that one would lead to another.

If a wife, for example, finally leaves her abusive husband, he may feel that his only recourse is to stalk her in an attempt to intimidate her back into the relationship. If she obtains a restraining order, he still won't quit until there is some resolution, good or bad. He is simply trying to bully her, just like some kids do on the playground. And, like the bully, he won't stop until the other kids take the victim's side or until the victim pops the bully in the nose.

One suggestion would be to secure a protective order as quickly as

possible. Then, every single time he violates the order—not sometimes, but every time—call the police. Believe me, most officers will
get tired of coming after the abuser, and they will get serious. If you
don't feel that is working, then set up an appointment with the police
chief, every Monday morning if you have to, and let him know that
you are dissatisfied with the performance of his officers in your case.
As a former police chief, I can tell you that police chiefs make every
effort to respond to public pressure.

What you do not want to do is project your values onto the perpetrator. We will explain what we mean through the same example.

Let's say the woman's stalker storms over to her apartment late at
night, banging on the door and yelling. She feels embarrassed because
the neighbors can hear him, and she doesn't want to be evicted. But
she also feels threatened. At that point, she might open the door, and
she might not.

If she doesn't, he might yell something like, "I promise. I just want
to talk to you one more time, then I will go away for good. This is the
last time. I promise."

Because of the mixed emotions running through her, she is
tempted to finally relent and let him in, thinking that she will finally
get him out of her hair if she agrees to talk to him one last time.

But it *won't* be the last time.

Projecting your values onto the perpetrator is a mistake. This
woman is the type who, when she makes a promise, she keeps it.
Therefore, she thinks that her stalker might also finally keep this
promise, even though he has broken thousands before. That's where
you have to almost take the humanity out of the equation and program
yourself to call the authorities every time, so he will finally get the
message.

Your best chance to beat the bully, or in this case the stalker, is to
get enough authorities on your side until he realizes he is not going to
win. Mike uses a perfect analogy to illustrate this principle to people
who think that nothing would stop a hate-filled man from attacking his
ex-wife: "If I put the ex-wife in the same room with the guy, yes, he

would attack her. But if I put ten fully armed cops in between him and her, he would walk away every time. Why? Because he is a bully who is only victimizing someone he thinks will continue to tolerate it."

The moral of the story is this: every time he violates the protective order, call the police. Surround yourself with as much help as possible. People will help. We know that most abused women don't think so, but in most cases, their abusers have psychologically tormented and manipulated them into believing that the only person they can rely on is the abuser himself.

It is the same principle that we discussed earlier in this chapter with Arvin Shreeve and David Koresh.

In conclusion, any life skill that you can add to enhance your safety or increase your chances of escaping a captive situation is well worth learning. Again, we will be honest: there are times when, no matter what, the victim is going to lose.

But the more you learn, the more you reduce the probability of victimization. We hope that, by understanding the mind of the abductor, you can take the proper preventive steps for you and your loved ones and learn from the experiences of those who have already lived through these nightmares.

9

THE END-ALL

HOMICIDAL PREDATORS

On a long stretch of desert highway, the tractor-trailer traveled deep into the night through the heart of West Texas. One could only guess the rig—whose cargo was a mystery to passersbys—was transporting perishables, furniture, or electronics. This trip had been particularly taxing on the driver, a middle-aged man with an outwardly friendly demeanor.

He had been hauling goods across the country for nearly twenty years and was well aware of the dangers associated with his occupation.

Despite the pressures of getting a load delivered on time, he knew that sleep deprivation was a trucker's worst enemy. He also knew that strange people traveled the highways, and he had definitely seen his share of them. But as the night wore on, Ben thought it best to stop and get some much-needed rest. He pulled over to the side of the highway and stretched out to get some sleep.

Just a few hours later, he heard a noise that startled him awake.

"Hello? Is anyone in there?" shouted two voices, a young man and a teenage girl.

Cautious, yet curious, the truck driver poked his head out the window.

279

"What can I help you with?" he asked them, being hospitable.

"We were wondering if you could give us a ride. You're headed south, right?"

"Sure, but you two look a little young to be out hitchhiking. That's dangerous for anybody, much less someone as young as you two. I've got a radio in here. Do you want to call your folks?"

The couple looked at each other for a moment then turned to the kind trucker. "It's our parents that we're trying to get away from."

The two hitchhikers seemed harmless enough. The girl had a soft, friendly way about her, and the young man had a calm and quiet demeanor. Ben didn't think that they would pose any trouble, and he decided to give them a ride.

"Well, I don't want to pry into your business. You two look like good kids. Why don't you get in, and I will take you as far as I can."

As they pulled onto the highway, the kind stranger began to make polite conversation with the young couple.

"My name is Ben. What are your names?"

"I'm Regina, and this is Ricky," the girl said.

"Well, it's good to meet you two."

As they traveled over the next couple of hours, the pair began to feel comfortable with the driver. He was very pleasant and wasn't at all judgmental. Things seemed to be going well, but Ben noticed that the young man was becoming fidgety and restless. The trucker stole a glance at him to make sure he wasn't carrying a weapon, but he determined that the boy was just trying to get comfortable. Still, Ben knew it could be dangerous to pick up hitchhikers, and he wanted to make sure the couple wasn't concealing anything.

When he was sure the couple was harmless, the driver abruptly pulled his Peterbilt over to the side of the road.

"What's going on?" they asked in unison.

"I'll tell you what's going on," he growled. "This is going on."

The couple was taken completely by surprise. In an instant, the face of a kind and helpful gentleman had abruptly taken on an expression of pure evil. While holding the gun on the young man, Ben handcuffed fourteen-year-old Regina Walters to the inside of the sleeper cab. He then ordered Ricky to get out of the truck.

"Do it slowly," he warned, following him out and keeping the gun fixed directly on the young man.

The hitchhikers, once on an exciting, romantic adventure, were now prisoners. Their romance had turned into horror.

From inside the cab, Regina heard gunshots in the distance, maybe a hundred yards or so off the sparse highway. Her heart sank, and she felt an immense lump in her throat. She knew Ricky wouldn't be coming back.

As she heard the footsteps draw closer to the truck, she had no idea what lay in store for her, but it wouldn't be good.

Had the couple known what they were dealing with, they never would have approached the truck of whom we believe will prove to be one of the most infamous highway killers in US history.

According to authorities, it was February 1990 when the truck driver, Robert Ben Rhoades, picked up the couple, eighteen-year-old Ricky Lee Jones and fourteen-year-old Regina Walters of Palestine, Texas.

After killing Jones, Rhoades turned his attention to Walters, whom he had imprisoned in a makeshift dungeon in the back of his cab. For over a week, he mercilessly raped and tortured the young girl before finally taking her to an abandoned old barn just off Interstate 70 in Illinois.

He cut her hair and shaved her pubic area, then he forced her to pose for photos in front of the barn in lingerie he had especially picked out for his victims. In the end, he strangled her, using a small piece of board that he had inserted through a double loop of baling wire. He twisted the board clockwise tightly around her neck until he was sure she was dead. He took the clothing from her body and left her in the barn. Her corpse was eventually found, badly decomposed, more than six months later.

In a chilling twist, Rhoades made two anonymous phone calls to Regina Walters's father just days after her murder, both at work and at his unlisted home number.

The cold-blooded killer told Walters, "I made some changes. I cut her hair."

He also told the grieving father that his daughter was in a barn loft, but he did not give Walters the location.

"Is my daughter still alive?" Walters desperately asked.

After a short pause, Rhoades hung up the phone without uttering a word.

That was the last the Walters family would hear about their daughter until she was found on September 29, 1990.

None of this information would have come to light, however, had it not been for one fateful night on an Arizona highway.

Arizona Highway Patrol trooper Mike Miller was patrolling Interstate 10, just outside Casa Grande, on April 1, 1990. Everything seemed normal until he noticed a parked tractor-trailer's hazard lights flashing on the side of the road. Because it was during the wee hours of the morning, Miller decided he would stop to lend a hand to a possibly stranded driver.

"Hello!" the trooper called out. "Is anyone here?"

When no one answered, Miller decided to see whether he could find the driver. As he walked around the rig, he couldn't find anyone around the vehicle or in the driver's area of the cab. But when he noticed that the cab door was unlocked and heard some commotion within the sleeper portion of the cab, Miller became suspicious and decided to investigate.

The trooper carefully climbed up onto the runner, pointed his flashlight toward the back, then nearly fell backward when he caught sight of a naked woman shackled and chained to the wall of the cab. She screamed uncontrollably when she saw the trooper.

Then he saw Rhoades scurry from behind the curtains that separated the sleeper cab from the driving area.

"Come out of the back and show me your hands!" Miller ordered.

"OK, OK, everything's cool, officer," Rhoades insisted. "I'm coming out."

"Keep your hands where I can see them and move slowly," the trooper reiterated.

"I am, I am," Rhoades said. "Look, just so you know, I have a gun with me. I just didn't want you to freak out, OK?"

"OK, let me see your hands," Miller said as he cuffed Rhoades and secured the weapon.

Through all this, the trooper couldn't believe what he was seeing. The woman, still in hysterics, was chained against the wall, her hands and ankles in handcuffs, and a horse bridle strapped around her neck, with a long chain padlocked to the horse bit. Miller noted the red welts on her body and blood trickling from the severe cuts on her mouth. She had clearly been whipped several times and orally tortured with the horse bridle.

"Hey, man, I promise, this isn't what it looks like," said Rhoades, trying to reassure Miller as the trooper led him to the patrol car. "She wanted me to do this to her. I swear. She told me she likes it this way. I was just playing along, then she started freaking out on me. That's when you got here."

"OK, sir, I need to sort this all out," Miller calmly told Rhoades, placing him in the backseat of the car. "I'm going to check on the lady. I'll be right back."

He cuffed the suspect—behind his back—and closed the door to the patrol car.

When he returned to the rig to check on the victim, she was still uncontrollably frantic.

"He's coming back!" she screamed. "Get me out of here! He's coming back!"

"Ma'am, I've got him locked up in my patrol car," Miller replied, trying to console her. "He's not going anywhere. Now, I'm going to get you out of here, but I want to cover you up with this blanket first, OK?"

"No! No!" she shrieked. "He's coming! He's coming! He's going to kill me!"

It was clear that the trooper wasn't going to be able to calm her anytime soon. Whatever had happened certainly wasn't consensual, Miller thought.

After he covered the woman with the blanket, he went back to check on Rhoades, who had slipped his hands, still handcuffed, from behind his body to the front and had just undone his seat belt when Miller returned.

"Hey, what are you doing?" he asked Rhoades.

"I was just a little uncomfortable, that's all."

Miller shuddered as he thought about the horrific scenarios that could have occurred had his suspect escaped.

"I'm going to need the keys to those handcuffs," he told Rhoades. "Where do you keep them?"

"They're in my pocket, on this side," Rhoades responded, motioning with his chin to the left.

The highway patrolman dug the keys out of the suspect's pocket and secured him in the vehicle. Just then, another police car pulled up. Officer Robert Gygax of the Casa Grande Police Department had gotten Miller's call for backup and had arrived within minutes.

"What do we have here?"

"You're not going to believe this," Miller said. "It looks like we've got a rape and torture victim. She's frightened out of her mind. Here, I've got the keys to the handcuffs. We're going to need them to get her out."

"The victim is handcuffed?" Gygax asked, somewhat perplexed.

"Yeah," Miller replied, glancing over at the suspect. "Thanks to him."

Gygax looked over at Rhoades, wondering just what they had on their hands.

Once the officers brought the woman to the Casa Grande Police Department, she began to calm down, finally realizing she was safe and that Rhoades was securely in custody. At the station, the twenty-seven-year-old victim, Jenny Harris, had regained enough composure to talk to the authorities about her ordeal. She described how she had met her attacker at a truck stop just north of Phoenix.

She told them that she often hitched rides to visit friends but that she was usually careful not to accept rides from "creepy" guys.

"He was very nice to me, very polite," Jenny told Rick Barnhart, the detective who questioned her. "He was more polite than most of the guys I usually meet there. But then all of the sudden, he changed."

"What happened?"

"I don't really know," she replied. "We were driving along toward Tucson, and we were talking. But I got tired and fell asleep. The next thing I knew, he pulled over, grabbed me, and shoved me into the back. Then he shackled me up like a wild animal. Then he took out this briefcase and started pulling things out of it."

"What kinds of things did he take out of the briefcase?"

"Handcuffs, a horse bridle, a whip, and these large pins."

"What did he do next?"

"He took off my clothes, chained me up, then he pulled out the scissors—"

At that, the young lady choked up and began to cry.

"It's OK, take your time," the detective reassured her. "Do you need to take a break?"

"No, no, I'm fine," Jenny sniffled. "I want to finish this."

After a moment, she continued.

"He took out the scissors, and he cut my hair short and clipped it. Then, he shaved the hair around my private area."

Jenny began to cry some more but motioned to the detective that she wanted to continue.

"I just want to get this over with." She paused. "Then, he put the bridle in my mouth and started to whip me."

As the interview continued, she related how she had been tortured on and off since he had picked her up earlier that day. For the purpose of collecting evidence, police photographed the long red welts that covered her chest and back from the vicious whipping, as well as the grotesque piercings of her nipples and labia.

Finally, Jenny said, "He told me he has done this for fifteen years."

"Did he tell you his name?"

"Whips and Chains. That's what he called himself. I think that was his CB radio name, too."

"OK, I think that's all for now," the detective said. "Is there anything else, anything that stands out, that you can tell me?"

"Not really. Just that it seemed like he really got off on the torture and bondage stuff. That turned him on more than anything."

"Jenny, I know this was difficult for you, but we really appreciate your cooperation," Barnhart told her. "You did great."

It was about 3 a.m. when Rhoades was ushered into the interrogation room. Immediately, the suspect began trying to minimize what he believed was circumstantial evidence against him. Upon entering the room, Rhoades casually slumped onto a nearby couch and let out a huge yawn, as if to say, "You guys don't have anything on me. This is no big deal because the whole thing was all her idea."

"Mr. Rhoades, why don't you start by telling me how you met up with Ms. Harris."

"I was just getting a bite to eat at the truck stop, and she came up to me and asked if I could give her a ride."

"Just like that, she asked you for a ride?" Barnhart asked.

"Well, no. She spent some time talking to me first, then she asked for the ride."

Barnhart didn't immediately respond, giving pause to allow Rhoades to keep talking. Then Rhoades leaned over, trying to be chummy with the detective.

"Look, I know you've got a job to do," Rhoades said. "But that lady is not playing with a full deck, you know what I mean? She's a lot lizard."

"What's a lot lizard?"

"You know, a woman who hangs out at truck stops trying to pick up on truckers. She gets around, if you know what I mean. That's what that woman is. I normally don't like to get involved with that kind because I've got too much work to do, and I don't want to get any diseases, you know what I'm saying? But I thought I'd give that woman a ride just to help her out. But she came on really strong, and, you know, I'm a man, so I thought I'd go along with her just this once, have a little fun on the side."

The detective continued to question the suspect about Jenny's injuries, but Rhoades never directly answered. The interrogation came to a halt when Rhoades made a crease in the couch with his hand and said, "I took you up to the point where I stopped the truck. Now, I'm not gonna cross that line. I stopped the truck."

The detective finally booked the suspect into jail for aggravated assault, sexual assault, and unlawful imprisonment, but he suspected that Rhoades had done far more, and Barnhart needed time to confirm his suspicions. Shortly after the interrogation, Barnhart sent a nationwide teletype, then he faxed a letter to a superior court judge in Florence, Arizona, to detain Rhoades at least until some information came in.

Then he called Rhoades's hometown police department in Houston, hoping for some kind of information.

It wasn't long before detectives from the Houston Police Department called to relate the details of a similar case that also involved Ben Rhoades. Rhoades had been suspected of kidnapping an eighteen-year-old woman in California and holding her captive for two weeks. As he did with Jenny Harris, he cut the victim's hair short and shaved her pubic hair. She, too, had been systematically tortured, and her captor had threatened to kill her. She eventually escaped when Rhoades forgot to close the handcuff that kept her chained inside the truck.

Unfortunately, the woman had been so brutalized that when officers brought her face to face with the detained Rhoades, she stared him down and told police that he was not her attacker. Without her testimony, police were legally unable to hold the suspect and were forced to release him. A few days later, the victim came forward and admitted that the man they had detained was indeed her attacker, but when she had to identify Rhoades, she had been too intimidated to implicate him. After two weeks of torture, in her mind, there weren't enough officers around to protect her.

Because of the inconsistencies in her testimony, authorities were unable to bring a case against Rhoades. The Arizona case, however, would prove to be a huge breakthrough for investigators, not only in Houston, but eventually in other parts of the country as well.

On April 6, 1990, police obtained a warrant to search Rhoades's apartment in Houston. The horror of what they found would stun even the most veteran law enforcement officer. During their search, they found numerous items of women's clothing, obscene magazines and books, instruments used for bondage, and white towels, some with blood on them.

The search also produced photographs of nude women, one of whom was Regina K. Walters. Some of the clothing that was found resembled that worn by Walters in other photographs in Rhoades's apartment, including one of the girl standing in front of the barn where her body was found.

Authorities also obtained phone records that linked the infamous calls made to Walters's father, tracing them to Oklahoma City and Ennis, Texas. Police were able to go through the trucker's work logs and pinpoint where he had been on the days the calls were made. The first call to Regina's father was from a pay phone at a truck stop in Oklahoma City on March 16. On that day, Rhoades had fueled up at the same truck stop. The next day, the logs indicated that Rhoades had been in Ennis, Texas. Ben Rhoades was indeed in both locations on the days in question, effectively proving that he made them. He had gotten the unlisted numbers from a notebook Regina had written them in.

Police found that notebook with the other items in the suspect's apartment.

In the notebook, Rhoades had written, "Ricky is a dead man," and had crudely drawn a picture of a gun and drops of blood next to the message. There were also other cryptic notations that seemed to indicate directions and other unknown meanings, such as "water tank, Fun and Hide," which could have meant he toyed with the young man before killing him.

Rhoades's wife was shown the handwriting and identified it as his.

Months later, these key pieces of evidence would be used to link Rhoades to Regina Walters and, in 1992, he was sentenced to life in prison in Illinois in connection with her death.

It was late 1997 when I presented this case to several dozen sheriffs and police chiefs at a police personnel convention in St. George, Utah. I went through all the evidence and behaviors of Ben Rhoades to illustrate the behavioral profile of the sexual sadist serial killer.

"To be clear, this type of offender is one who is outwardly friendly," I told the audience. "He is not going to outwardly appear or behave in a deviant manner, like the quiet, creepy guy who keeps to himself in the movies. Ben Rhoades's victims said that when they first met him, he was a very nice, polite man. That's how he cons his prey. But once he secures and isolates his victims, the sexual sadist will use torture devices and scare tactics. He uses a voice that is nonemotional to unsettle his victims. If you can find him, evidence is usually easy to obtain, because sexual sadists tend to keep trophies, and they love to photograph or tape their victims so they can fantasize to their memories. The key is that the sexual sadist is very difficult to distinguish from the rest of society because he can fit in so well."

I then walked over to the video screen and made one last, unsettling point. Pointing to one photo in which Rhoades's teenage victim wears an expression of deep despair, I said, "The most telling characteristic of sexual sadists is that they usually tell their victims what they're going to do to them ahead of time."

As I began to finish the presentation on Rhoades, I went through the victimology of a person most likely to be taken by this type of killer.

"When you look at the victims Rhoades selected," I began, "you will find that there are some commonalities among them. Both of the victims who survived his attacks were especially vulnerable: Either they'd had emotionally upsetting incidents around the time they were abducted or were very young and naive, or they had physical afflictions such as dyslexia or other learning disabilities. In the case of Regina Walters and Ricky Lee Jones, there is no question that Rhoades preyed on their naiveté."

I concluded that portion of the presentation by showing some photographs collected at Rhoades's apartment and tracking on a map the cross-country routes he had taken. Using his trucking logs, investigators had tracked approximate dates for the portions of the country that he traveled through, especially during the early months of 1990, when it is believed that he went on an abduction and killing rampage. The authorities who worked most closely on the Rhoades case believe he was attacking as many as three girls a month by early 1990.

"Those who investigated this case believe, as do I," I told the audience, "that Ben Rhoades left several victims in his wake. There are still nearly fifty missing people or unidentified bodies for which investigators cannot rule out Rhoades as a potential suspect."

After the conference, I was approached by Sheriff Ed Phillips from the Millard County Sheriff's Office, a rural area in central Utah. Ed and I had worked together twelve years before, when I was a police chief in Delta, a small town located in that county. Incidentally, Millard County is, geographically, the largest county in the state.

"You know, I was looking at those photos and that map, and I wanted to talk to you for a minute about a case we haven't been able to close since 1990," Ed said. "Do you have a minute?"

"Sure. What's up?"

"Well, I'm not entirely sure. But the scenery in those pictures of Regina Walters is similar to some of the landscape in Millard County. And in October of 1990, a couple of hunters found a badly decomposed body in some bushes right off I-15 by Fillmore."

"Do you think this victim might have been one of Rhoades's?" I asked him.

"I'm not sure, but I think we should look into it."

About a year later I got a call from John Kimball, a detective from the Millard County Sheriff's Office. He asked if Mike and I would facilitate a UTAP review of this case as part of a multi-state joint task force conference we were conducting to look into unsolved homicides in the Great Basin area. The conference included more than fifty law enforcement professionals from five states. Our aim was to put our heads together to see if we could, as a collective group, solve some of these cold cases.

We presented his case before the group and John was able to get some good information about Ben Rhoades. He followed those leads up and, in 2003, finally caught a break in the case.

Amazingly, one of the bloody towels found in Rhoades's Houston apartment contained the Utah victim's DNA on it. After some jurisdictional legal issues were resolved, the matter finally went to court in Texas. Rhoades was charged in 2006 with the murders of the twenty-four-year-old woman, Patricia Walsh, and her husband, twenty-eight-year-old Douglas Zyskowski, two newly wed Christian missionaries who were hitchhiking in Alabama when Rhoades picked them up.

Authorities believe the trucker shot and killed Zyskowski then dumped his body near I-10 outside of Ozona, Texas.

They also think that Rhoades then kept Walsh for about a week before shooting her multiple times in the head and dumping her naked body in Millard County, Utah. This was a difficult case to solve because, although Zyskowski's body had been discovered months earlier, he wasn't identified until 1992. And because his wife's body had never been identified, the two slayings were not linked until 2003, when authorities were finally able to identify her through dental records. In 2006, after exhaustive legal analysis, authorities from the states of Utah and Texas agreed that it would be best to try Rhoades for both homicides in Texas, where there would be a greater chance for the death penalty. Texas prosecutors were hoping for the case to go to trial in 2007.

Though this case is one of the most sensational we have included, there are some important things to point out in terms of reducing your risks, especially if you cross paths with someone like Rhoades.

One, it is important to realize that the murderer is the end-all, meaning he has also committed other crimes and has worked himself up to this point. Homicide is the pinnacle of the career criminal. That's why serial killers are horrifying and fascinating at the same time. They represent our darkest fears and our greatest curiosities. Someone like Ben Rhoades or Jeffrey Dahmer has exceeded all limits of acceptable human behavior. At the same time, they have the ability to appear to live a moral life.

In chapter 5, we introduced you to Terry Donnelly, the man who killed five elderly women. This is what he had to say about protecting yourself from predatory killers based on appearances alone: "We put on an act. It's not like TV. You don't have Christopher Walken with the crazy eyes and all that. You have a [seemingly] normal person."

With that understanding, if you apply the same principles we have discussed to reduce your risks of becoming a victim of lesser crimes, then you will most likely avoid homicidal predators as well. But if you base your self-protection strategy on appearances alone, then you're going to be in trouble.

It's also important to understand that serial killers don't start out as serial killers.

They introduce things into their lives that draw them into that kind of thinking. Pornography is almost always the number-one trigger for someone psychologically predisposed to random murder. It is the ultimate objectifier. That's why the vast majority of people who get involved with pornography usually don't stop with soft porn. They usually feel the need to get more hard-core, until a beautiful nude human body isn't enough. The body then becomes merely an object used as nothing more than to satisfy their desires. For someone like Ben Rhoades, that includes torture and murder. To him, his victim isn't even a human being. She's just part of a series of fantasies that he has lived over and over in his mind through pornography.

That's partly why we are seeing more and more sexual child victimization.

People kidnap children and auction them off over the Internet for the most horrible purposes imaginable. Why would someone do that? Because these predators have objectified the body so much in their minds through pornography that even a child becomes just another object used to satisfy their wants and desires. That's what makes it possible for NBC's *To Catch a Predator* to be a weekly show—there are so many predators to choose from. It's no coincidence that the Internet is the common denominator. It is a medium that allows, at once, the perpetrator to fantasize, and it provides a mechanism for acting out those fantasies. For example, a sexual perpetrator and/or serial killer can turn on the Internet, open one window to fantasize over photographed children then, with the click of a mouse, start bidding on other children for sale in another window. As we said at the outset of the book, the crime itself is nothing new, but technology has sped up the process.

Once hooked, serial killers, like anyone who becomes expert at their craft, spend a lot of time studying and practicing. Sexual sadists, like Rhoades, rehearse their crimes mentally several times over before they ever carry them out physically.

As criminal profilers, that's how we know what we're dealing with. If a killer is messy in the way he commits a murder, we know he hasn't had much experience. If he is well organized, however, then we anticipate that he has done it before.

That is the point of difference between M.O. (the method with which a criminal operates) and signature for a serial killer. An M.O. can change, and often does, because a murderer gets more proficient and organized with time. Signature is that which gives the criminal a sense of psychosexual gratification. It seldom changes.

The signature aspect of the Ben Rhoades cases, for example, was excessive bondage and the photographing of his victims. It's interesting to note that sexual sadists do not like to talk about the signature aspect of their crimes. Mike and I have talked to a few who are in custody, and they refuse to discuss their bizarre rituals. It's deeply personal to them, too deep to discuss. But that's how we catch them.

Now, how does this knowledge help you reduce your risk level?

One, know that serial killers are still opportunists. They, like many of the criminals we have discussed throughout this book, rely on their victims giving them the chance to isolate them.

Case in point, in 1997, John Douglas and I conducted a criminal behavior seminar in Salt Lake City. One attendee was a lady who had been charmed and picked up by highly publicized serial killer Ted Bundy at a Salt Lake–area shopping mall. As they were walking toward his now-infamous VW Bug, her brother happened to see her and demanded that she go home with him, not the stranger. In that moment, Bundy's plan was foiled because he had no recourse. He was in a public place, and his method of capture—charming girls into his car and taking them to an isolated location—had been quashed. He was forced to let his intended victim go.

This is a classic case of opportunism. Had this good woman's brother not intervened and insisted on taking her home, she probably wouldn't have been here to tell her story. Unfortunately, later that week, he claimed another young Salt Lake City woman as a victim, luring her in just as he had this young woman.

So, first thing, if at all possible, don't allow yourself to be compromised into a situation in which you are isolated with someone you don't know or trust, no matter how trustworthy and normal that person seems. Remember, the serial killer has fantasized his intended acts over and over in his mind. If you don't give him a concealed place to act those fantasies out, he is powerless to do anything to you.

Second, don't make the mistake of thinking that, if an individual doesn't look "weird" or "creepy," it means you can trust him. Mug shots, which are what we usually see in the newspaper, are pictures taken after the killer has been caught. Of course they look creepy. To look at a mug shot of Ben Rhoades, one of the most sinister-looking men imaginable, you would wonder why anyone would go anywhere with that guy. But serial killers don't look that way while they are enticing their victims into trusting them. Again, they appear to be normal and friendly.

Third, don't allow yourself to be put in a situation where you don't have control over your circumstances. Let's take our focus off the Ben Rhoadeses and Ted Bundies of the world for just a minute. One of the most common misconceptions about predatory murderers is that they are strangers whom we don't know. We have stereotyped them into the psycho mold of the stranger who snatches people in the night and carries them off to their personal torture chambers. Of course, sometimes it does happen that way, but the overwhelming majority of the time, the victim must in some way ignorantly provide an attacker the opportunity to attack.

While it is sometimes true that predatory killers are strangers, the most common murderer is one who is usually involved in drugs and trying to get you or a loved one to do the same. He might be the local drug dealer or gang member, or he could be the college kid whom students go to for a "quick fix" or a "quick high."

When I was the chief of police in Provo, Utah, I helped work an especially sad case that illustrates this principle very well.

It was a Saturday morning when I was called out to a local church.

Two kids had been riding their bikes around the parking lot when they spotted the body of a young lady lying in a flower bed behind the church.

"What do you think happened here?" asked one of the sheriff's investigators.

"Let me take a look," I answered.

I walked over to the body and looked for anything on or around it that might indicate traces of signature behavior. The first thing I noticed was that whoever had done this had not desecrated the body in any way. I also noted the positioning of the girl's body, and I immediately came to a rough conclusion.

"Whoever did this," I told the detectives, "was probably an acquaintance."

"How do you figure?"

"Well, for one, look at how the body is displayed. There are no visible bruises, so whoever placed her here was very gentle with her, which suggests there was no violent attack on the victim. Also, the location of the body is very telling."

"In what way?"

"They placed her behind the church in a bed of flowers, almost as if they were memorializing her," I answered. "If they were out to make a statement, they would have just dumped the body or displayed her out in front of the church so everyone could see the corpse. That's what someone who had coldly killed her would have done. Whoever did this knew her, and, even if they killed her, must have had some feelings of affection toward this young lady."

"I agree," he said. "What a shame."

"It sure is," I concurred.

"I would start with her circle of family and friends. It won't be long before someone comes forward with some information."

And it wasn't.

Within twenty-four hours, police had apprehended two suspects, Jess Ferris and Jonathan Jamison, who were eventually convicted for the seventeen-year-old girl's death.

Nancy Ferris was a high school student just finishing her junior year. She had been in trouble off and on throughout her teenage years but had finally gotten out of the drug scene, had improved her grades, and was headed in the right direction. It had been almost a year since she had taken drugs or had even taken a drink of alcohol.

But along came two old pals, Jess and Jonathan, who just couldn't stand to see her "wound up too tight and not having any fun." Of course, what they were really concerned with were their pocketbooks and selfish desires. They were going to be at a party that night, and they wanted Nancy to go with them.

"I don't know," she said. "I finally got out of rehab, and I'm just not into the party scene anymore."

"Oh, come on, babe," Jess teased. "That's what rehab's for, so you can still party and keep it under control."

After several more minutes of being badgered by her two old buddies, Nancy finally acquiesced.

"Well, I guess a couple drinks wouldn't hurt. But none of the hard stuff, OK?"

"That's it, baby! We're gonna have a good time tonight!" Jess exclaimed.

"No, Jess, I mean it. No hard stuff, promise?"

"Hey, baby, it's us you're talking to," said Jess, quickly winking at Jonathan. "You don't have to do anything you don't want to do."

"OK, then I'll see you guys there."

Nancy did more than just have a couple of drinks; Jess and Jonathan made sure of that. Two drinks turned into six, and six quickly evolved into a few hits of marijuana. Finally, when Nancy had lost her inhibitions, Jess and Jonathan pulled out the big stuff, the heroin.

"You remember your old friend here, don't you, baby?" said Jess, waving a loaded syringe in front of Nancy's face.

"Oh, yeah, baby!" she said with a laugh. "But that's for you guys. I think I've had enough."

"Oh, come on," Jonathan urged. "You're here. You've gotta go all the way now."

"But I'm too wasted to shoot up," Nancy protested.

"That's OK, baby," said Jess. "I'm in control. Just give me your pretty little arm, and we'll do the rest."

Nancy didn't have a comeback for that one. Heroin had been the hardest drug for her to kick. She had spent months in rehab and therapy just to get over the nagging need for the narcotic. If she took it now, she knew what kind of climb she had in front of her. But before she could utter another protest, Jonathan had rolled up her sleeve, exposing her vein, and Jess was injecting her with the needle.

Nancy felt that familiar sudden surge of adrenaline. She knew the rush that was coming next. At least, she thought she did.

But before she knew what was happening, she began gasping for air. Her chest felt so tight that she could feel her heart stop beating. Everyone in the room got a great laugh from her reaction. It was like seeing a first timer. But when Nancy started going into convulsions, the group knew something was wrong, terribly wrong.

"Nancy, what's going on, baby?" asked Jonathan, sobering up quickly at that point. "Come on, Nancy. Just sit up, and you'll come out of it. Come on."

But Nancy couldn't sit up. She couldn't do anything. The convulsions had stopped, and so had the young lady's breathing. Someone tried to administer CPR, but it was too late. Nancy's heart had stopped, and she was dead.

A stunned silence filled what was once a festive room.

"She's dead, man," said Jonathan, beginning to panic. "What are we going to do? She's dead!"

"I don't know," Jess said. "Let me think for a minute."

"Dude, what's there to think about? She's dead!" Jonathan blurted.

"Hey! I'm not taking the fall for this, dude, so keep your mouth shut and let me think," yelled Jess, pinning Jonathan to the wall, before realizing another dozen or so people had witnessed the crime. "No one says a word to anybody about this. Do you understand?"

"But what do we do?" Jonathan said meekly, tears rolling down his cheeks.

"OK, if anybody asks, she OD'd," Jess said. "That's the story, OK?"

After everyone in the room, including Jonathan, had half-heartedly nodded, Jess came up with an idea.

"All right, let's get her out of here," he said.

"We can't just dump her, dude," Jonathan protested.

Jess was angry and immediately wanted to slap Jonathan. But, seeing that everyone agreed with his friend, he managed to contain himself.

"No, dude, you're right. Nancy deserves better than that. I've got an idea. We'll take her some place nice, like a church. It's a spiritual place, and there are flowers there. It will be like a memorial. I think she'd like that."

"I don't know, man," Jonathan said, still tearful and shaking his head.

"Dude, that's what she'd want," pleaded Jess, trying to convince his friend and the others that it was the right thing to do. "Look, we were friends, right?"

"Yeah."

"OK, then, she wouldn't want her friends to get in trouble over something that was just an accident. Nancy was great that way. She was always looking out for her friends. It's not like we're dumping her in any old place. It's a church, man. She would want us to do this. It's the best thing we can do for her now."

Jonathan finally went along with the plan, but somehow, he and Nancy's other acquaintances at the party that night felt terribly wrong about it.

I knew that the detectives needed to act quickly and question Nancy's circle of friends as soon as possible, while their emotions were still running high. It took only a few hours for investigators to find some of the partygoers. Within the day, some had confessed to what they had seen, and police arrested Jess and Jonathan, who were eventually convicted of manslaughter.

Again, the lesson from this experience is to avoid entrusting your well-being to those who do not have your best interest in mind, drug dealers being foremost among them. They will try to convince you that they are looking out for you, but in the end, they will leave you behind when you are all used up.

From a parental perspective, Ferris's father told us that he wished he had kept better track of his daughter's acquaintances and whereabouts—something all parents should do with the utmost regularity.

"I just wish I would have been more involved," he said. "I should have been more consistent about knowing where she was and knowing who she was with. That's what I would tell parents, especially anyone with teenagers. Just care enough to get into their business, even if they don't want you to."

The final principle of reducing your risks is to look for people or things that are out of place. We talked earlier about using your sixth sense. Even if the person isn't visibly out of his element, if something he does or says seems even the slightest bit odd to you, then don't give into his request for your trust. If he says he needs help, for example, make sure there are people around when you give him that help. Avoid being alone with such an individual.

One example occurred in the college town of Logan, Utah. Early one weekday morning, Milton Peterson was lying underneath a tree outside a religious education building when he noticed sixty-year-old Jim Hansen arriving for work. It was about 5 a.m., and Peterson, about eighteen at the time, raised his head and leered at Jim as he sauntered along the sidewalk to the building's entrance.

"Good morning," Jim said casually, waving from about thirty yards away.

The young man nodded as if to return the well wishes. But, in his mind, he had an entirely different wish for the religious education administrator.

"It's time," Peterson muttered to himself. "It's time for the old man to die."

With that, he made his way into the building and found Jim's office.

"Can I help you with something?" the kindly old man asked. Jim always made time for adolescents who seemed troubled. He had been counseling and instructing youth in the area for the better part of forty years, and he could tell something was bothering this young man.

"Yeah, I need to talk," Peterson said flatly.

"OK, young man, I'm glad you came to me. What would you like to talk about?"

"This!"

The young man suddenly yanked a hunting knife from inside his coat and stabbed Jim as hard and as furiously as he could. The episode lasted only a few minutes, but by the time Peterson was done, the father of five and grandfather of nine lay dead on the floor next to his desk, with more than fifty stab wounds covering his body.

After Peterson caught his breath, he concealed the weapon and quickly fled.

"The old man deserved what he got," he said, taking little care to clean the incriminating blood off himself.

It wasn't long before police caught up with Peterson. Based on the statements of witnesses who placed him at the scene early that morning, detectives quickly identified the young man. They found him a short time later and, through plenty of blood trace evidence, were able to tie him to the murder.

It appeared that prosecutors had a solid case against the suspect, but Peterson's attorney was bent on using an insanity defense. Based on the young man's behavior leading up to the murder, he certainly had a chance of swaying a jury in his favor.

Peterson was widely known around town as an unstable kid.

He listened to the grisliest satanic music imaginable, constantly walked around town singing his favorite tunes, and wandered the streets at all hours muttering to himself. He was also known to meander around town with his face painted in a variety of designs and colors, usually mimicking musicians from his favorite bands. Once, he even paid the Logan Police Department to take a mug shot in which he was handcuffed and flashed a wicked smile.

In addition, there didn't seem to be a reasonable motive for the murder. Peterson didn't take anything from his victim, which ruled out robbery. And before their meeting that fateful morning, nothing tied the perpetrator and the victim together.

On the surface, the homicide was so random that it seemed the defense could make a legitimate case for insanity. So, prosecutors agreed to institutionalize Peterson for a period of five years, at which time he would undergo further evaluation.

As the date of Peterson's potential release neared, authorities feared that he would pose an imminent danger to the community. Prosecutor Scott Wyatt, who had not assisted in the original case, was particularly concerned. He asked me to assess a motive for the crime, Peterson's potential danger to the community, and to make a recommendation to the judge based on my assessment.

I agreed. As I began the process, I first did a thorough study of the victim.

As I studied the victim, I could find nothing about him that would provoke such a random, violent attack. By all accounts, he was friendly, helpful, and noncombative. Such a passive person wouldn't willingly engage in a physical confrontation.

I then turned my attention to the perpetrator. I studied his life, previous statements he had made to authorities, and his interests. Still, I couldn't come up with anything. Finally, as I was going through his family background, I came across the answer. I compared the lifestyle of Peterson's father to that of the victim.

The two men were very similar.

As I reread the police report, it turned out that Peterson had engaged in a heated argument with his father the morning he killed Jim Hansen. Peterson stormed out of the house, walking several blocks until he finally lay down on the front lawn outside the religious education building. The young man had written and talked openly about his deep desire to kill his dad, but like many predatory killers, he couldn't work up the courage to attack the real object of his ire. Instead, he needed a substitute. But not just any substitute. He needed one that he could work up the gumption to kill yet still be able to legitimately fantasize that the victim was his father. Who better than a man who looked like his dad?

The report I provided to that end contributed to the judge's decision to institutionalize Peterson indefinitely.

Again, the lesson is that, if a person is out of place, avoid being alone with that individual. In this case, Jim Hansen could have locked the door behind him and waited for other instructors or students to arrive before unlocking the door. I'm sure he thought it was odd to see Peterson lying in front of the building at 5 a.m., but because this man had spent his adult life nurturing the community's youth, he probably thought he could help Peterson. It's important to remember, though, that sometimes we need help to be able to give help.

Remember, predatory killers don't avoid killing because you've been nice to them. This is what Terry Donnelly told us about people who try to use loving kindness to deter predators: "Animals like me use people like that. We exploit their kindness. That's what we do."

Ben Rhoades apparently took advantage of the kindness of a Christian missionary couple who had been volunteering at a home for wayward men in Georgia before he picked them up.

While we want to help you protect yourself from these predators, we don't want to discourage you from being kind to strangers. Still, it is important to realize that, once you have been targeted, the only thing that dissuades a predatory killer from acting on his impulses is increasing the likelihood that he will get caught.

In Jim Hansen's case, the arrival of a group of people would have turned Peterson away, at least in the moment. There would have been witnesses.

Granted, once Peterson locked onto his intended victim, he probably would have stalked him. At that point, the thing to do would have been to remain in open, public areas, then to have notified the authorities.

Because stalking is such a difficult crime to prove, it's important to realize that, if you find yourself in such a situation, you will probably have to contact law enforcement multiple times in order to enforce a restraining order. If you feel threatened by a stalker, then your safety has to take priority. Yes, it is inconvenient to constantly have to alter your life because of a stalker, but your safety supersedes the inconvenience.

The best way to cut off any power a stalker might try to usurp from you is the same for most other predatory crimes—avoid being alone and involve as many people as possible.

If you find, for example, that you are arriving late for work because of a stalker, enlist the assistance of your employer. More often than not, he will help, especially if you bring proof that shows him you are taking the appropriate steps to resolve the situation. Then, he will probably not only be more understanding of the situation but also be able to assist you in helping police get the stalker off the streets.

Finally, we want to say one last word about the predatory killer.

We conclude with a chapter on homicidal predators because we want you to understand that murder is the pinnacle of a predatory criminal's resume. It's what he works his way up to.

Think of all the offenders we have discussed. Whether they were kidnappers, rapists, drug dealers, child abusers, elderly abusers, or domestic abusers, many escalated to murder during the commission of other crimes.

Carl Steven Moseley went from petty crimes to rape to the murders of two young adult women. Brandon Wilson became involved in marijuana and LSD, drugs that enhanced his delusions of grandeur to the point where he decided to take the life of an innocent nine-year-old boy—simply because Brandon thought he was chosen by a higher power to do so. Brad Morrison didn't kill anyone, but he had traveled well down that path. He started as a drug user who turned to burglary to support his habit. After four years of burglarizing, he became a notorious rapist, one who became increasingly violent toward the end of his criminal career. Timothy McVeigh was actually considered a war hero at one time. But he let a seething anger build inside him to the point that he was willing to take the lives, en masse, of innocent people, including children. Mark Wing went from being a petty criminal/drug user to a domestic abuser to someone who tortured and killed his infant child. He did so because he had an image in his mind of an ideal family that consisted of only two children, not three. Terry Donnelly was another misdemeanor criminal who escalated to rape and murder. He got to the point that he was willing to take advantage of the kindness of elderly women to satisfy his thirst for blood. Ben Rhoades, Dale Wayne Eaton, Ted Bundy—the list goes on.

In the chapter I wrote for Sheila Kimmell's book, *The Murder of Lil Miss*, I address the nature of serial killers the only way I know how, by explaining them as I always do:

> I have come to the realization that these human predators are the exception, not the rule. They are emotionally dysfunctional creatures who occasionally surface and inject their narcissism into a generally stable world. Fortunately, they represent only a tiny fraction of the population.
>
> Understanding the serial killer is even more difficult because we presume that they are "like us." They are not "like us." They don't think or feel like you and me. They regard other people as things or possessions for the taking and satisfaction of their own selfish and distorted needs. They have no sense of responsibility to society and are completely void of empathy. Society at large becomes the host, and they are the parasite. They perpetually feed off of the naiveté and trust of other people.
>
> Another common error we make when trying to understand this predator is to project our value system into theirs and seek common ground. We must recognize that there is no common ground. This type of offender is akin to a piranha among a school of guppies. The nature of the piranha is to seek out and destroy. The guppy will never change the piranha's motivation.

And neither will we change the motivation of the predatory killer.

That is the only explanation we have for the serial murderer, and the key to protecting yourself from these piranhas is to understand that predatory killers are capable of anything. To try and stop them on even footing is, more often than not, going to be a losing battle. Please don't wait until you find yourself in a situation where you are already vulnerable. Train yourself now to recognize a vulnerable situation and keep out of it.

In this chapter, we have gone over some ideas for keeping yourself safe from these predators. Again, it's important to remember that there is no one list of do's and don'ts that will completely protect you.

You have to create a mind-set, a lifestyle, for yourself that will have you constantly thinking (not worrying, but thinking) about what you can do to reduce your risks of being victimized. If you can avoid setting yourself up as a target for the lesser crimes, then more than likely, you will also avoid becoming a target for a more heinous crime.

CONCLUSION

PLAN TO HAVE A HAPPY ENDING

Jim Bridges sat in his car, listening to talk radio. It was a great way to kill time while he was on the lookout for his prey.

Hunting, he called it.

He liked to listen to talk radio, especially political shows, because it was the one thing he could listen to that entertained him and kept his mind sharp at the same time.

"Stinking politicians," he muttered to himself. "All they want to do is raise our taxes. I can barely afford to fill up my tank, and these schmucks are busy giving themselves six-figure raises."

As he contemplated the many ways that society had dealt him a bad hand, his attention turned to the eight-year-old boy on the sidewalk across the street from him. The boy had been playing with a group of friends, but it seemed that everyone had been called home for one reason or another. He was dressed in a T-shirt and blue jeans and was meandering quite slowly when Bridges decided that he would be the next target.

"Finally, he's alone," he thought. "OK, Jimmy, make your move."

With that little self–pep talk, he pulled alongside the boy and began to talk to him.

"Hey, do you know where the nearest 7-Eleven is?" he asked the boy.

"No. I'm not sure," he answered, wondering if he should scream like he had been taught in his third grade class.

"Stranger danger" was what the teacher called it. A local police officer came to the school and taught various techniques for escaping dangerous strangers. Although the lesson piqued Tommy's interest, he was more curious about the officer's gun and if he had ever shot anybody. Besides, the techniques seemed obvious to him. The kids in the movie were so dumb. Certainly, he would never be that dumb.

"What kind of a stupid head would get into a car with someone they don't know?" he joked with his friends.

But now he was faced with that very situation.

"I have an address here, but I think it's wrong," said Bridges, interrupting Tommy's thoughts. "Do you think you could come over here and tell me if I have the right address? I just need to know if this street is nearby here."

"Sure. I guess so," the boy replied.

When he approached the car, the man quickly opened his door and grabbed Tommy, trying to pull him into the vehicle.

At that point, the boy began to scream, and an alert neighbor, seeing what was going on from her kitchen window, simultaneously grabbed her phone in one hand and a rolling pin in the other. She dialed 9-1-1 as she bolted out the door and toward Bridges's car.

"Let him go!" she yelled. Then she heard a voice on the other end of the line.

"9-1-1 operator, how can I help you?"

"There's a creepy guy trying to kidnap a boy!" she told the operator about a second before she cracked the would-be kidnapper's windshield with her rolling pin. "Let him go!"

By then, such a fuss had been made that other neighbors had started toward the vehicle.

Bridges let Tommy go and began to drive off. Fortunately, there was a patrol officer nearby the Sacramento-area neighborhood who quickly cut Bridges off and apprehended him.

As it turned out, Bridges had served time for child molestation and had recently been released. Because his release stipulated that he was not to be around children, he had no natural opportunity to get a child alone. Therefore, he had hoped to get the boy alone by abducting him and taking him to an isolated area. Luckily, the boy lived around some alert neighbors and had been trained to make a lot of noise in that situation.

Curiously, after Tom McHoes, who was a local newspaper reporter for the *Roseville* (California) *Press-Tribune* at the time, had written up the arrest in his police beat column, Bridges hired an attorney to threaten Tom, the newspaper, and the police department with a defamation of character lawsuit. The premise: entrapment.

"My client feels he was entrapped into this situation," the attorney told Tom.

Tom's reply: "Good luck with your lawsuit. It's pretty hard to entrap someone into kidnapping a child."

These neighbors saved this boy because they stayed alert. They took control of the situation. More important, they snatched the advantage away from the predator.

That is exactly what we hope you have come away with—a sense for what it takes to take back control from these people we call predators. They prey on us, hoping we are fearful and counting on us to be lazy with our personal safety. But, as we have said again and again, the best way to stop a predator of any kind is to swing the Risk Continuum in your favor.

Put yourself in situations where you can cut off the predator's opportunities by reducing your risks and, at the same time, enhancing the predator's risk of being caught. That means you just need to make a few simple changes in lifestyle, as well as in the way you think. We hope that we've been able to show you some practical, yet easy, ways to do just that.

Remember, hypothetically speaking, if you learn to think like the criminal who wants to victimize you, and if you can learn to analyze like the detective who would be working your case, then you stand a good chance to avoid becoming the victim.

It's all about being prepared, not scared.

INDEX